I CALL MYSELF A CHRISTIAN...
AM I?

I CALL MYSELF A CHRISTIAN...
AM I?

Hallmarks Of A True Follower
Of Jesus Christ

KATHLEEN SHIMSHOCK-LYONS

XULON PRESS

Xulon Press
2301 Lucien Way #415
Maitland, FL 32751
407.339.4217
www.xulonpress.com

Paperback ISBN-13: 978-1-6628-3214-7
Ebook ISBN-13: 978-1-6628-3215-4

DEDICATION

To my brothers and sister—Leonard,
Maria, George, Andrew, and Stephen—
whose lives will always be interwoven
with mine by the thread of love.

CONTENTS

Acknowledgments

MOST OF US ARE FAMILIAR WITH THE SAYING, "it takes a village" when referring to all the people who help shape the life of a child. I contend "it takes a village" to complete a book! I am humbled and honored by those who have graciously devoted their time and attention to reading through my work to contribute in some way. The posture of their hearts in giving of themselves has caused my own heart to overflow with gratitude. It is because of their collective efforts that this book is now in your hands.

First and foremost, I give thanks to God. Though my limited understanding falls short of being able to fully comprehend the magnitude of God's grace, there is no doubt I am the recipient of it. I have been blessed beyond measure. Thank You, Father, for Your incredible love for us; thank You for the sacrifice of Your Son who died in my place. It is only by Your love and grace that eternal life is possible. Blessed be the Father and the Son, the Lord Jesus Christ!

I want to thank my husband, Steve. Your love and unwavering support continue to be limitless. You have been my greatest cheerleader throughout my journey, supporting and encouraging me in every endeavor since the day we met. You truly are a walking example of the love Christ has for His Church. Your love for me has been and continues to be, selfless and sacrificial. Your devotion to making my needs a priority allows me to rest securely in the knowledge that you always have my highest good at heart. I am truly blessed to be your wife.

Many thanks to Retired Assistant Pastor, Gary Thomas, of Calvary Chapel, Olympia. As I wrote this book, it was my heart's desire to accurately represent the Word of God. Gary, you graciously accepted the task of reviewing my work for just that purpose. Your diligence and careful examination regarding my presentation of the truths found in God's Word allowed me to fulfill my goal. Although I presented you with many changes along the way, you did not waiver in your dedication to seeing this project through to the end. Your time and attention to detail as you poured over my manuscript is something for which I will always be grateful. Your wise and discerning comments prompted careful consideration of God's truths, ultimately leading to greater clarity as I conveyed my message. The value of your feedback was immeasurable. My book is the better for it.

I also want to thank Richard & Diane Allard, and Kevin Koester. The three of you graciously gave of your time as you read through my manuscript with an editor's eye. I am so appreciative of your willingness to spend countless hours giving thoughtful attention and consideration to the material. Your comments and suggestions were invaluable and helped shaped my book. Thank you!

I want to thank my niece, Stephanie Colborn. You have a heart of gold and you are always ready and willing to help others. Thank you for the many hours you spent making sure the Bible "addresses" and Strong's numbers were accurate. That was quite the undertaking and I am grateful you were up to the task.

I also want to thank Mark and Cathy Lewandowski for being among the very first to read my work and provide feedback. Thank you for your support and encouragement along the way.

Special thanks to Almaz Berhe and Gail Lupien whose friendships I truly cherish. Almaz, throughout this project you always had an ample supply of edifying and encouraging words. Your support has meant so much. Gail, thank you for steering me to Precept Bible study—the catalyst in which God, in His sovereignty, removed the blinders from my eyes, making my heart ripe to receive His gift of salvation.

Lastly, I want to thank Kay Arthur of Precept Ministries, International. I am grateful you were faithful to the calling God gave to you and your husband, Jack. You have successfully given millions of people around the globe the skills to study and learn God's Word for themselves. It was through your Bible studies that I came to truly know the Lord. Your studies took me straight to the heart of God, and His Spirit did a work in me. Through the redeeming work of Jesus Christ, God grabbed a hold of my heart, and now my heart is fully His. I am forever grateful. I am forever changed.

Foreword

"I CALL MYSELF A CHRISTIAN...AM I?"

H OLDING THIS BOOK IN YOUR HANDS INDI-
cates that you, or someone in your life, recognizes the importance of this question.

So often, transcendent life-shaping questions fade into the background while physical needs and activities constantly demand our
attention. Our lives are filled with work, school, shopping, driving,
sports, and all sorts of projects, but if that is all, we fall short of
experiencing the deep meaning and lasting value that God intends
for our lives.

A few years ago, on a trip to Fiji, I was part of a group that built
homes and provided medical assistance to people in need. The
families were grateful for the physical help. But I got to see a far
deeper gratitude and joy spring from their hearts when our discussion turned to God's deep love. We were all reminded that He has
not forgotten any of us and that life is really about knowing Him.
Our minds and hearts were lifted from life's struggles and

came to rest in the knowledge that God is present and He meets us in our needs.

Jesus said, *"Come to me, all you who are weary and burdened, and I will give you rest. Take my yoke upon you and learn from me, for I am gentle and humble in heart, and you will find rest for your souls"* (Matthew 11:28-29, NIV). It is in Christ, and Christ alone, that we find what our soul needs.

This call of Christ is often misunderstood. Some think the call is to church membership, baptism, or agreeing to a statement of faith. Instead, Jesus is simply asking us to come to Him personally to find rest for our souls. Part of finding this rest includes taking on His yoke which, in turn, requires laying down our own. For this reason, coming to Jesus is an act of repentance, as we turn from our own ways in order to take on His. When we do so, He powerfully, yet gently reorders our lives and transforms our relationships, filling us with His love, joy, hope, and peace.

As our culture rapidly moves away from viewing life through the lens of biblical truth, it is ever more essential that we keep sight of the person and work of Jesus Christ as revealed in Scripture. This is why Kathleen's work is so timely. To stand firm in our cultural moment, professing Christians must become well-grounded in the Gospel.

As the missions pastor at our church, I long for people to understand God's good and loving purpose for their lives. I have witnessed Kathleen's passion for the in-depth study of God's Word and her heart to teach its precepts. Through the years, she has developed a rich familiarity with the truths of the Bible, which enables her to accurately draw from Scripture and present us with an understanding of what it means to follow Christ. Kathleen has done this in no ambiguous terms. She is clear and pointed in what it means to be a Christian, which prompts us as readers to reflect on our faith both deeply and practically.

In the Apostle Paul's second letter to the church in Corinth, he exhorts, *"Examine yourselves to see whether you are in the faith; test yourselves. Do you not realize that Christ Jesus is in you—unless, of course, you fail the test?"* (2 Corinthians 13:5, NIV). Each chapter of Kathleen's book considers an essential element of the Christian faith, helping us to gaze into the mirror of God's Word and undertake a humble and sincere self-examination.

If you are considering whether to follow Christ or wondering if your life exemplifies being His follower, then this book is definitely for you. As you read, I encourage you to approach each chapter with a humble openness to the Scriptures and to what God may teach you about what it means to call yourself a Christian.

Bill Dunning
Missions Pastor
Calvary Chapel of Olympia

Preface

"He who is not with Me is against Me; and he who does not gather with Me scatters." (Matthew 12:30)

THIS IS ONE OF THE MOST PROFOUND STATE-ments made by Jesus. Essentially, Jesus is saying there are only two forces in the world—one that is for Him and gathers to Him, and one that is against Him and scatters away from Him. It is not possible to sit on the fence when it comes to the person of Jesus Christ. Many people believe in a god or a creator of the universe or some higher power, but if you mention the name of the Lord Jesus Christ, you can practically see the scattering. Jesus will divide. He said so Himself (Luke 12:51).

The division Jesus spoke of is that which is created by attaching your "wheel to His wagon," so to speak. If you follow Him, He will be a dividing line that separates you from others. Oftentimes, this will include members of your own family. In Matthew 12:46-50, Jesus was told that His mother and brothers were seeking to speak to Him. Jesus responded, saying,

"Who is my mother and who are My brothers?" And stretching out His hand toward His disciples, He said, "Behold My mother and My brothers! For whoever does the will of My Father who is in heaven, he is My brother and sister and mother."

Jesus made it clear that His true family members are those who do the will of His Father. For all who are members of God's family, we are brothers and sisters in Christ, having a rich inheritance in the kingdom of God, one that is imperishable, undefiled, and will not fade away (1 Peter 1:4). But there is a cost that comes from being a follower of Jesus, a cost He encourages us to count (Luke 14:28-31).

A true follower of Jesus Christ is to be *with* Him 100%, whatever the cost. If you are not *with* Him, Jesus's statement is quite clear: you are *against* Him. So what exactly does it mean to be *with* Christ? If you are *with* Jesus Christ, you are indelibly "stamped" as belonging to Him. Those who belong to Christ *are* with Christ. The question becomes, how can we know for certain that we belong to Jesus Christ?

This book will provide you with an in-depth, biblical understanding of what it means to be *with* Christ—in other words, what it means to be a Christian. The basis for writing this book is to demonstrate to the reader that there are foundational elements and distinguishing characteristics—hallmarks—clearly noted in the Scriptures that identify us as Christians. Some hallmarks are indisputable components of being a Christian. This means that without them, it's not possible to be a Christian. Others arise as a result of becoming a Christian. Therefore, the degree to which those hallmarks are present in the life of a Christian will vary. The further along a Christian is in his or her spiritual walk with the Lord, the more prominent those hallmarks become. But regardless of whether one has been a Christian for a day or ten years, the Holy Spirit dwelling within the life of a believer will produce a desire for the things of God that is unmistakable and evident to others. This book highlights those hallmarks that let us know for certain that we belong to Jesus Christ. If one professes to be a Christian, the evidence, or lack thereof, will be apparent.

There are countless numbers of people who profess to be Christians, many of whom fill our churches each week. But are they truly Christians? More importantly, are *you* truly a Christian? We are going to take an in-depth look at God's Word and learn what it means to be a true follower of the Lord Jesus Christ.

The Apostle Paul tells us in 2 Corinthians 13:5, *"Test yourselves to see if you are in the faith; examine yourselves! Or do you not recognize this about yourselves, that Jesus Christ is in you – unless indeed you fail the test?"* The Corinthian Church was a group of people who had been discipled by Paul and who had put their faith in Jesus Christ. Though Paul was aware the majority of those he was writing to were genuine believers and thus, true followers of Christ, his exhortation implies he suspected that some among them were not. Therefore, he strongly urged them to examine themselves to see if they were in the faith.

My exhortation to you is the same. Examine yourself! See if you are in the faith. It is my prayer you are indeed so. However, if you discover you are not in the family of faith, my prayer is that you give yourself fully to our Lord and Savior, Jesus Christ.

Introduction

MANY PEOPLE CALL THEMSELVES CHRISTIANS. Yet few are probably ever asked to define what that means. If professing Christians were asked about their faith, and what it means to follow Christ, I'm guessing there would be as many different answers as those who were asked. While that may be a bit of an exaggeration, I expect the variation in answers would be fairly high.

I am someone who always believed I was a Christian. However, if I had been asked to share my faith with someone before I truly became a Christian, my response—whatever it might have been—would have followed my initial reaction of a blank stare. I can't say for sure what I would have said, but I can assure you it would have been based solely on my own reasoning. Though I had considered myself a Christian my entire life, only in recent years have I learned what that truly means.

Many people belong to various groups and organizations. They may join for a specific reason or a variety of reasons. Regardless of the reason, I doubt you would find any who have no idea why they belong. Many could probably tell you what the group stands for and some may even be able to recite the organization's mission statement. Most would likely be able to accurately convey to you why they belong and could probably convince you to belong as well. Can those who claim to belong to Jesus Christ do the same? Given the importance of our mission as followers of Christ, if we profess to follow Him, it is vitally important that we understand what following Christ means. More importantly, do our lives express that we truly belong to Him?

My purpose for readers of this book is two-fold: First, it's a call to examine yourself, to see if you are truly in the faith. There are many people sitting in churches today who assume they are Christians. Yet if they don't know what the Bible teaches about being a Christian, then it is quite likely they are not. Second, I want to provide you with a solid, biblical understanding of what it means to be a true follower of the Lord Jesus Christ. As Christians, we are called to be ready to make a defense to everyone who asks us to give an account for the hope that is within us (1 Peter 3:15). If someone were to ask us, "Why did you become a Christian?," it is imperative that we be prepared to answer that question—without hesitation—accurately, and according to God's Word.

If you are not a follower of the Lord Jesus Christ as you begin this book, it is my prayer that you'll be one by the time you are finished. For those of us who have already surrendered our lives to Christ, may our lives bear the marks—the hallmarks that define us as His.

Helpful Notes to The Reader

Located in the Appendix, you will find a Definition of Terms. There are different words and phrases the Bible uses that identify people as followers of Jesus Christ. Therefore, to provide clarity, I have defined and included them in the Appendix. These words and phrases are Christian, Follower, Disciple, Believer, Born Again, Born of the Spirit, and Born of God. I use these words and phrases interchangeably; they are synonymous. Though each word or phrase may connote something slightly different, essentially they all mean the same thing—they refer to individuals who are true followers of Jesus Christ. Every time these words are used throughout this book, they refer to those who have repented of their sins and have put their faith in Jesus Christ as Lord and Savior. They believe that Jesus is the only begotten Son of God, who lived and died, was buried, and rose again on the third day. They believe that Jesus is Truth, His words are Truth, and without Him, there is no hope of eternal life.

Unless otherwise indicated, Scripture references are from the Holy Bible, New American Standard Version, NASB 1995. I strongly encourage you to look up noted Scripture verses as you move along in your reading. This book is rooted and grounded in God's Word; it is based on Biblical truth. So grab your Bible, and join me as we journey together through the hallmarks of a true follower of Jesus Christ.

Chapter 1

I CALL MYSELF A CHRISTIAN...AM I?

Am I a Christian? Today I can most assuredly answer, "yes!" But I've called myself a Christian my entire life. So even if you had asked me that question thirty, twenty, or even ten years ago, I would have said yes. But I now know it wasn't always true. Something changed.

A few years ago I was having a conversation with someone in our women's Bible study at church and she had asked me, "When did you become a Christian?" Though that is certainly a reasonable question, it took me a bit by surprise because no one had ever asked me that before. At the time, I was fifty-one years of age. While I wasn't able to provide her with an exact date, I did give her an approximate time because I knew the point at which a change had occurred. But I also told her that though I had always called myself a Christian, I had come to realize that for most of my life I was not. It wasn't until I began to study God's Word, the Book of 1 John in particular, that the fallacy I once had of my Christianity, and hence, my salvation, truly came to light.

1

I was raised in the Catholic faith. Both of my parents were Catholic and instilled their faith in my brothers and sister and me. We were faithful Catholics. All of us kids were baptized as infants, made our First Confession, First Holy Communion, and received Confirmation. We went to church every Sunday and all the Holy Days of Obligation as required by the Catholic Church, and we regularly attended catechism classes during our formative years up through about the tenth grade. It was there that we learned some of the more well-known Bible stories and about such things as forgiveness, the Trinity, penance, and the Sacraments. Together we regularly prayed the Rosary, and we always partook in the practice of Lent. There was no question, that as a family, we were faithful Catholics. But was I a Christian?

As a teenager, I remember responding to an evangelist giving an altar call. It's only a vague recollection now and I can't remember if it was something I was watching on TV or listening to on the radio. But I do remember accepting that call and confessing my sins to God and asking Jesus to be my Lord and Savior. Did that altar-call experience make me a Christian?

I also prayed—nearly every night. Many times my prayers were scripted and repetitive, but not always. There were certainly plenty of times I just spoke to God and poured out my heart to Him. Did that make me a Christian?

I believed in God and that Jesus was the only Son of God. I believed that Jesus died, was buried, rose again on the third day, and then ascended into heaven. Did that make me a Christian?

As an adult, going to church was something I continued even though I was no longer forced to attend by my parents. I went regularly for quite some time and was even part of the music ministry for many years. Did that make me a Christian?

As one looks at this list, one might be inclined to answer, "yes," to the question I posed at the beginning, "Am I a Christian?" Perhaps you may be inclined to answer "yes" because of Romans 10:9, which states, "… if you confess with your mouth Jesus as Lord, and believe in your heart that

God raised Him from the dead, you will be saved." But if you're someone who has an understanding of the full counsel of God's Word, you couldn't answer that question just based on what I've told you thus far. You would need to know more about me. For you to know whether or not I was a Christian, you would have to know two things. First, you would have to know what God's Word teaches about being a follower of Jesus Christ. Second, you would need to know if my life expressed that I was a follower of Jesus Christ.

Contained within the Scriptures are specific hallmarks that identify us as Christians. That is the subject of this book. We are going to look at what the Bible teaches about what it means to be a Christian.

My Story

Before we dig into the heart of the matter, I believe it will be helpful for you to know the backstory—the story of how it came to be that I sit here penning this book. A transformation is best understood when we know the place from which one started.

I began attending a Bible-based church in early 2010. I had just met Steve, my future husband, and he had invited me to go to church with him. Before that time, I had only attended Catholic churches as that's what I had done all my life; it was all I knew. When I first began attending church with Steve, I admit that some things seemed odd to me. For instance, the words to the songs we sang were projected up on a big screen and there was a lack of formality during the service. But nothing was odd in and of itself. It was simply different from my experience with the Catholic Church. Had I not grown up with that background, I would not have had any preconceived ideas about what to expect at a church service, and therefore, I doubt I would have thought anything to be "odd."

The biggest contrast between what I had known and what I was now experiencing was the teaching of God's Word. The church I was now attending opened up the Bible and would read and teach from it, verse by verse. A Catholic service will have an Old Testament reading, a New

Testament reading, and a reading from one of the four gospels during a given Mass. But during my years of attendance, those readings were never really expounded upon. Occasionally a priest would give his sermon based on one of the readings, but honestly, not that often. Now I certainly can't paint with a broad brush stating the Catholic Church as a whole doesn't expound on the Scripture that is read during a Mass. I'm simply sharing my own experience.

Another difference was tradition. One can attend a Catholic service just about anywhere in the world and no matter where you go, the format is the same. Frankly, it's part of what makes attending a Catholic church somewhat comforting. The familiarity of the Catholic Mass can have the effect of making one "feel at home" based on the traditions that have been carried down throughout the years. At the Bible-based church I attend, there are no formal traditions. We do regularly partake in Communion and one might put that into the category of tradition. However, I don't see it simply as a tradition. Rather, we are obeying what Christ told us to do; "do this in remembrance of Me" (Luke 22:19).

Given my years of affiliation with the Catholic Church, the transition from attending a Catholic service to a Bible-based teaching service carried with it some minor emotional adjustments. Growing up Catholic was, in a sense, a way of life. What was once a comfortable "old sweater" of familiarity, was now a new venture that I was approaching with a cautious eye. Yet, despite the differences, the transition was actually quite easy. The most welcome change for me initially, as well as to this day, was that I *wanted* to go to church. I enjoyed the time of worship through music and the style of teaching—expounding on the passages in the Bible. Though I was unfamiliar with the Bible, I was now being taught what was in it and gradually became interested to know more.

As time passed, I began thinking it might be nice to join a Bible study. A friend I had made at church was in one of the Bible study groups that were offered. With her encouragement, I decided to join the group she attended. That was the fall of 2013, about two-and-a-half years after I began attending our church.

I had turned forty-seven that summer and up until that time I had seldom read any of the Bible, let alone studied it. There had been some times in my life that were emotionally difficult and I had opened up my Bible and read some verses here and there. It's funny how many of us tend to do that in times of stress or heartache. But that was all I did, and then I would close it and move on.

As I reflect on my upbringing in the church, one of the most shocking things to me now is that I had never really read the Bible, nor did I truly know what was in it. The stories from the Bible that were familiar to me were vague at best. I did know that some people believed it to be the Word of God. But apart from that, I have to say, I had very little knowledge of the Bible. The question that came to my mind was, "why?" Given that I had attended church for so many years, why didn't I know even a little bit of doctrine regarding the Christian faith?

As we began our Bible study that fall, I had no idea at the time what I was getting myself into. But let me just say, "Wow!" Unbeknownst to me, I had joined the group that offered the most in-depth and consequently, time-consuming study. In addition, our study at that time was in the Book of Isaiah, a book that quite frankly, can be difficult to understand, especially for a Bible neophyte such as myself.

During that first year of study, there were a number of times I wanted to quit. I often put off my homework until the last minute as the study required a fair amount of time as well as concentrated effort. I remember how I felt when I discovered our study of Isaiah was in two parts. As Part 1 was drawing to a close, I thought, "now's my chance!" If I wanted to quit, doing so at the end of Part 1 would have been an opportune time. But something kept pushing me forward. Though I had contemplated quitting, I often found myself amazed at what I was learning. Prior to joining the study, I had almost no idea what God had to say in His Word. But now I was seeing and learning of God in a way I had never known before. Little did I know at the time, the Holy Spirit was bringing conviction to my heart. He was revealing to me who I was apart from God, as well as the person God wanted me to be.

I completed the study of Isaiah the following spring and even joined a summer study. By the end of the summer, there was a shift. I no longer put off doing my homework as a standard practice. I now found myself wanting to study, eager to learn what God was going to say next.

That fall, our group began our study in the Book of Exodus. Admittedly, I wasn't exactly thrilled to study Exodus. I would have preferred to delve into a book from the New Testament. But if there is one thing I learned during my first year of Bible study, it's that God's timing is perfect. It was lesson nine of an eleven-lesson study that "sealed the deal" for me. I was so blown away by what I discovered during that lesson, that from that point forward, there was no going back. I had a hunger for God's Word and a transformation of my heart was taking place. For the first time in my life, I truly desired to know God and to live a life that was pleasing to Him.

As someone who now wanted to live a life that was pleasing to God, that begs a couple of questions. One, what kind of a life had I been living? And two, what caused the transformation of my heart to occur? I'll begin with the first question. What kind of life had I been living? Well, by today's standards, a pretty good one. I was what most people would call a "good person." And when I compared myself to others, it was easy for me to come to that same conclusion! But I learned something during that first year of study, something profound. Other people are not the standard by which I am to measure whether or not I am a good person. That measuring stick is fluid and can change with seasons, generations, and cultures, just to name a few. Jesus is the standard. Jesus lived a perfect, sinless life (Hebrews 4:15). So how did I measure up against the true measuring stick? Not well. Not well by any stretch of the imagination. The Bible tells us in Romans 3:23, *...for all have sinned and fall short of the glory of God.* Romans 3:10 tells us, *there is none righteous, not even one.* My bubble had burst. I wasn't even close to being a "good person." There were many areas of sin in my life, both overt and covert, and it seemed as though each day brought more revelation; the light that was being shed on my sinful habits continued to grow brighter. I began to see those areas in which I was turning a blind eye to inappropriate things in my thoughts and my behavior. For example, there were the things I read, the shows or movies that I watched, inappropriate talk that came out of my mouth or engaging with others who spoke the same way. Then there were the jokes I laughed at or the jokes I told. Worse yet, were the sins that weren't visible to others, such as the thoughts I had and fueled in my mind. It became clear to me that I was far from being a "good person," and I would never, of my own volition, be able to attain such a status. Romans 7:18 says, *For I know that nothing good dwells in me, that is, in my flesh; for the willing is present in me, but the doing of the good is not.* No matter how hard I tried and no matter what steps I took, such as going to church, doing good deeds, being kind to others, etc., I would never be able to measure up to God's standard based on anything I could ever do, say, think or feel.

In case you might be feeling unsettled and thinking, "Oh great, if we can't do anything based on our own merit to ensure that we measure up to God's standard, what hope is there for anyone?" Let me just say...there is a way! We can be reconciled to a perfect and holy God, and we will look at that in the following chapters.

Now let's look at the second question. What happened to me that awakened the desire within me to know God and to now want to live a life that was pleasing to Him? Unequivocally, it is the Holy Spirit now residing within me. What a sharp contrast between how I used to think and behave before the Spirit was within me, versus how I think and behave now that the Spirit guides and directs my thoughts and actions.

If I called myself a Christian my entire life, but clearly did not have the Holy Spirit dwelling within me, was I a Christian? Romans 8:9 states, *...you are not in the flesh but in the Spirit, if indeed the Spirit of God dwells in you. But if anyone does not have the Spirit of Christ, he does not belong to Him.* This verse leaves no room for doubt. The Holy Spirit must reside within us for us to belong to the Lord Jesus Christ.

The more I learned about what God's Word had to say about being a true follower of Jesus Christ, the more I came to realize that for most of my life I hadn't been. Looking back, I would consider myself to be what many people would call a fan of Jesus, but certainly not a follower. I believed in

Jesus as the Son of God, but I had never truly repented of my sins, nor had I submitted to Him as Lord and Savior. In the Gospel of Matthew, Jesus gives us an example of what a "fan" of His looks like.

Matthew 7 is the third chapter of what is commonly known as Jesus's Sermon on the Mount. Jesus was teaching His disciples many things regarding what it means to be kingdom seekers. Verses 21 through 23 are very sobering for someone like me who always considered myself to be a Christian. Jesus said,

> *"Not everyone who says to Me, 'Lord, Lord,' will enter the kingdom of heaven, but he who does the will of My Father who is in heaven will enter. Many will say to Me on that day, 'Lord, Lord, did we not prophesy in Your name, and in Your name cast out demons, and in Your name perform many miracles?' And then I will declare to them, 'I never knew you; depart from Me, you who practice lawlessness.'"*
> (Matthew 7:21-23)

Sad to say, this described me. I was certainly not doing the will of the Father, nor did I care to know the will of the Father. Yet I truly believed I was a Christian. I believed in God and Jesus, I went to church, I listened to Christian music, I tried to be a "good person," and when I prayed, I prayed in Jesus's name. But God's will wasn't even on my radar. And yes, I often practiced lawlessness. I had no regard for the Law of God and therefore, had no problem engaging in habitual sin.

As I came to realize that for many years I was not the child of God I thought myself to be, the more I felt God impressing upon my heart to share with others what His Word teaches about being a follower of His only begotten Son, the Lord Jesus Christ; in other words, what His Word teaches about being a Christian. Let's dive in!

Chapter 2

AN ACKNOWLEDGEMENT OF SIN

WHENEVER ONE BREAKS DOWN THE BASICS of what it means to be a Christian, it will, without a doubt, include the recognition we are all sinners. We are sinners by nature and sinners by choice. In this chapter, we will begin by taking a look at what is meant by the word *sin* given that it has a dual meaning. We'll use the Book of 1 John to both explore the dual meaning and examine why the acknowledgment of sin is so important. John lays out for us, in no uncertain terms, why this acknowledgment is essential for the Christian.

In Scripture, the word *sin* can either be a noun or a verb. It is used as a noun when referring to the sin nature. The sin nature resides within us and refers to the spiritual condition in which we are born. We will look at what that means shortly. The word *sin* is used as a verb when referring to acts of sin. Acts of sin are those sins we commit by choice, all of which stem from the influence the sin nature has on our mind, our will, and emotions.

Let's begin by defining *sin*. The Greek word for *sin* is *hamartia*. It means to miss the mark. It can also mean to wander from

9

the path of uprightness and honor, to do or go wrong (Strong's G266). *Hamartia*, at its roots, is an archery term. The mark in archery would be the bull's eye. But what does it mean when spoken of in the Bible? If it means to 'miss the mark,' what mark are we missing? The mark we are missing is God's standard of righteousness. God's standard is Himself; He is perfectly just (Isaiah 30:18) and right (Psalm 92:15).

All Have Sinned

As previously noted, the Bible tells us in Romans 3:23, *...for all have sinned and fall short of the glory of God.* The word 'all' in that sentence means just that—all. We *all* fall short of "the mark." Not one person, living or dead, except for Jesus Christ, has ever lived a sinless life. Accepting the fact that we are all sinners isn't always easy. In fact, many deny it. I was someone who denied it for most of my life simply because I compared myself to the population at large and found myself to be a "good person." Yes, there were some things I had done that I knew God considered a sin. But since I didn't really know God, my ignorance made it easy for me to presume that God was accepting of my sin. Through that lens, it really wasn't sin. Besides, He made me the way I am; at least that was the rationale that allowed me to continue sinning. In my mind, if there was any responsibility for my "sin," it was on Him. If God didn't want me to sin, He wouldn't have made me with a propensity to sin. Talk about wrong thinking! When you think wrong, you do wrong!

The saddest part of what I just admitted was that I didn't know God. I had no idea of His character or His nature. When we don't know someone very well, it's hard to love them and it's hard to trust them, let alone put our faith in them. That's why knowing God's Word is so vitally important. If we don't know God, we have no plumb line for what is right. Without Him, it is easy to justify whatever we say and do as being "right" and thus, deceive ourselves into believing that the truth we have invented in our minds, is in fact, Truth. In this instance, we essentially violate God's Second Commandment. We create a god in our own

10

image, one we have formulated in our minds, a god that suits our life-style, our beliefs, and our standards. This is why many people, including many who profess to be Christians, aren't interested in knowing God. If you profess to be a Christian, yet you do not know God, your account-ability to Him is a moot point. You will remain a slave to your sinful nature (Romans 6:20).

Most people prefer the god they've created in their own image. This way they can either view their sin in a favorable light, feeling "good" about who they are and how they behave, or they can keep their sin hidden, defending, excusing, or rationalizing their behavior. When we create a god in our own image, we do not have to be accountable to anyone for our immorality except ourselves. If we are the ones setting the standard for what is right, it's doubtful we will ever violate our stan-dards. We will do what is right in our own eyes.

Let's face it. It can be hard to admit we are sinners. For many of us, it's hard to admit because we like our sin. If we didn't like it, we wouldn't be doing it. The Bible even tells us there are fleeting pleasures in sin (Hebrews 11:25). On the other hand, some people don't like their sinful habits and perhaps wish they could stop sinning. But until we reach a place of acknowledging we are sinners, there's no real "fix." A strong desire to be free from a sinful habit is nearly impossible to achieve when we do not have a clear understanding of the sin nature. And our culture does nothing to help us triumph over our sinful behavior. Our culture tends to cast aside and dismiss our sin and instead, label our sin as a disease, a lifestyle, a hang-up, a disorder, a predisposition, etc. Discontinuation of sinful behavior, whether we enjoy our sin or hate our sin, will either remain a "non-issue," or will be difficult to prevail over without first recognizing that what we are doing is sinful. However, the good news is that, unlike a predisposition or disorder, sin can be overcome. There is a way to overcome sin and that comes through Jesus Christ, the very One who died for our sins.

Our acknowledgment of sin, or lack thereof, reminds me of what Jesus said when He was dining at a table with tax collectors and sinners.

The scribes of the Pharisees were questioning Jesus's disciples as to why Jesus would eat with people known for their immoral behavior. In His response to their question, Jesus said, "I did not come to call the righteous, but sinners" (Mark 2:15-17). We learn two things from this. One, since we already know there are none righteous, not even one (Romans 3:10), the only kind of righteousness that remains is self-righteousness. Two, Jesus calls sinners. The good news is that all who admit they are sinners can be set free from the bondage of the sin nature by coming to the very One who can forgive their sins. The bad news is when we are self-righteous and do not acknowledge we are sinners, there is no solution for our sin problem. Whether we enjoy the fleeting pleasures of sin or hate the bondage that sin brings, until we come to know there is only one standard of righteousness and we all fall short, we will never come to a place of being able to admit we are sinners. And our need for the One who can cleanse us from our sin will remain unmet.

The Sin Nature Within

Let's now go to the Book of 1 John and see what the Apostle John tells us about sin and the sin nature.

> *If we say that we have no sin, we are deceiving ourselves and the truth is not in us. If we say that we have not sinned, we make Him a liar and His word is not in us.* (1 John 1:8, 10)

Wow! There is no doubt that John's words hit us hard. Let's look at each verse separately.

If we say that we have no sin, we are deceiving ourselves and the truth is not in us (v. 8). The word *sin* in this verse is in its noun form. Therefore, it is a reference to the sin nature. The sin nature is the inward element in each of us which influences and entices us to produce acts of sin. The sin nature is the root of our sinful behaviors. We commit acts of sin because we are sinners by nature. Consider a dog's bark. When we hear a dog bark, we don't conclude that the barking sound generated by the dog is what makes it a dog. A dog barks because it is a dog by nature. The root of the barking is the fact that it's generated by a dog. It's the same concept regarding sin. We commit sins because the root—the sin nature—already exists within us. John makes it clear that if we say we do not have a sin nature, meaning we do not acknowledge that as being inherent within us, we are deceiving ourselves and the truth is not in us.

That begs a couple of questions: what truth are we talking about here that's not in us and how is it that we even have a sin nature? To answer the first question, let's quickly look at what is meant by the word *truth* in this verse. The word *truth* in the Greek is *alētheia*. In verse 8, it has a definite article in front of it. The definite article *the* tells us it is a specific truth, not just a generic truth. The word *truth* in this verse is defined in the Greek as *the truth*, as taught in the Christian religion, respecting God and the execution of His purposes through Christ, and respecting the duties of man; the truth which is the gospel or which the gospel presents (Strong's G225). We learn from this definition that the truth referred to here is God's objective truth concerning who He is and all that He has purposed through His Son, Jesus Christ. To put it simply, the definition of *the truth* can be summed up in one word...Truth. If we claim we do not have a sin nature, John tells us we are deceived in our thinking. This means we lack understanding concerning the effect the indwelling sin nature has on our mind, will, and emotions, all of which can lead to sinful behavior. If we willfully refuse to acknowledge the sin nature within, then the objective truth of God, in all its fullness and scope regarding who He is and all that He has purposed through His Son, Jesus Christ, is not in us. If we don't understand the nature of our sin problem, we will not understand the solution for our sin problem.

Now let's answer the second question. How is it that we even have a sin nature? Romans 5:12 states, *Therefore, just as through one man sin entered into the world, and death through sin, and so death spread to all men, because all sinned....* The remainder of Romans 5 tells us that

Adam was the one man by whom sin entered into the world, and with that sin came death as a consequence. The evidence of our sin nature lies in the fact that we have one very convincing proof—we all die. Romans 6:23 tells us, *the wages of sin is death*. Death, in and of itself, is evidence we have a sin nature. Let's explore this a bit further to get a better understanding.

Understanding the Sin Nature

Many people, Christian and non-Christian, are familiar with the story of Adam and Eve. In its most simplistic form, Adam and Eve ate the fruit of the one tree in the Garden of Eden of which God told them not to eat. In Genesis 2:16-17, God told Adam, *"From any tree of the garden you may eat freely; but from the tree of the knowledge of good and evil you shall not eat, for in the day that you eat from it you will surely die."* Genesis 3 tells us that Eve was deceived by Satan in the garden, and she took of the fruit to eat it. She then gave the fruit to Adam for him to eat, and he did so. At that moment, the sin nature entered the world and the consequence thereof...death. We are all sinners by nature because of that one act of rebellion in the garden. The sin nature was then passed down to all humanity through Adam. The Bible tells us that Adam was made in God's likeness and image (Genesis 1:26, 27). But after Adam's sin, his son Seth was then born in Adam's likeness, according to Adam's image (Genesis 5:3). When Adam sinned, God's image in him became distorted. Adam then begat a son in his own sinful, corrupt, and fallen image, and consequently, so has all humanity been brought forth, except for Jesus Christ. Jesus was conceived by the Holy Spirit (Matthew 1:18; Luke 1:35) and therefore, did not inherit the sin nature.

If God told Adam, *"for in the day that you eat from it you will surely die,"* and Adam didn't physically die at that moment, what died? Ultimately, the consequence of their sin would culminate in physical death just as God said. But something did occur at that very moment. The spirit within them "died," not in the sense that it ceased to exist, but rather in the sense that it became corrupted by the intrusion of sin, and their perfect fellowship with God was severed. Their actions after eating the fruit of the tree give us insight into what occurred. After they both ate of the fruit, here is what we learn: *Then the eyes of both of them were opened, and they knew that they were naked; and they sewed fig leaves together and made themselves loin coverings* (Genesis 3:7). In verse 5, we learn that the serpent told Eve, *"For God knows that in the day you eat from it your eyes will be opened, and you will be like God, knowing good and evil."* Both references to their eyes being opened are used metaphorically. Their physical eyes were functioning just fine; verse 6 states that Eve saw that the tree was good for food and that it was a delight to the eyes. Therefore, when we read that the eyes of both of them were opened, it's a metaphor for something taking place outside of their control that allowed them to see something that was coming from within them, and that something was the wickedness of their hearts. Their consciences had just alerted them that they had violated God's standard, and as a result, they experienced guilt. Their guilt caused them to feel shame, which prompted them to want to "cover up." For the first time, they experienced self-conscious awareness, and their perfect fellowship with God, the source of their everlasting, life-giving spirit, was broken.

Human beings are tripartite beings, meaning we have a spirit, a soul, and a body (1 Thessalonians 5:23). When Adam and Eve sinned, something happened to their spirit component; it became corrupted by the intrusive sin nature and died in the sense that everlasting life was no longer possible if left in that unregenerate state. The corrupted spirit within Adam and Eve is evident by the fact that they felt uncomfortable in their nakedness and took matters into their own hands. They thought that by covering themselves up with fig leaves, they could "cover up their sin." Ephesians 2:1-3 gives us a great picture of how we live our lives when operating from a position of being ruled by the flesh (the sin nature). Adam and Eve went from having the mind of the Spirit of God working and ruling within them, to being governed by the mind of their flesh—their physical desires, needs, and wants. In other words, they were now being ruled by the sin nature. Their broken state of fellowship with God, which occurred as a result of the Spirit of God being dead within them, is what has been passed down to every generation from that point forward. This is why when Jesus came onto the scene, He told Nicodemus in John 3:7, "you must be born again." We will take an in-depth look at what that means in chapter five. But for our purposes here, the following will suffice. For the spirit within us to be restored back to life, in which our fellowship with God is no longer broken, Jesus told us that we must be born again. This means we must have a spiritual birth that comes from God that restores our spiritual condition.

As a consequence of what took place in the garden, we are all born with a sin nature, and we all act on that sin nature. This is evident no matter where we look. One never has to teach a child to lie, or to be selfish or stubborn. These behaviors, among a whole host of sinful behaviors, stem from the sin nature—that natural bent we have for behaving sinfully. It's our state of being governed by the flesh in which we allow our bodies to "call the shots." In Romans 8:3, Paul calls the flesh *sinful flesh*, indicating that the sin nature is a part of every fiber of our being. We have a natural bent toward sinful behavior because of the indwelling sin nature within us. It began when Adam sinned and since then, has been carried forward with every generation. The psalmist David tells us in Psalm 51:5, *Behold, I was brought forth in iniquity, and in sin my mother conceived me.* David isn't saying his conception was brought forth in sin because his parents had sex outside of marriage. He is saying that his sin problem—being born with a depraved nature that influences and entices him to sin—dates back to when he was conceived. The sin nature is that part of us that gives rise to the desire within us to always do our own thing—to rebel against God's will for us. Given the choice to do God's will or to do as we wish, the sin nature fosters the desire within us to choose our own path, following after our sinful ideas, desires, and passions.

God's Law Shows Us Our Sin

You might be saying about now, "okay, I get that I have a sin nature. But how do I know which behaviors are sinful?" The answer is simple, we have God's Law. God's Law is His perfect standard. Anything that goes against God's Law and His righteousness is sin.

We read in Exodus 20 the account of God giving His Law to Moses, who in turn, gave it to the Israelites. God gave Moses the Ten Commandments on top of Mt. Sinai while the Israelites were wandering in the wilderness shortly after they had left Egypt. The Law is what shows us our sin. Romans 3:20 tells us, *...because by the works of the Law no flesh will be justified in His sight; for through the Law comes the knowledge of sin.* The Law was never given to save us; it was never intended to make us right or declared innocent before a holy God (Acts 13:38-39; Galatians 3:11). Rather, it was given to show us our sin. It's like an x-ray of our heart, who we are on the inside, in our inner being. The Law can be likened to a mirror. When we look in a mirror, the mirror reflects our image, allowing us to see if something is wrong with our hair or face. But it can't fix our hair or wash our face. It only shows us that our hair needs fixing and our face needs washing. The mirror simply reveals our condition, but the mirror itself cannot remedy our condition. The Law, like a mirror, lacks the power to change the heart of a person. It can only reveal what is in the heart.

We also learn in Galatians 3:19 why the Law was given. *Why the Law then? It was added because of transgressions, having been ordained through angels by the agency of a mediator, until the seed would come to whom the promise had been made.* The Law was given not only to show us our sin but also to point us to Christ. A careful study of Galatians 3:19 clearly shows that the seed referred to in this verse is Jesus Christ. Jesus was the promised seed. The Jews knew that one day a Messiah would come, and until He came, they had God's Law as their standard for how they were to behave.

Your next question might be, "now that Jesus has come, do we have to keep the Law?" Regarding moral law, the short answer is, "Yes!" There were three kinds of laws handed down to the Israelites. There were Ceremonial Laws, Civil Laws, and Moral Laws. Jesus was the fulfillment of all the Law and the Prophets. This means He lived His life such that He completely fulfilled every law. He did so by living a sinless, righteous life, and His arrival into the world fulfilled all the prophetic Scripture that pointed to His first coming. Jesus said in Matthew 5:17, *"Do not think that I came to abolish the Law or the Prophets; I did not come to abolish but to fulfill."* In other words, Jesus came to accomplish their purpose. Out of the entire history of mankind, Jesus was the only human who completely fulfilled all the Law as He was the only one to ever live a sinless life. Given that Christ fulfilled the Law, let's look at how that translates to how we are to live.

Loving God and Others Fulfills God's Law

While we are no longer under the Law (Romans 6:14; Galatians 5:18), meaning we are not under the old covenant of the Law, we can conclude we are not without Law. Proverbs 19:16 states, *He who keeps the commandment keeps his soul, but he who is careless of conduct will die.* Psalm 119:1-3 reads, *How blessed are those whose way is blameless, who walk in the law of the Lord. How blessed are those who observe His testimonies, who seek Him with all their heart. They also do no unrighteousness; they walk in His ways.* First John 2:3 says, *By this we know that we have come to know Him, if we keep His commandments.* And in John 14:15, Jesus was speaking to His disciples and said, *"If you love Me, you will keep My commandments."* God's Law—all His commandments—give us a picture of God's standard for moral behavior, and they are a reflection of His holiness. They also reveal to us His nature and character. God's moral laws are how we learn what it means to live righteous lives and how we learn to love one another.

In Matthew 22, we find Jesus having a conversation with a lawyer. The lawyer asks,

> *"Teacher, which is the great commandment in the Law?" And Jesus said to him, "You shall love the Lord your God with all your heart, and with all your soul, and with all your mind. This is the great and foremost commandment. The second is like it, You shall love your neighbor as yourself. On these two commandments depend the whole Law and the Prophets."* (Matthew 22:36-40)

Jesus told him that if you love God with all your heart, soul, and mind and love your neighbor as yourself, you will essentially be living a life that upholds God's Law. The Apostle Paul tells us the same thing:

> *...for <u>he who loves his neighbor has fulfilled the law</u>. For this, "You shall not commit adultery, you shall not murder, you shall not steal, you shall not covet," and if there is any other commandment, it is summed up in this saying, "You shall love your neighbor as yourself." <u>Love does no wrong to a neighbor; therefore love is the fulfillment of the law</u>.* (Romans 13:8b-10)

Let's look at this in terms of application. If we love God with all our heart, soul, and mind, we are not going to create a god in our own image that suits our lifestyle and sinful nature. We are going to desire to honor and worship the true and living God and seek to please Him by living according to His righteous standard. If we love our neighbor as ourselves, we will naturally not want to do anything that would violate God's commandments toward others. For example, we will not want to steal from our neighbor or covet anything our neighbor might have. Our love for God and others is what fuels our obedience to His Word, and in so doing, we fulfill the Law of God.

Jesus Came to Save Us from Our Sin

Now that we have looked at how we inherited the sin nature, let's go back to the Book of 1 John and continue with what John tells us regarding acts of sin. *If we say that we have not sinned, we make Him a liar and His word is not in us* (v. 10). Ouch, this really packs a punch! The word *sinned* in this verse is referring to our acts of sin. As briefly noted earlier, the root of all acts of sin is found in the sin nature. That's where all acts of unrighteousness stem from—the root. The fruit—behaviors that we manifest—of the sinful nature within us, are the acts of sin we commit. You can liken sin to a fruit-bearing tree. The sinful fruit produced comes from having a sinful root—the sin nature. John states that if we say we have not committed acts of sin, then we make God a liar, and God's Word is not in us. This is a very serious indictment. Why the severity in John's statement? If we do not admit we are sinners, we make God a liar because we are in fact, denying the entire reason He sent His Son Jesus to this world—to take the punishment for our sin. In Matthew 1:21, an angel of the Lord said to Joseph, *"She* (Mary) *will bear a Son; and you shall call His name Jesus, for He will save His people from their sins."* We also see that when John the Baptist was baptizing people in the Jordan River, he saw Jesus coming to him and said, *"Behold, the Lamb of God who takes away the sin of the world!"* (John 1:29). And in John 12:27, Jesus tells us in His own words that for this purpose—to be our sin-bearer on the cross—He came. Jesus's death was for the express purpose of saving us from our sins and the consequence thereof... eternal death. To deny this fact is to call God a liar. If we call God a liar, His Word can't be in us. The Bible tells us in John 1:1 that Jesus is the Word. If we refuse to acknowledge our sin, it is clear that Jesus is not in us; there is no need for Him.

Summary

A Christian, by definition, will acknowledge that he or she is a sinner. Without this acknowledgment, it is not possible to be a true believer and follower of our Lord Jesus Christ; it denies the entire reason God sent His Son to this earth. Jesus came for the express purpose of saving people from their sins. If you do not acknowledge that you are a sinner, you will never believe you need a Savior, and therefore, you will never think you need Jesus.

Chapter 3

A REPENTANT HEART

REPENTANCE IS A MAJOR THEME OF THE BIBLE. It was the message of many of the Old Testament prophets as they prophesied God's Word to the nation of Israel, and it's a vitally important message we see repeated many times in much of the New Testament. So what exactly is repentance? If a person repents, what are they repenting from? What is accomplished by repentance? Finally, is it necessary to repent if one professes to be a Christian? These are the questions we are going to answer as we learn why a repentant heart is necessary for the Christian.

The first time we see the word *repent* in the New Testament is in Matthew 3:2. John the Baptist was preaching in the wilderness of Judea, saying, *"Repent, for the kingdom of heaven is at hand."* The word *repent* in the Greek is *metanoeō*. It means to change one's mind. It comes from the word *meta*, meaning "after," implying "change" (Strong's G3340). It's where we get the English word *metamorphosis*. It implies a change from one thing to another. As we see the word *repent* in Scripture, it involves a heart of contrition, in which one turns away from sin and toward God.

It is important to note there is a difference between two related words: confess and repent. To confess means to say the same thing as another, i.e. to agree with, assent (Strong's G3670). When you confess to God, essentially you are saying you agree with God regarding His view on a matter. To repent means to turn in the opposite direction—away from sin and toward God. Repentance is a one-hundred-and-eighty-degree turn. It has two aspects to it: an inward change of heart and an outward change in behavior. When we repent of our sins, there should not only be a confession of those sins but there should be an intentional turning away from those sins. Repentance always includes confession, and it is always followed up with action. When we change our view on a matter, we have a change of heart, a change of mind. A change of heart will inevitably lead to a change in behavior. This is why John the Baptist, in Matthew 3:8, was exhorting his Jewish brethren to *"...bear fruit in keeping with repentance."* John was saying that since they had repented of their sinful behaviors, their lives should now reflect their changed hearts. A person who has repented of his or her sins will give evidence of a changed life (2 Corinthians 5:17; Galatians 5:19-23; James 2:14-26). When we truly repent, we will have an internal resolve and determination to turn away from our sins and toward God.

The second time we see the word *repent* in the New Testament is in Matthew 4:17. Jesus had recently been baptized and then led by the Spirit into the wilderness. It was there that He was tempted by Satan, yet did not sin (Hebrews 4:15). Shortly thereafter, we see Him beginning His earthly ministry in the same fashion as John the Baptist. Jesus said, *"Repent, for the kingdom of heaven is at hand."* Both John the Baptist and Jesus were telling their Jewish brethren to repent. Given that the first account of Jesus speaking in Matthew is a call to repent, two things are made evident. One, it is clear there is sin in our lives, and two, repentance is imperative.

We learned in the previous chapter that all have sinned and fallen short of the glory of God (Romans 3:23). This means there isn't a single one among us who hasn't sinned. We are sinners by nature and sinners by choice. The fact that we all commit acts of sin are the evidence for Jesus calling us to repent. Now let's take a look at why repentance for our sins is imperative.

Repent or Perish

If we remain in our sin, meaning we do not repent of our sins, there is a consequence.

> But *your iniquities have made a separation between you and your God*, and your sins have hidden His face from you so that He does not hear. (Isaiah 59:2)

> ...dealing out retribution to *those who do not know God* and to those who do not obey the gospel of our Lord Jesus. *These will pay the penalty of eternal destruction, away from the presence of the Lord* and from the glory of His power. (2 Thessalonians 1:8-9)

And in Luke 13:5, Jesus Himself said, *"unless you repent, you will all likewise perish."* These verses make it clear that our sin is what separates us from God. It not only separates us from God when we sin, but without repentance, sin will separate us from God eternally.

Let's look at a passage in the Book of Acts. When the Apostle Paul was in the province of Achaia during his second missionary journey, he gave a sermon while in Athens, Greece. He was brought to the Areopagus (a rock outcropping) by the Epicurean and Stoic philosophers who wanted to hear more about the new teaching of the gospel message that Paul was proclaiming. Paul stood in the midst of the Areopagus and began proclaiming the gospel of Christ to the crowd. Those present were primarily Gentiles who did not know the history of the Jewish people nor anything about their God. The people of Greece were idol worshippers and worshipped many gods. Since they did not know the Scriptures, Paul approached his message from the standpoint of God as Creator of the world and everything in it—a message they could understand based on what they saw and experienced in nature. Given their pagan customs of idolatry, Paul closed his message with this:

> *"Being then the children of God, we ought not to think that the Divine Nature* (his reference to God) *is like gold or silver or stone* (a reference to the idol images of their gods made by human hands), *an image formed by the art and thought of man. Therefore <u>having overlooked the times of ignorance, God is now declaring to men that all people everywhere should repent, because He has fixed a day in which He will judge the world in righteousness through a Man* (Jesus)</u> *whom He has appointed, having furnished proof to all men by raising Him from the dead."* (Acts 17:29-31)

This passage in Acts is a clear indication that the days of being ignorant about God are over. Ignorance of any kind can greatly impact our lives, but ignorance about God has the greatest impact. We see this even in the Old Testament. God said, *"My people are destroyed for lack of knowledge"* (Hosea 4:6). God told the Israelites that their lack of knowledge—ignorance of Him and His Word—is what was literally killing them and creating great iniquity among them. The word *destroyed* in Hosea 4:6 means to cease, to be cut off (Strong's H1820). Their lives were becoming a complete disaster because there was no knowledge of God in the land. As a result, they were destroyed. Scripture is clear that ignorance of God ultimately leads to our destruction.

As we turn our focus back to Acts 17, Paul tells us that God is declaring to men that all people everywhere should repent because there is coming a day in which Jesus Christ will judge mankind. If we do not repent, we will be judged as unrighteous and will be eternally separated from God. Non-repentance of our sins separates us from God because

God is holy, and in Him, there is no unrighteousness. Therefore, we must be holy and righteous to be in His presence. The only way we are declared righteous is by repenting of our sins and putting our faith in His Son.

As we keep in mind the definition of repentance—turning away from sin and toward God—it's important to point out that repentance and faith can be understood as two sides of the same coin. When you turn away from your sin, it means you've had a change of mind about your sin and thus, a change of mind about who Jesus Christ is and what He accomplished on your behalf. As you turn toward God, you are placing your faith in the finished work of His Son, Jesus Christ, as Lord and Savior. This is clearly seen in the Gospel of Mark. *Jesus came into Galilee, preaching the gospel of God, and [said], "The time is fulfilled, and the kingdom of God is at hand; repent and believe in the gospel"* (Mark 1:14-15). When you look at the relationship between repentance and reconciliation with God, and hence, eternal salvation, you are changing your mind from rejection of Christ and wanting to remain in your sin, to faith in Christ and walking in righteousness.

Christ, Our Substitute Sacrifice

Let's look a little more closely at how repentance and faith in Christ allow us to be declared righteous, thus bringing reconciliation between us and God.

From the beginning, God set into motion a plan of atonement for the sins of man—substitutionary sacrifice. We first see this in the Garden of Eden. In Genesis 3, after Adam and Eve sinned, they suddenly felt shame at their nakedness (Genesis 3:7); their open fellowship with God had just been severed. In their guilt and shame over violating God's command, Adam and Eve sewed fig leaves together to cover themselves. However, the coverings they made were neither sufficient to restore their broken fellowship with God nor cleanse them of their guilt. They had to come to God in His prescribed manner. After God confronted them with their sin, He made clothing from animal skins for Adam and his wife (Genesis 3:21). The garments God made allowed them to live in their new fallen environment, and more importantly, they were garments of His salvation that adequately covered the guilt of their sin, thus restoring their fellowship with God. For God to clothe them with animal skins implies that an animal had to give up its life. The animal was the substitute sacrifice for their sin.

The Bible tells us that without the shedding of blood, there is no forgiveness of sins (Hebrews 9:22). God's plan for atonement/remission of sins, as set forth from the beginning, requires the shedding of blood. God established sacrifice as His method for mankind to come back into right-standing with Him. This is clearly seen in the Book of Leviticus. The first seventeen chapters of Leviticus describe in great detail the requirements for making atonement for the sins of the people via animal sacrifices. The offerings and sacrifices were required by God as a way for the Jews to atone for their sins, and it was the method by which they were made right with Him. The only way for them to approach God and be in His presence was through sacrifice. Keep in mind, the sins being atoned for were not the sins of the animals, but rather, the sins of the people. The animals were the substitute. This substitutionary sacrificial system all pointed to what God would ultimately do—sacrifice His Son, the Lamb of God, who takes away the sin of the world (John 1:29).

The literal translation of the word *atonement* in Hebrew means to cover (Strong's H3722). Prior to Jesus's death, burial, and resurrection, animal sacrifices for sin had to be made continually (Hebrews 10:1) and could only cover, but not remove, the sins of man. Hebrews 10:4 states: *For it is impossible for the blood of bulls and goats to take away sins.* Therefore, for the sins of man to be removed, there had to be a greater sacrifice...a human sacrifice...a perfect, sinless human. Since the righteous judgment against sin is death, only one without sin can be a sufficient substitute sacrifice to remove the sins on behalf of others, and thus satisfy, the righteous demand of a holy God (Hebrews 2:17). Given that every human born since the time of Adam and Eve had been born with the sin nature, no one qualified except Jesus. His conception was not from the seed of man but by the Holy Spirit (Matthew 1:18). As such, He did not inherit the sin nature. He was the only One to ever meet the standard of God because He was God in human flesh (John 1:14; Colossians 2:9). Therefore, when Jesus—our substitute sacrificial Lamb—came, His blood was shed for our sins and His sacrifice was all-sufficient in that it actually *removed* our sins (Hebrews 10:12); it didn't just cover our sins. This means that Christ's sacrifice didn't merely pacify God's wrath toward sinful man, it appeased/satisfied God's wrath. As a result of Jesus's death and resurrection, animal sacrifices are no longer required. Jesus's sacrifice was sufficient for all sins; a sacrifice made once, for all people, for all time, when He offered up Himself.

By this will we have been sanctified through the offering of the body of Jesus Christ once for all. (Hebrews 10:10)

Reconciliation With God

The shedding of Jesus's blood is the "cure" for sin and the sin nature that resides within us. In other words, His sacrifice overcomes the sin nature and the effect it has on our lives. On the cross, the sins of man were heaped upon Jesus, the sinless, perfect sacrifice, a lamb unblemished and spotless (1 Peter 1:19). It is by His blood that the propitiation (appeasement/satisfaction of God's wrath) toward sinful mankind was made. All of humankind can now be made right with God through the shed blood of Jesus Christ. We learn in 2 Corinthians 5:18-21 that God reconciled us to Himself through Christ. Verse 21 tells us that God made Jesus, who knew no sin, to be sin on our behalf, so that we might become the righteousness of God in Him. Jesus is the answer to how all sinners—everyone—who fall short of God's righteous standard, can become reconciled to a holy God. When we repent of our sins and put our faith in Jesus Christ as our Lord and Savior, God imputes Christ's righteousness to us (Romans 4:11, 24). All our sins were put upon Christ as He hung on the cross, and in exchange, by repentance and through faith in Him, we get His righteousness. Wow! That is one deal that leans ever so undeservedly in our favor. How great a love our Father has for us! The Bible tells us in 2 Peter 3:9 that God does not wish for any to perish but for all to come to repentance. The truth of God's Word is that we will indeed perish and live eternally separated from Him if we do not repent. But if we repent of our sins and put our faith in Jesus Christ, we become the recipients of God's abundant, amazing grace. God no longer sees the sinful nature within us; He sees Christ's righteousness. As such, believers in the Lord Jesus Christ have everlasting life and assurance of entering God's kingdom (1 John 5:13).

I noted earlier the first part of Romans 6:23; *the wages of sin is death.* The remainder of that verse reads, *...but the free gift of God is eternal life in Jesus Christ our Lord.* God, because of His mercy and grace, has given us the most profound and precious gift. All we have to do is receive it. We receive it by repenting of our sins and putting our faith in His Son, Jesus Christ.

Summary

We are all sinners who have fallen short of God's righteous standard. Our sins, if not repented of, will eternally separate us from God. To repent of our sins is to turn away from our sins and toward God by putting our faith in Jesus Christ. It is through Christ alone that it is made possible for those who repent to have everlasting life. Only a person who has repented and placed his or her faith in the finished work of Jesus Christ can truly be a Christian.

Chapter 4

A Life Not Marked
by Habitual Sin

W E HAVE SEEN THAT ONE OF THE HALLMARKS
of true followers of Jesus Christ is an acknowledgment that
we are sinners. We also learned that repentance of our sins is necessary
for the Christian. When we repent, it doesn't mean we will automatically
stop sinning altogether. But it does mean we will turn away from our sins
and toward God. Given that we know we will sin again, what does that
mean in terms of habitual sin? Is it possible for a Christian to willfully
continue to sin as a lifestyle? To quote Romans 6:15: *What then?*
Shall we sin because we are not under the law but under grace? May it
never be! Let's take a look and see what we can learn about whether or
not a Christian can live a lifestyle of habitual sin. We will do so by
using the Book of 1 John 3:4-9 as our outline.

Can A Christian Live in Habitual Sin?

Everyone who practices sin also practices lawlessness; and sin
is lawlessness (1 John 3:4). To practice sin means to sin

habitually. We are told that if we habitually sin as a lifestyle, we also practice lawlessness. The Greek word for *lawlessness* is *anomia*. It means contempt and violation of law, iniquity, wickedness (Strong's G458). Essentially, the Apostle John is saying that those who make a practice of sin have no desire to be accountable to God and His laws.

Now let's look at 1 John 3:5-9.

> *5 You know that He appeared in order to take away sins; and in Him there is no sin. 6 No one who abides in Him sins; no one who sins has seen Him or knows Him. 7 Little children, make sure no one deceives you; the one who practices righteousness is righteous, just as He is righteous; 8 the one who practices sin is of the devil; for the devil has sinned from the beginning. The Son of God appeared for this purpose, to destroy the works of the devil. 9 No one who is born of God practices sin, because His seed abides in him; and he cannot sin, because he is born of God.*

As one reads these verses, it may prompt a response of, "wait...what?" We just learned in chapter two that 1 John 1:8 states, "If we say we have no sin, we are deceiving ourselves and the truth is not in us." Yet here we see the Apostle John saying that no one who abides in Him (Jesus) sins. Careful observation of the text in its proper context, along with the verb *sins* being in the active present tense, shows us that John is referring to an habitual practice of sin. Let's examine John's statements line-by-line.

You know that He appeared in order to take away sins; and in Him there is no sin (v. 5). The *He* and *Him* referred to in this verse is Jesus Christ. This statement says that as believers in Christ, we know that His purpose for coming to earth was to take away sins. As a quick reminder of what we learned in chapter three, to *take away sins* means that the sacrifice of Jesus on the cross was sufficient to satisfy the wrath of God toward mankind for the transgressions committed against Him. The second part of verse 5 reiterates that there is absolutely no sin found in Jesus. Jesus did not inherit the sin nature, nor did He ever commit a single act of sin. This drives home the point that Jesus's sacrifice was sufficient to take away our sins. Only the shed blood of a perfect, sinless human could satisfy the righteous demand of a holy God.

No one who abides in Him sins; no one who sins has seen Him or knows Him (v. 6). An explanation of what it means to abide in Christ will be covered more thoroughly in a later chapter. For our purposes here, only a short explanation of the word *abide* is all that is necessary. The Greek word for *abide* is *menō*. It means to remain, not to depart, to continue to be present (Strong's G3306). Let's also look at the words *seen* and *knows*. The word *seen* in the Greek is *horaō*. It means to see with the mind, to perceive, to know, to discern clearly (Strong's G3708). The word *knows* in the Greek is *ginōskō*. It means to get a knowledge of, to understand, to get acquainted with (Strong's G1097). John is saying that as believers in Jesus who abide in Him, we remain with Him as followers and do not depart from Him. Therefore, we will not make a practice of sin. If we do, then it is clear we are not remaining with Him. If we are not remaining with Jesus, then the implication is that we have departed from Him. As someone who has departed from Him, that person is not able to clearly discern Him for who He is and does not have an understanding or knowledge of Him.

Little children, make sure no one deceives you; the one who practices righteousness is righteous, just as He is righteous (v. 7). John begins this verse by cautioning believers to be on the lookout for those who might deceive us. He tells us that those who practice righteousness are righteous, just as He (Jesus) is righteous. The word *righteous* in the Greek is *diakaios*. It means observing divine laws; keeping the commands of God (Strong's G1342). Vine's states: In the New Testament it denotes "righteous" as right conduct, judged whether by the Divine standard, or according to human standards, of what is right. Said of God, it designates the perfect agreement between His nature and His acts [in which He is the standard for all men] (Vine's Expository Dictionary). God's expressed actions are a demonstration of His righteous nature. Since

Jesus always did the will of the Father (John 6:38, 14:31), there was complete agreement between God's nature and Jesus's acts. Jesus is God's righteousness because there is no sin in Him (1 John 3:5). Therefore, if we make a practice of obeying God's Law, we, who have the righteousness of God in us, via the Holy Spirit through Jesus Christ, are in fact, righteous. Our righteous actions are a demonstration of Christ's nature within us. As a reminder from the previous chapter, Jesus's righteousness is imputed to us the moment we repent of our sins and put our faith in Him as our Lord and Savior.

As we move along through the text, we are struck with a hard truth. The first sentence of verse 8 says, *...the one who practices sin is of the devil; for the devil has sinned from the beginning.* This is one of those truths in which John reduces the facts of the matter to their irreducible minimum; he bottom-lines it for us. He tells us that the one who practices sin, meaning it is one's lifestyle, is of the devil. The devil has sinned from the beginning; this is his nature. If we willfully continue in sin, we are expressing his nature. There are no shades of gray here. As a believer in the Lord Jesus Christ, one cannot practice an habitual lifestyle of sin. If we do, God's Word is clear—we are of the devil. Now I understand how that statement can go against the grain of one's pride, even for those who claim to be Christians. It tends to spark a knee-jerk reaction of offense. Before I became a Christian, though I hadn't heard this verse specifically, I had heard enough to know that my sinful lifestyle was not pleasing to God. And whenever I was reminded of it, it grated against my pride and sensibilities. I blew it off with a, "Yeah, right!" attitude. Rather than deciding to obey God, I made a god in my own image who agreed with my behavior because I wanted to continue in sin. But a lifestyle of habitual sin is an act of direct rebellion against God and His righteous standard.

Let's look a little more closely at what it means to be *of the devil*. The Greek word for *devil* is *diabolos*. It means prone to slander, accusing falsely (Strong's G1228). Vine's states: It is one of the names of Satan; being the malignant enemy of God and man, he accuses man to God

(Vine's Expository Dictionary). We see that the devil, who is Satan, is an enemy of God. Therefore, one can conclude from this statement that if you are *of the devil*, you are acting in accordance with Satan, who is God's enemy and acts in opposition to Him. If you are in opposition to God, you cannot be *for* God or *of* God; you are of the devil. The first part of verse 8, in principle, can be understood as the one who practices sin is in direct opposition to God.

The second sentence of verse 8 states, *The Son of God appeared for this purpose, to destroy the works of the devil.* We already saw in verse 5 that Jesus came in order to take away sins. Now we are given another reason He came. The word *destroy* in the Greek is *lyō*. It means to loose one bound, i.e. to release from bonds, set free (Strong's G3089). In Scripture, we see several ways in which Satan works. He makes accusations against God's people (Zechariah 3:1; Revelation 12:10), he tempts us with evil (1 Thessalonians 3:5), and he entices believers to sin (2 Corinthians 11:3), just to name a few. Unless we are born again, we are still slaves to the sin nature, and therefore, have no power over the works of the devil. Jesus came to set us free from that bondage; He triumphed over Satan's power (Colossians 2:15). If our identity is in Christ, then we are loosed from Satan's power over us. This means that for the Christian, sin is a choice; we are no longer slaves to the sin nature (Romans 6:6).

The Unrighteous Will Not Inherit The Kingdom of God

The New Testament lists habitual sins and states that those committing them will not inherit the kingdom of God. These can be found in Galatians 5:19-21 and 1 Corinthians 6:9-10. Both of these epistles were written by the Apostle Paul. Let's take a look at both passages.

Now the deeds of the flesh are evident, which are: immorality, impurity, sensuality, idolatry, sorcery, enmities, strife, jealousy, outbursts of anger, disputes, dissensions, *factions, envying, drunkenness, carousing, and things like these, of which I have forewarned you, that <u>those who practice such things will not inherit the kingdom of God</u>.* (Galatians 5:19-21)

Or do you not know that <u>the unrighteous will not inherit the kingdom of God</u>? Do not be deceived; neither fornicators, nor idolaters, nor adulterers, nor effeminate, nor homosexuals, nor thieves, nor the covetous, nor drunkards, nor revilers, nor swindlers, will inherit the kingdom of God. (1 Corinthians 6:9-10)

Keep in mind that though Paul listed specific habitual sins that were commonplace among the two groups of people to whom he was writing, habitual practices of sin are not limited to what is noted in these two passages. This is evident based on what Paul said in Galatians, *...and <u>things like these</u>, of which I have forewarned you.* However, Paul made it clear that of the specific sins listed here, if one commits these sins habitually, he or she will not inherit the kingdom of God. A person living in habitual sin will be eternally separated from God.

Given my personal experience with habitual sin, I am going to briefly touch on two of the sins listed in both the Galatians and Corinthians passages: immorality and fornication. Immorality and fornication cover a multitude of sexual sins. The bottom line is that the only sexual lifestyle ordained by God is the sexual union between a man and a woman within the bonds of marriage. Jesus confirmed this when He answered the Pharisees' question in Matthew 19 after they asked, "is it lawful for a man to divorce his wife for any reason at all?" Contained within His answer, Jesus quoted Old Testament Scripture from Genesis 1:27 and 2:24. He confirmed that since the beginning of time, God's plan regarding the sacred bond of marriage was one man and one woman for life because God has joined them together as one flesh.

Not long after I met the man with whom I had my first long-term relationship, he and I began a sexual relationship. Though I felt guilty at times for sexually engaging with him given that we weren't married, apart from those fleeting moments of guilt, I never really had a reason nor a desire to stop. Eventually, we moved in together and continued our sexual relationship. What is so heartbreaking to me now is that I didn't give any attention to the inner voice within me that alerted me that what I was doing was sinful. Though the Spirit of God was convicting me, I chose to disregard those promptings and suppress God's Truth. I didn't care enough about the God who created me to learn more about Him and what He had to say about what I was doing. I can't recall wondering, even for a moment, if He had a plan and purpose for my life that was different than the one I was choosing. Oh yes, I continued to go to church, thinking I was a "Christian." After all, why would God create me with sexual desires and passions if He didn't want me to engage sexually with another person? Well, this is a great example of how easily we are deceived. We can go to church, claim to be followers of Christ, yet be so disconnected from Him that we don't even realize we are sinning against Him. This is why it is so important to know God, know His Word, and know His Truth.

The idea of a sexual relationship only within the confines of marriage, to most people, seems like an antiquated notion. Sex outside the bonds of marriage is so commonplace today that hardly anyone questions the possibility that it could be a sin. If one doesn't view it as sin, one certainly wouldn't view it as a lifestyle that would prevent a person from entering the kingdom of God. As long as people create a god in their own image like I once did—a god who turns a blind eye to their sin, who accepts their sin, or who doesn't consider anything other than the true and living God's righteous standard as sin—then all is well, right? We can keep living our lives the way we please and don't have to worry that what we are doing is sinful. In fact, we can become so far removed from the notion that a lifestyle of sin is not acceptable to God, that it doesn't even cross our moral radar as anything less than "normal" or "healthy." With that type of thinking, a professing "Christian" might also deem it acceptable by God Almighty! It's very easy to dull our conscience in those areas of our lives in which our personal desires and wants are more important to us than knowing and obeying God. We are warned of this distorted type of thinking in Scripture. In Peter's second epistle, he wrote to Christians stating that we are to be found spotless and blameless when the Lord returns. He refers to Paul's letters, stating, *...in which are some things hard to understand, which the untaught and the unstable distort, as they do also the rest of the Scriptures, to their own destruction* (2 Peter 3:16). Sadly, I know this to be true because I was someone who once did exactly that; I distorted Scripture. I chose to only see God as a God of love, mercy, and grace because those are His attributes that worked well with everything I wanted to do. Therefore, in my distorted way of thinking, whatever I thought, He thought. Whatever I chose to do, He agreed. Whatever I considered to be the path to life eternal, it was so. I feel like I need a big flashing neon sign right here: Warning! Warning! Warning! *Do not be deceived, God is not mocked; for whatever a man sows, this he will also reap* (Galatians 6:7).

God's Love Demands Justice

There are many professing "Christians" who live lifestyles of sin. But rather than repent of their sin, there are countless ways in which they choose to justify it. In so doing, one might hear statements such as, "I know God's hand is in this," or "I really feel like the Holy Spirit is leading me to...," implying that God is directing them to engage in or commit sin. I recall these types of phrases coming out of my own mouth at times when what I wanted, and presumed that God also wanted for me, was more important to me than actually getting to know who He is and obeying Him. I would even pray for a desire of my heart that if granted, would only draw me further away from God. As I look back, the arrogance and audacity of my own heart blow me away. The Bible tells us in Jeremiah 17:9, *The heart is more deceitful than all else and is desperately sick; who can understand it?* How true that is. When we are ignorant of God's Word, we are so vulnerable and can be easily deceived by the lusts of this world. Regardless of what one may believe to be true, I can assure you that God will never bless that which He has denounced. He can't. God is perfectly righteous and holy and will never lead us down a path of sin. If we live a life of sin, we can never expect God to condone it, nor look favorably on us, nor empower us with His Holy Spirit to live a lifestyle that He opposes. Oh, we may justify our sinful behavior as being fine with God since the proclivities we have toward certain sins can be arrogantly rationalized in our minds as, "He made me this way." But make no mistake, God cannot bless sin, nor can He disregard it.

Another common phrase often made by professing "Christians" engaged in a lifestyle of sin, or perhaps defending a loved one's lifestyle of sin, is, "I see God as a loving God and He would never send anyone to hell." That statement alone is evidence they truly do not know God. It displays an ignorance of the seriousness of sin, and it assumes we bear no responsibility in our eternal destination. There are two things to keep in mind. Yes, God is a loving God. But God is also just. A God of love cannot be anything less than a God of justice—One who upholds His righteous standard. If you are unfamiliar with God's written Word, then naturally, the god you believe in will be whatever you have determined him/her/it to be in your own mind. God is certainly a loving God; as an outpouring of His great love and mercy toward all mankind, He made a way for all who repent of their sin and put their faith in His Son, to live with Him eternally. His love for us is the very reason He upholds His righteous standard. He would not be a loving God if He allowed us to sin without consequence. God desires to be in fellowship with us and our sin separates us from Him. Therefore, He chastens us (Hebrews 12:6) for our good, so that we may share His holiness (Hebrews 12:10).

True love demands justice. It's why we feel a sense of relief when someone who has deliberately harmed an innocent child or animal is found guilty and receives a just punishment. It's why we are glad to learn when someone who has lived a life of crime is finally held accountable.

It's our love for innocent victims that calls us to demand and execute justice for those who violate our laws. We also see this concept played out every day within our own families. A parent's love for their children is the very reason they correct, chasten, and punish bad behavior. I would think that for most parents, Christian or not, the goal for their children is that they grow up to become productive members of society—well-mannered people, doing the right thing, and having a love for others. Well, that's God's goal for us too. This is why He upholds His standards. He wants us to become productive members of His family, using the gifts and talents He has given us to serve others in love, to walk in righteousness, and to bear the image of His Son.

We must always remember that anything we do will never escape God's notice (Hebrews 4:13). We are all accountable to Him whether we believe it or not (Leviticus 5:17). Many of us desire God's blessings upon our lives. But how many of us also desire to be under God's authority? You can't have one without the other. To fully reap God's blessings, we must submit to His rule and His Lordship. The idea of submitting to anyone's authority can oftentimes cause us to take a defensive posture. But God's rule and authority benefit us; His laws are for our protection and our highest good (Joshua 1:8; Psalm 119:1, 165). If we esteem God's authority and treasure His Law in our hearts, obedience to God's Word not only becomes the desire of our hearts, but His Word serves as a preventive that keeps us from sinning. The psalmist says, *Your word I have treasured in my heart, that I may not sin against You* (Psalm 119:11). Obedience is key to receiving God's greatest blessings (Luke 5:4-7).

No One Who is Born of God Practices Sin

Let's now shift our focus back to where we left off in 1 John 3. *No one who is born of God practices sin, because His seed abides in him; and he cannot sin, because he is born of God* (v. 9). The phrase *born of God* is similar to the phrase *born again* found in John 3:3, which we will examine more thoroughly in the next chapter. The word *born* in the Greek is *gennaō*. It has both a literal meaning and a metaphorical meaning. The literal meaning is to be physically born, referring to men who have fathered children; of women giving birth to children. The metaphorical meaning is that of God making mankind His sons and daughters through faith in Christ's work (Strong's G1080). Anyone who is *born of God* is born into God's family. This is accomplished through repentance of our sins and faith in the finished work of Jesus Christ. It is through faith in God's Son that we become God's children (Galatians 3:26).

First John 3:9 tells us that anyone who is born into God's family does not make a practice of sin. The reason is that God's seed, the person of Jesus Christ, through the Holy Spirit, is now residing in that person. Christ's righteousness is now a part of that person's DNA, so to speak. And the job of the Holy Spirit, once indwelling you, is to guide you into all Truth (John 16:13) and bring glory to Jesus (John 16:14). As such, a person who is born of God will no longer be comfortable living a lifestyle of sin because doing so goes against God's Truth and does not glorify His Son. If the Holy Spirit is indwelling you, His job of guiding you into Truth and bringing glory to Jesus will begin to override your sinful proclivities. You will always be unsettled or ill-at-ease when going down a path of habitual sin. This is not to say a Christian will never sin. A Christian will sin. We saw that in chapter two. What is being said here is that Christians will not habitually sin as a lifestyle. The Holy Spirit living within us is now the stronghold that directs our steps; it is not our fleshly desires (Galatians 2:20). Yes, Christians still live in a body made of flesh, but no longer do the desires of our bodies guide our mind, our will, or our emotions. It is now the Holy Spirit living within us. And here's the clincher, a person who is born of God no longer even has a desire to let sin rule over him or her. As Christians, the desires of our hearts change because the Holy Spirit living within us causes us to want to live a life pleasing to God (2 Corinthians 5:9). Christians give the reigns of governance over our mind, our will, and emotions to the Holy Spirit so that we are Spirit-led. The reason the Apostle John states, *and he cannot sin, because he is born of God*, is because anyone who is born of God will no longer be able to live a lifestyle of sin and be comfortable with it. A lifestyle of sin goes against the perfect righteousness of God and the two are incompatible.

God is Faithful to Cleanse Us From All Unrighteousness

Now the good news! Whew! *If we confess our sins, He is faithful and righteous to forgive us our sins and to cleanse us from all unrighteousness* (1 John 1:9). What a wonderful verse of Scripture. I love it! Though we are all sinners, we have a promise of God—a guarantee—that if we confess our sins to Him, He is faithful and righteous to forgive us our sins. And the good news doesn't stop there. It goes on to say in the following two verses:

> *My little children, I am writing these things to you so that you may not sin. And if anyone sins, we have an Advocate with the Father, Jesus Christ the righteous; and He Himself is the propitiation for our sins; and not for ours only, but also for those of the whole world.* (1 John 2:1-2)

John is saying that when we do sin—and we will—we have an Advocate (Jesus—the perfect, righteous Lawyer) who pleads our case to God the Father. Our Advocate is the propitiation for our sins. This means that because of His sinless nature, Jesus was the One and only person who was able to appease the Father's wrath toward us. He was the perfect substitute sacrifice. John goes on to say, *not just for our sins,* meaning those who are already believers and followers of Jesus Christ, but also *for those of the whole world.* The good news is that Jesus Christ is the propitiation for anyone who believes in Him and surrenders his or her life to Him, honoring and obeying Him as Lord and Savior.

Summary

A Christian will not make a habit of a sinful lifestyle. For all true followers of the Lord Jesus Christ, the Holy Spirit indwells us and actively alerts us when we fall into sin. As a result, we will no longer be comfortable living in habitual sin. It will grieve our hearts. We will begin to see our sin the way God sees it—so grievous that His Son had to die for it. As such, we will either never go down the path of habitual sin, or if we do, the Holy Spirit will frustrate our course with God's Truth to the point that we will resolve to put an end to it, repent, and turn back to walking in obedience.

Chapter 5

BORN AGAIN

I REMEMBER AS A KID HEARING THE WORDS *BORN again*. I had no idea at a young age what those words meant but they seemed to carry a negative connotation. I had heard statements such as, "Oh, so and so is one of those types of Christians, one of those *born again* kind." It was as if being born again was its own sect of Christianity or some type of separate "religion." In my young mind, it conjured up thoughts of people who were "out of control" or flagrant in how they expressed their passion for the Lord. I'm not sure why I had those thoughts. I certainly hadn't been exposed to people who behaved that way. But there were a number of preachers on television at that time who were quite boisterous in their preaching. I think I just assumed they were probably those "born again types."

As the years passed and I became an adult, though I rarely heard the phrase *born again*, it still brought up the same thoughts as in my childhood. Being of the Catholic faith, it seemed a sharp contrast from what I witnessed in people who attended Catholic churches. On the one hand, I envisioned people who were born again as being demonstrative and a little "crazy," and people who were Catholic as more stoic and "together." Given what I thought it meant versus who I saw myself to be, it didn't seem like anything I wanted to become.

What is notable about my assumptions is that they were antithetical to the true meaning of being born again. In 1 Corinthians 14, the Apostle Paul was speaking to the Corinthian Church regarding the gifts of the Holy Spirit. In verse 40, he said, *"But all things must be done properly and in an orderly manner."* The Bible also tells us that self-control is one of the characteristics of the nine-fold fruit of the Spirit (Galatians 5:23). The thoughts I had made up in my mind and the behaviors I had seen on TV were in direct opposition to what would be evident in a person who is born again.

I don't know why the phrase *born again* conjures up misconceptions in the minds of non-believers and even some professing Christians. It also seems the more we hear these words, the more "ordinary" they become. Sadly, our familiarity with them tends to diminish the weight of what they truly mean. To be born again is more powerful than most of us realize. These are not just two words to casually describe a person. Being born again is the crux of the Christian faith! Without it, there is no Christian faith. As something so vital and important to Christianity, it's puzzling to me how so many of us who grew up in the church had no idea what it meant. Well, let's change that. Let's take a look at what it means to be born again.

The phrases *born again, born of the Spirit, born of God,* and *born of Him* all mean the same thing—a spiritual birth. The word *born* in the Greek is *gennaō.* Put simply, it means to be born. It can be used in two ways: one is to denote a physical birth, and the second is metaphorical, denoting causing something to arise (Strong's G1080). The word *again* is *anōthen.* It means from above, from a higher place, of things which come from heaven or God (Strong's G509). Putting these two words together, *gennaō anōthen* means to be born/arisen from a higher place. As we take a look at the narrative in the Gospel of John in which Jesus tells us that we must be born again, we will draw the same conclusion; *born again* denotes a spiritual birth that comes from God, by His Holy Spirit.

Jesus Speaks With Nicodemus

John 3 tells the story of a conversation between a man named Nicodemus and Jesus. Nicodemus was a Pharisee and came to Jesus by night to speak with Him. Jesus told Nicodemus that unless one is born again, he cannot see the kingdom of God (John 3:3). Nicodemus then responded:

> *"How can a man be born when he is old? He cannot enter a second time into his mother's womb and be born, can he?" Jesus answered, "Truly, truly, I say to you, unless one is born of water and the Spirit he cannot enter into the kingdom of God. That which is born of the flesh is flesh, and that which is born of the Spirit is spirit. Do not be amazed that I said to you, 'You must be born again.' The wind blows where it wishes and you hear the sound of it, but do not know where it comes from and where it is going; so is everyone who is born of the Spirit." (John 3:4-8)*

Nicodemus, like all Jews living during the time of Jesus, believed he was guaranteed entrance into heaven based on his Jewish lineage. God had made a covenant with Israel, and Nicodemus, being born into the Jewish bloodline, was part of that covenant. So when Jesus told him that unless one is born again, he cannot see (v. 3) nor enter (v. 5) the kingdom of God, it took Nicodemus by surprise, and he questioned Jesus as to what He meant.

Based on Nicodemus's question regarding entering his mother's womb for a second time, we observe that Jesus was not referring to a physical birth when He said that one must be born again. He was referring to a spiritual birth. Jesus made that clear when He said, *"That which is born of the flesh is flesh, and that which is born of the Spirit is spirit."*

Before we explore this passage of Scripture, let's do a quick review of what we learned in chapter two regarding being born with a sin nature so that we understand why Jesus said, *"You must be born again."* We are born with a sin nature because of what took place in the Garden of Eden. Adam and Eve sinned by eating the fruit of the tree of the knowledge of good and evil—the one tree of which God had forbidden them to eat. The moment Adam ate, through him, sin entered the world. As a direct result of his sin, death also entered. The Spirit within Adam and Eve died in the sense that it became corrupted by the intrusion of sin, and their perfect fellowship with God was broken. From that point forward, all humanity, except for Jesus Christ, has been born with a sin nature. Therefore, in order for the consequences of sin and death to be overturned, a rebirth of our spirit is required to restore our spiritual condition. Then, and only then, is our fellowship with God restored, and we are granted eternal life.

Born of Water and The Spirit

Let's now go back to our passage in John 3. In verse 5, *born of water and the Spirit* are coupled together. There are several interpretations of what Jesus meant when He said, "born of water and the Spirit." I will briefly cover a few of them to help provide you with a better understanding.

Baptismal Regeneration is the name given to the doctrine held by some denominations in which salvation is linked to baptism; meaning, you have to be baptized (born of water) in order to be saved (born of the Spirit). This doctrine is quickly ruled out because it does not explain what occurred with the thief on the cross. Luke 23:39-43 is where we see this narrative. At Jesus's crucifixion, He was hung on a cross between two thieves. One thief said, "Jesus, remember me when You come into Your kingdom!" Jesus then said to him, "Truly I say to you, today you shall be with Me in Paradise." The thief on the cross had no time to be baptized, and yet, Jesus told him that *today* he would be with Him in Paradise. Also, Nicodemus would not know of Christian baptism as Jesus had not yet instructed His disciples to baptize those who come to believe in Him. It wasn't until after His resurrection, when Jesus appeared to His disciples on a mountain in Galilee, that He told them to baptize those whom they make disciples (Matthew 28:19).

We also see in 1 Corinthians 1:17, Paul said, *"For Christ did not send me to baptize, but to preach the gospel, not in cleverness of speech, so that the cross of Christ would not be made void."* If a person's salvation was dependent upon baptism, Paul would have said something very different, and Paul's goal during his missionary journeys would have been very different. If Paul believed that salvation was linked to baptism, then he, as well as Jesus during His earthly ministry, would have baptized as many people as possible.

Some believe that "born of water" is a metaphor for the Word of God. Ephesians 5:26 tells us that one can be cleansed by the *washing of the water of the word*. With that in mind, "born of water and the Spirit" refers to being born again, as accomplished by the written Word of God, together with the workings of the Holy Spirit. But it is unlikely that Nicodemus would have associated "born of water" with the Word of God. Also, the *washing of the water of the word* found in Ephesians is in the context of sanctification. God's Word sanctifies us, it has a cleansing effect on our hearts and minds.

There are two more highly held views. Some believe that "born of water and the Spirit" refers to two types of birth. "Born of water" is viewed as a reference to physical birth, such as when a woman's water breaks just before giving birth. "Born of the Spirit" is viewed as a reference to spiritual birth—a rebirth of the spirit which comes from God, by His Holy Spirit. This possibility carries some weight given what Jesus said in verse 6, *"That which is born of the flesh is flesh, and that which is born of the Spirit is spirit."* This statement indicates that Jesus is speaking of two types of births that are separate and distinct. Given the context of Nicodemus's question about entering his mother's womb a second time, and the sentence structure in John 3:5 in which a conjunction is used (the word *and*, indicating one thing occurs and then another), this seems a plausible conclusion. This indicates that only after a physical birth is it possible to be born a second time in which a spiritual birth takes place. True as that may be, it is rather self-evident, and *born again* (v. 3) seems to be synonymous with *born of water and the Spirit* (v. 5). The Greek text, *gennaō anōthen*—to be born/arisen from a higher place—indicates a singular action. Also, water is never referred to in this same fashion elsewhere in Scripture.

Others postulate that "born of water and the Spirit" refers to spiritual regeneration. In this manner, the regenerative nature and role—cleansing and purifying—of the Holy Spirit, is that which describes a singular birth of the spirit. This is based on Ezekiel 36:25-27.

> *Then **I** will sprinkle clean water on you, and you will be clean; **I** will cleanse you from all your filthiness and from all your idols. Moreover, **I** will give you a new heart and put a new spirit within you; and **I** will remove the heart of stone from your flesh and give you a heart of flesh. **I** will put My Spirit within you and cause you to walk in My statutes, and you will be careful to observe My ordinances.*

We also see in Psalm 51:2, a reference to being cleansed from sin by washing. David was speaking to God and said,

> *"<u>Wash</u> me thoroughly from my iniquity <u>and cleanse me</u> from my sin."*

Taking into account the passage in Ezekiel and Psalm 51:2, "born of water and the Spirit" strongly suggests a washing of regeneration and renewal/rebirth of the spirit, especially in light of John 3:10 in which

Jesus answered Nicodemus, saying, *"Are you the teacher of Israel and do not understand these things?"* Jesus was clearly holding Nicodemus, a high-ranking religious leader of the Jewish people, to some accountability of what is written in Old Testament Scripture regarding the concept of being born of water and the Spirit.

Though there are differing views on what is meant by the phrase, "born of water and the Spirit," one thing is clear, only God can bring forth a spiritual birth. As seen in Ezekiel 36:25-27, it is God who cleanses us; it is God who gives us a new heart and puts His Spirit within us. To be born again is strictly a work of His doing.

> *He saved us, not on the basis of deeds which we have done in righteousness, but according to His mercy, by the washing of regeneration and renewing by the Holy Spirit.* (Titus 3:5)

> *"...to those who believe in His (Jesus) name, who were born, not of blood nor of the will of the flesh nor of the will of man, but of God.* (John 1:12-13)

These verses make it clear that a spiritual birth can only come from God. We cannot achieve it through any works of our own. In our flesh, we can only bring forth that which is flesh. To be born spiritually is a work of God and nothing less. It is God who regenerates our spirit; it is God who makes our spirits alive (Ephesians 2:4-5).

You Must Be Born Again

In light of what we have learned, if one professes to be a Christian, is a spiritual birth necessary? Absolutely! Of this, there is no doubt. Let's look again at Jesus's words. In verse 3, He said to Nicodemus, *"Truly, truly, I say to you, unless one is born again he cannot see the kingdom of God."* Then in verse 5, Jesus said, *"Truly, truly, I say to you, unless*

one is born of water and the Spirit he cannot enter the kingdom of God."
Jesus let Nicodemus know, in no uncertain terms, that he would not see,
nor enter, God's kingdom unless he had a spiritual birth. Jesus wanted
Nicodemus to grasp the fact that entering heaven would require more
than his Jewish lineage. He had to have a second birth—a rebirth of
the Spirit—to enter God's kingdom. Furthermore, as we look at verse
7, Jesus said, *"Do not be amazed that I said to you, 'You must be born
again.'"* The Greek word for the verb *must* is *dei*. It means it is necessary; a necessity in reference to what is required to attain some end
(Strong's G1163). Jesus Himself told Nicodemus that he *must* be born
again. There is no other way to interpret the meaning of the word *must*
other than what it actually means. Being born again is, without a doubt,
a necessary requirement for entering God's kingdom. If you are a professing Christian but have not been born again, meaning you have not
had a spiritual birth, Jesus's words are clear:

> *"Truly, truly, I say to you, unless one is born of water and
> the Spirit he cannot enter into the kingdom of God. ...<u>You
> must be born again.</u>"* (John 3:5-7)

Born Again by Faith

So how does one obtain a spiritual birth? We'll answer this question
by looking further through the same narrative in John 3. Jesus was still
speaking with Nicodemus about being born again and said this:

> *As Moses lifted up the serpent in the wilderness, even
> so must the son of Man be lifted up; so that whoever
> believes will in Him have eternal life. For God so loved
> the world, that He gave His only begotten Son, that who-
> ever believes in Him shall not perish, but have eternal life.*
> (John 3:14-16)

In verses 14 & 15, Jesus was referring back to the Old Testament Book of Numbers. He took Nicodemus to a specific time in their history when Moses made a bronze serpent for the Israelites.

> *And Moses made a bronze serpent and set it on the standard; and it came about, that if a serpent bit any man, when he looked to the bronze serpent, he lived.* (Numbers 21:9)

The verses leading up to verse 9 give us a little of the backstory. This passage takes place as the Israelites were wandering through the desert after leaving Egypt. They regularly grumbled and complained during their desert experience as they often felt discouraged. They did not have any of the foods they were used to, nor was there an ample supply of water. The Israelites assumed they would die in the desert. Here we see yet again, in their unbelief, they murmured against God and Moses for bringing them out of Egypt. Given their continued lack of faith in God to provide for their needs, the Lord sent fiery serpents that bit them so that many people of Israel died (v. 6). Upon realizing their sin of speaking out against God and Moses, the people asked Moses to intercede with the Lord on their behalf. After having done so, the Lord told Moses, *"Make a fiery serpent, and set it on a standard* (a signal pole)*; and it shall come about, that everyone who is bitten, when he looks at it, he will live"* (v. 8).

So why this passage? Why did Jesus refer to this Scripture and how does it relate to what He was saying to Nicodemus? Let's break down what transpired in the wilderness. The people spoke out against God and Moses, and God sent judgment. As a result of the judgment, the Israelites recognized their sin and knew they needed forgiveness. They pleaded with Moses as he was the mediator between them and God. God then offered a remedy for their transgression. The remedy was such that the Israelites had to trust that simply looking at the serpent on the standard would allow them to live. In other words, if they trusted in the solution, they would be cured of their disease which was caused by their sin. The Israelites had to admit they had a disease (sin) and that the disease had a consequence (death). But if they looked up at the serpent on the standard (believed in the cure), they would be saved from death. Wow, talk about something that on the surface sounds completely ridiculous to our ears! God took human logic and turned it upside down. This reminds me of what the Apostle Paul wrote: *But God has chosen the foolish things of the world to shame the wise* (1 Corinthians 1:27). The Israelites were probably looking at each other with puzzled stares wondering how looking at the serpent on the end of the standard could cure anything, let alone save them from death. But that was the remedy. Their cure in this particular situation didn't require seeking a doctor's solution for their disease, nor any kind of self-help "pull-yourself-up-by-the-bootstraps" strategy. The Israelites could not do anything based on their own merit to cure their disease. Their cure was completely based on their faith in what God instructed them to do. For them to live, they had to come to God, God's way.

Jesus used this passage in Numbers 21 to help Nicodemus understand how it is that a person is born spiritually. He demonstrated to Nicodemus that based on the principle of faith, a spiritual birth takes place. One must first admit that he or she has a disease (a sin problem) and that the disease has a consequence (death). But if one looks up at the raised standard (Jesus's finished work on the cross in which He took the punishment for our sin), then by faith (believing in Him and what He accomplished on our behalf), he or she will be saved from death and have eternal life.

We are born again, meaning we are born spiritually, when we realize we have a sin problem and believe that our corrupt spiritual condition can only be overcome by putting our faith in the finished work of Jesus Christ. Only then are we justified and declared righteous, and will not perish in our sins but have eternal life (Romans 3:21-26).

For God so loved the world, that He gave His only begotten Son, that whoever believes in Him shall not perish, but have eternal life. (John 3:16)

Keep in mind that the meaning of the word *believe* in John 3:16 is not simply an acknowledgment that Jesus Christ existed. As noted in the Definition of Terms, the word *believe* in this verse means to fully surrender to, adhere to, rely upon, and put one's trust in. To be born spiritually means we believe, by faith, in what Jesus Christ accomplished for us on the cross. We believe that only Jesus can overcome the sin nature within us; He is the solution for our sin problem. By His death and through His resurrection—His power over sin and death—we are now in right-standing before a holy God. And since Jesus was raised from death to life, we too will be raised from death to eternal life (Romans 6:4; 1 Corinthians 15:42, 44).

I love what Ephesians 2:8 tells us. *For by grace you have been saved through faith; and that not of yourselves, it is the gift of God.* Let's read this verse again but this time with a little amplification.

> *For by grace*—God's unmerited favor toward us, in which He, out of His great love for us and desire that we be reconciled to Him, sent His only begotten Son to earth to take the punishment for our sins
>
> *you have been saved*—from eternal death; from eternal separation from God
>
> *through faith*—believing in Jesus Christ as our sin-bearer;
>
> *and that not of yourselves*—we cannot earn our salvation; it's nothing we have done, it's everything that Christ has done,

> *it is the gift of God*—salvation by faith is nothing we
> can purchase or earn, but like any gift, we must receive it.

We are born again when we accept God's precious and gracious gift of salvation and put our faith in the finished work of our Lord and Savior, Jesus Christ.

The Holy Spirit Within—Our Assurance of Everlasting Life

We have learned how it is that a person becomes born again. Now what? What happens to us after our spiritual birth? When we repent of our sins and put our faith in Jesus Christ, our spiritual birth is inaugurated, so to speak. The Holy Spirit of God is birthed within our spirit and resides within us. The Spirit of God cannot enter a person who has only been born once. As we learned in a prior chapter, we are born with a sin nature and our bodies are made of corruptible, sinful flesh. Unless we have been cleansed by the blood of Jesus Christ, in which a spiritual birth takes place, the Holy Spirit of God cannot enter into us. However, the moment we are born again, Christ's righteousness is imputed to us (Romans 4:24). As such, God no longer counts our trespasses against us (2 Corinthians 5:19). Our sins—past, present, and future—are removed and the Holy Spirit of God is now able to enter into us. In this process, we, who through our physical birth were born spiritually dead in our trespasses and sins (Ephesians 2:1), are now spiritually alive (Ephesians 2:5) and reconciled to our heavenly Father (2 Corinthians 5:19), who is perfectly holy and righteous (Psalm 92:15). We will be able to stand blameless before Him, enter His kingdom, and live with Him eternally. Without the indwelling Holy Spirit, this would not be possible; we would perish in our sins.

In Acts 2:38, Peter was speaking to the crowd in Jerusalem shortly after the disciples in the upper room had received the Holy Spirit, and he said, *"Repent, and each of you be baptized in the name of Jesus Christ for the forgiveness of your sins; and you will receive the gift of the Holy Spirit."* In Ephesians 1:13-14, the Apostle Paul tells us: *In Him* (Jesus), *you also, after listening to the message of truth, the gospel of your salvation – having also believed, you were sealed in Him with the Holy Spirit of promise, who was given as a pledge of our inheritance.* These verses tell us that when we repent and put our faith in Jesus as our sin-bearer, we are sealed with the Holy Spirit. This is vital for the Christian. The only righteousness that God accepts is Christ's righteousness. When God examines our spirit after our physical death, only a born-again spirit, in which His Spirit resides, will be granted entrance into His presence for eternity. Without the presence of the Holy Spirit within our spirit, the righteousness of Christ will not be found in us. The Holy Spirit is our pledge—our guarantee, our down payment—of everlasting life with our Savior.

The Holy Spirit Gives Rise to Change

To be a Christian means we have been born again with a spiritual birth that comes from God. As soon as that happens, we are sealed with the Holy Spirit who takes up residence within us. He is our guarantee of eternal life. The question now becomes, how can we be certain we have been born again and that the Holy Spirit of God is actually living within us? Simply put...a changed life.

The Holy Spirit doesn't enter into us and then just sit idly by and leave us the way we are—far from it. We will be moved. At the moment a person is born again, one may not necessarily feel or think considerably differently. In fact, several days may pass, perhaps even a week or two, and it may seem as if nothing has changed. But I can assure you, based on the Word of God, that once the Spirit of God is in you, He moves within you, and you will not remain the same.

One of the very first verses in the Bible states, *The earth was formless and void, and darkness was over the surface of the deep, and the Spirit of God was moving over the surface of the waters* (Genesis 1:2). There is something about this verse that generates in me a humble, awesome reverence for the power and sovereignty of God. Our very first introduction to the Spirit of God is energy. When we consider how vast and powerful the waters are on this earth, the Spirit must be a mighty force as He moves over the surface of the waters. The Spirit is not static. The Spirit is dynamic. As we follow the movement of the Spirit throughout Scripture, one thing is evident, the Holy Spirit is powerful and moves with strength and intensity in the lives of God's people to accomplish His purposes.

Summary

A Christian is someone who has been born again. To be born again is to have a spiritual birth that comes from God, by His Holy Spirit. This spiritual birth is brought about when we realize we have a sin problem, we repent of our sin, and put our faith in Jesus Christ as our sin-bearer. God then cleanses us and puts His Spirit within our spirit. As a result of our spiritual birth, we have a right-standing before God. The Holy Spirit dwelling within us is our guarantee of everlasting life and causes change to occur in our lives.

Chapter 6

A CHANGED LIFE

W E LEARNED IN THE PREVIOUS CHAPTER that a Christian is someone who is born again. When we are born again, the Holy Spirit indwells us and begins to move in our lives. That movement may not be detectable at first, but once the Spirit is in us, He will move, and in turn, we will move! That movement is what causes change to occur. The question becomes, what kind of change and to what end? For the Christian, the answer is simple. Our lives should begin to reflect, more and more, the nature and character of Jesus Christ.

The Agent of Change: The Holy Spirit

Given that the Holy Spirit is the agent of change in a believer's life, we will begin by looking at the ministry of the Holy Spirit. We will then take a look at what makes the change process possible, what it entails, and what it looks like practically. Before we dive in, let's answer a question. Can a believer know, beyond a shadow of a doubt, that he or she is indwelt with the Holy Spirit? Jesus answers that question for us.

Let's turn once again to our passage in John 3 that we looked at in chapter five. Jesus said to Nicodemus, *"The wind blows where it wishes and you hear the sound of it, but do not know where it comes from and where it is going; so is everyone who is born of the Spirit"* (John 3:8). The word for both *wind* and *Spirit* in this passage is the same word in the Greek—*pneuma*. It has a dual meaning. When capitalized, it means the third person of the triune God, the Holy Spirit, coequal, coeternal with the Father and the Son. When it is not capitalized, it is a movement of air, hence the wind itself (Strong's G4151). In John 3:8, Jesus was describing the invisible effect of the Holy Spirit. He explained that the evidence of the Holy Spirit in a person's life is like the evidence of wind as it is blowing. Though we cannot see the wind, there is evidence that wind exists. As Jesus mentioned, we can often hear the sound created by the wind. And though we cannot see the direction it is moving, we can discern the direction when we see something being moved by it, such as sand or debris. In other words, we can see the effects of wind when something has been caught up by its power. If strong enough, we can see damage to homes or the scattering of broken limbs off of trees. Wind has an effect. Jesus likened the effect of the wind to the effect of the Holy Spirit in the life of a person who is born of the Spirit. The Holy Spirit changes people's lives the same way wind can change places or structures. And just like the wind, though we cannot visibly see the Holy Spirit, we can clearly see and often feel His effect.

The Ministry of The Holy Spirit

We are going to examine why change occurs as we take a look at the ministry of the Holy Spirit. The role or "job" of the Holy Spirit is rather specific and laid out for us in the Scriptures. In the Gospel of John, there are five clear objectives the Holy Spirit accomplishes regarding His role as the third person of the Triune God. They are listed below. I will go through each one in some detail to present a clear picture of the role the Holy Spirit plays in a person's life. This will also provide insight as to how one can know for certain that he or she is indwelt with the Holy Spirit.

1. The Holy Spirit will teach you all things, and bring to your remembrance all that I said to you (John 14:26).

2. The Holy Spirit will testify of Me (John 15:26).

3. The Holy Spirit will convict the world concerning sin and righteousness and judgment (John 16:8).

4. The Holy Spirit will guide you into all the truth (John 16:13).

5. The Holy Spirit will glorify Me (John 16:14).

It is important to note that the Holy Spirit is not limited to these five objectives. The Bible lists many other ways in which the Holy Spirit operates in our lives, such as giving gifts to those in whom He dwells (Romans 12; 1 Corinthians 12; Ephesians 4; 1 Peter 4), sealing us for the day of redemption (2 Corinthians 1:22; Ephesians 1:13-14), and the source of power that believers need to accomplish God's purposes (Acts 1:8). Some of the other roles of the Spirit will be noted as they arise in this study.

The Promise of Another Helper

The role of the Holy Spirit found in the Gospel of John was given to us by Jesus. In each instance, Jesus was speaking to His disciples and told them about the Spirit who would come in His place once He was no longer physically with them. Jesus told them in John 14:18, *"I will not leave you as orphans; I will come to you."* In John 14:16, He said, *"I will ask the Father, and He will give you another Helper, that He may be with you forever."* Jesus was letting His disciples know that once He was no longer physically with them, He would, in essence, still be with them. And not just for a little while, but forever. Apart from function, the essence of Christ in the form of the Holy Spirit is no different than Christ Himself. When Jesus told His disciples the Father would give them *another Helper*, He meant another Helper just like Himself. Let's dissect a couple of words in John 14:16.

There are two words for the word *another* in the Greek: *allos* and *heteros*. *Heteros* denotes another of a different kind (Strong's G2087). But the word *another* used in John 14:16 is *allos*. *Allos* in the Greek denotes another of the same kind (Strong's G243). Vine's states: Christ promised to send "another Helper/Comforter," meaning another like Himself (Vine's Expository Dictionary). Jesus told His disciples that once He would no longer be physically living among them, they could expect that He Himself would be living within them in the form of the Holy Spirit. The Holy Spirit is another of the same divine nature.

The word *Helper* in the Greek is *paraklētos*. It means an intercessor, helper, succorer, aider, assistant. Regarding the Holy Spirit, He is the Helper destined to take the place of Christ with the apostles (after His ascension to the Father), to lead them to a deeper knowledge of the gospel truth, and give them divine strength needed to enable them to undergo trials and persecutions on behalf of the divine kingdom (Strong's G3875). With this definition in mind, we can surmise that the Holy Spirit is the divine Helper who assists us in gaining a deeper understanding of Christ and who fuels our inner being, enabling us to carry out God's will and plan for our lives.

1. The Holy Spirit will teach you all things, and bring to your remembrance all that I said to you (John 14:26).

As we begin our study regarding the role of the Holy Spirit, keep in mind that Jesus had just told His disciples about the Holy Spirit who would come and serve as a Helper to them. John 14:26 in its entirety is as follows: *"But the Helper, the Holy Spirit, whom the Father will send in My name, He will teach you all things, and bring to your remembrance all that I said to you."* In John 14:26, the role of the Holy Spirit is twofold:

to teach us all things and to remind us of all that Jesus has spoken. "All things" refers to the totality of the persons or things referred to (Strong's G3956; Vine's Expository Dictionary). In this instance, the person referred to is Jesus Christ. Jesus told His disciples that when the Father sends the Holy Spirit, they could expect that He would teach them all things concerning the totality of Himself.

As believers, we can discern a distinct difference within ourselves before and after the Holy Spirit takes up residence within us. That distinction becomes abundantly clear as we read Scripture and begin to understand it like never before. It's like the blinders have been removed from our eyes. Our understanding becomes illuminated because the Holy Spirit is our resident Teacher (1 John 2:27). When Jesus was speaking to His disciples after His resurrection, we are told that He opened their minds to understand the Scriptures (Luke 24:45). As you read and study Scripture, you will know if the Spirit of God is in you because you will begin to gain understanding, wisdom, and knowledge regarding the person of Jesus Christ. The Holy Spirit will illuminate all that Jesus taught and all that God has spoken through His Word.

Let's look at 1 Corinthians 2:14:

> *But a natural man does not accept the things of the Spirit of God, for they are foolishness to him; and he cannot understand them, because they are spiritually appraised.*

Paul, the author of the Book of 1 Corinthians, tells us that the things of the Spirit of God are not understandable by the natural man. A *natural man* is a reference to someone who is not born again. The things of God are spiritually appraised (discerned) and therefore, one needs the Holy Spirit to understand them. This is why many people, even professing Christians, have difficulty understanding God's written Word. If you are someone who struggles with understanding Scripture and there is nothing about God's Word that captures your attention, that is often a good indication you are not indwelt with the Holy Spirit. This is not to say that once you are born again every passage of Scripture will be easily understood. But when you are born again, you will gain an understanding of what is said in the Scriptures. God's Word will come alive and penetrate your heart like never before. This is the Holy Spirit at work, teaching you all things concerning Jesus Christ.

You will also see evidence of the latter part of John 14:26 come alive in your life. You may have experiences of sharing the Gospel with someone or simply having a conversation, when unexpectedly, a Scripture verse you didn't even realize you knew, comes to mind. Without a doubt, that is the Holy Spirit at work, bringing to your remembrance all that Christ said.

2. The Holy Spirit will testify of Me (John 15:26).

"When the Helper comes, whom I will send to you from the Father, that is the Spirit of truth who proceeds from the Father, He will testify about Me" (John 15:26). Another role of the Holy Spirit is that He testifies about Jesus. This is a very significant truth and one of the most notable things the Spirit does in the life of a believer. I use the word notable because it's what I would call one of the most proof-positive things that let us know we indeed have the Holy Spirit within us. The Holy Spirit reveals to those who have been born again exactly who Jesus is—He is God in human flesh, He is the Christ, He is our Lord, and He is our Savior. In other words, the Spirit testifies that Jesus is exactly who He says He is.

Before a person is born again, he or she may have a worldly view of Jesus—that He was just a good teacher, a prophet, or one among the "greats." Or your view may be similar to what mine had been, a belief in concept only, that Jesus is the Son of God and that He is God. But the unsaved don't know Him. Let me clarify what I mean by the word saved. To be saved is synonymous with being born again. As we looked at in the last chapter, when we are born again, we are saved from the consequences of sin, which is spiritual death—eternal separation from God. I did not know God before I was saved. I knew of Him and I believed that Jesus was the Son of God, but I only knew God intellectually. I didn't know Him personally. I did not acknowledge Jesus as Lord, nor as Savior. Honestly, I didn't even really know what the words Lord and Savior meant. And sadly, I never cared enough to find out. Given my ignorance, I just casually agreed with what many church-goers believe about Jesus, that "He is God." I had never put my trust in Him nor submitted my life to Him. Once you have been indwelt with the Holy Spirit, the Spirit goes to work within you and is constantly testifying about Jesus—He is indeed God in human flesh, our Lord and Savior, God with us.

3. The Holy Spirit will convict the world concerning sin and righteousness and judgment (John 16:8).

Jesus said to His disciples, *"And He, when He comes, will convict the world concerning sin and righteousness and judgment"* (John 16:8). He went on to expound on what He was saying in verses 9-11, *"...concerning sin, because they do not believe in Me; and concerning righteousness, because I go to the Father and you no longer see Me; and concerning judgment, because the ruler of this world has been judged."* These three things Jesus spoke of all pertain to the role of the Holy Spirit in the life of a person who is not yet born again.

Let's begin by taking a look at what is meant by *the world*. When we see the word *world* in Scripture, it can have several meanings. It can mean the literal earth, it can mean the world system of government and world affairs, or it can mean the inhabitants of the earth, the human race. In this verse of Scripture, it is referring to the human race.

The role of the Holy Spirit in the lives of people who are not yet born again—those in whom the Spirit is not residing—is to convict them of sin, righteousness, and judgment. The word *convict* in the Greek is *elegchō*. It means to convince, to bring to light, to expose (Strong's G1651). It is a conviction in the sense that when one is measured against the Law of God, one is found guilty. Jesus tells us that one of the roles of the Holy Spirit is to convince those who have not been born again, that in and of themselves, they are unable to be made right with God. It is the Spirit of God who convinces us that something is not right with us—that we have a problem, a sin problem.

We saw in a previous chapter that we are born with a sin nature. The indwelling sin nature separates us from God. In order for us to be brought back into right-standing with God, our righteousness must match God's righteousness. This is why the Holy Spirit convinces us we are sinners. Until we come to this recognition, we will never look for, nor be in need of, a Savior. For many people, admitting we are sinners isn't always easy. Most people don't see themselves as sinners. I was once one of those people! The god of my imagination "graded on a curve." When I compared myself to others, I saw myself as a "good person." On my own "scale of righteousness," I placed myself pretty high on the scale. Well, we've already learned how far that notion was from the truth. There is one standard—God's standard—and we all fall short. It is only when we realize we are sinners that we will ever find ourselves in need of a Savior.

Concerning Sin...

Jesus said, *"And He, when He comes, will convict the world concerning sin...concerning sin, because they do not believe in Me."* (John 16:8, 9). In these verses, the word *sin* is in the singular form. This is because it is referring to the sinful nature within us, not our acts of sin. Our conscience will do a fairly good job of convicting us of specific sins, such as stealing, lying, or cheating. But our conscience alone will not convict us that God's righteous judgment has us indicted as transgressors of His Law. It is the Holy Spirit who brings this to light. Most people understand when they break some sort of rule in a general sense, but despite that, they see themselves as "good people." They do not recognize that the sinful spiritual condition within them has them indicted, and a guilty verdict has already been rendered against them. A person's unbelief in their need for a Savior to restore their spiritual condition is the sin that will damn them. It is the sin of unbelief. *"He who believes in Him is not judged; he who does not believe has been judged already, because he has not believed in the name of the only begotten Son of God"* (John 3:18). Unbelief in our need for Jesus prevents us from reconciliation with God. Without reconciliation with God, there is no possibility of eternal life with Him. None of our acts of sin can be forgiven if we don't believe we need a Savior who can forgive those sins.

You might be asking yourself, "how does the Holy Spirit convict us of sin?" It is God's Word that will convict us, and the method by which that is accomplished is often carried out through people. The Holy Spirit works primarily through people who have been born again. And sometimes, though less often, He'll convince people of their sin and their need for a Savior through dreams, visions, or even promptings of the heart/mind in our conscious awareness. God is not limited to using human instruments to accomplish His purposes. However, as we go through New Testament Scripture, we discover that we are His primary source for getting His will done here on earth. Based on the instructions Jesus gave to His disciples in what is commonly referred to as the Great Commission, we see that God uses people to carry out His will. *"Go therefore and make disciples of all the nations, baptizing them in the name of the Father and the Son and the Holy Spirit"* (Matthew 28:19). God uses Spirit-filled people to lead others to a saving faith in Jesus Christ.

We see this pattern throughout the Book of Acts. God used Jesus's disciples, who were filled with the Holy Spirit, to bring others to recognizing their need for a Savior. In the second chapter of Acts, we see Peter preaching his first gospel message after having just been filled with the power of the Holy Spirit. Luke, the author of the Book of Acts, tells us in Acts 2:37 that the people who heard Peter's message were *pierced to the heart*. God used Peter as His instrument to preach His Word, but it was the conviction of the Holy Spirit that pierced their hearts. That's how God still works today. As believers share God's Word or their testimony of coming to saving faith, it is the Spirit who brings conviction to the hearts and minds of others.

There may also be times when non-believers are around Spirit-filled Christians and have a sense of conviction in their presence. Non-believers will pick up on the righteousness of Christ residing within the believer and experience a realization they fall short. As you might imagine, it's not always easy for non-believers to be around Christians. The reason for that can be due, in part, to the non-believer's experience. They can interpret their feelings of conviction in a way that causes them to think the Christian is coming across as "holier than thou" or "better than" them. And let's be honest, that can sometimes be true. But I would venture to say that it is more likely to be the non-believer's interpretation of their experience rather than the Christian projecting that type of behavior in word or deed. I say this because self-righteousness within anyone, Christian or not, isn't typically threatening or unsettling to another's conscience. Though it may be irritating, it usually doesn't bring about a sense of something impending. It is Christ's righteousness within believers that will cause non-believers to see their own unrighteousness, thus giving them the sense that something is not right with their spiritual condition.

Concerning Righteousness...

The next thing Jesus said was, *"...concerning righteousness, because I go to the Father and you no longer see Me."* It was Jesus's ascension into heaven, after His death, burial, and resurrection, that showed us that God's only acceptable righteousness was Christ's righteousness. Our own righteousness, apart from Christ, will never be enough; all our righteous deeds are like a filthy garment (Isaiah 64:6). We must possess Christ's righteousness in order to be in the presence of God. His righteousness within us guarantees our salvation and eternal life.

Concerning Judgment…

The last thing Jesus said in verse 11 is, *"…concerning judgment, because the ruler of this world has been judged."* The Holy Spirit will convict the world that the judgment of God is real and we are accountable to Him. God's solution for our sin problem is repentance of our sins and faith in His Son. For all non-repentant sinners who reject God's solution, the Spirit of God lets us know that the consequence for that rejection is God's righteous judgment. We can know there is judgment because of what happened to Satan, the ruler of this world. Colossians 2:13-15 shows us Jesus's triumph over Satan. Jesus defeated Satan and his power over sin and death at the cross. Satan's only power was effectively stripped away when Christ died for our sins because the payment for sin had been paid in full. From that point forward, all who put their trust in Christ Jesus have eternal life.

Let's quickly take a look at what happened to Satan and how it came to be that he is currently the ruler of this world as Jesus noted in John 16:11.

God created the heavens and the earth; all of it belongs to Him (Genesis 1:1; Deuteronomy 10:14; Psalm 24:1; 89:11), and He is sovereign over all (Psalm 103:19, 135:6; Isaiah 45:5-7, 46:10). With that being true, why did Jesus refer to Satan as the ruler of this world? While we know for certain God is sovereign and nothing happens on earth or in the heavens that is outside of His control, we also know the rulership of this earth was given to Satan when he and a third of the angels rebelled against God (Isaiah 14:12-15; Luke 10:17-18; Revelation 12:7-10).

Luke 4 gives the account of when Jesus was in the wilderness for forty days and nights being tempted by Satan. In verses 5-6, Luke speaks of the conversation between Satan and Jesus. Satan tempted Him, saying, *"I will give You all this domain and its glory; for it has been handed over to me, and I give it to whomever I wish"* (Luke 4:6). The domain Satan was referring to was the domain of this earth—*all the kingdoms of the world* (Luke 4:5). In His reply, Jesus did not refute Satan's claim that he had the authority to turn over that which had been handed over to him.

Let's look at a few other passages that also speak to this. *And you were dead in your trespasses and sins, in which you formerly walked according to the course of this world, according to the prince of the power of the air, of the spirit that is now working in the sons of disobedience.* (Ephesians 2:1-2) Second Corinthians 4:4 states, *...in whose case the god of this world has blinded the minds of the unbelieving so that they might not see the light of the gospel of the glory of Christ, who is the image of God.* In John 12:31, Jesus was speaking and said, *"Now judgment is upon this world; now the ruler of this world will be cast out."* And in 1 John 5:19, we are told that the whole world lies in the power of the evil one. The 'prince of the power of the air,' the 'god of this world,' and the 'evil one' are references to Satan. Satan is currently the ruler of this world. But do not fear! If you haven't yet read the end of the Bible, the Book of Revelation, God tells us that the rulership of this earth will one day return to Jesus Christ, where He will rule and reign for a thousand years (Revelation 20:4-6). At the end of the thousand-year reign, though Satan will be released from his prison to deceive the nations (Revelation 20:7-8), it won't take long before he will be devoured and thrown into the Lake of Fire for eternity (Revelation 20:10).

Therefore, when we read, *"...concerning judgment, because the ruler of this world has been judged,"* part of the role of the Holy Spirit is convincing the non-believing world that judgment is real and one day, everyone will face that judgment. For believers who have put their faith in God's Son, our sentence of judgment has been legally dismissed (Colossians 2:14). Christ took the punishment for our sins upon Himself (2 Corinthians 5:21), defeating Satan's power over sin and death on the cross. As long as we have put our faith in what Christ accomplished for us through His death, burial, and resurrection, then we too can count ourselves as defeating Satan. Satan no longer has a spiritual hold on us. *Greater is He who is in you than he who is in the world* (1 John 4:4). But for those who do not put their faith in Christ, they, like Satan, will receive the judgment of God and will be cast, along with Satan and his angels, into the Lake of Fire, *where their worm does not die, and the fire is not quenched* (Mark 9:48).

4. The Holy Spirit will guide you into all the truth (John 16:13).

John 16:13 in its entirety is as follows: *"But when He, the Spirit of truth, comes, He will guide you into all the truth; for He will not speak on His own initiative, but whatever He hears, He will speak; and He will disclose to you what is to come."* Notice the definite article *the* before the word truth. This is to indicate a specific truth. The words *the truth* are a reference to the truth that is central to the person and work of Jesus Christ. The Holy Spirit of God is the One who guides a believer into the truth of Jesus Christ. All that Jesus said and taught becomes living Truth in the life of the believer and will begin to resonate within the believer whenever Truth is heard. The believer will develop discernment between what is and is not Truth, meaning God's Word versus everything else. In my life personally, this has been one of the biggest indicators that the Holy Spirit is indeed living within me. Let's look at a passage of Scripture that speaks to this.

> *...but just as it is written, "Things which eye has not seen and ear has not heard, and which have not entered the heart of man, all that God has prepared for those who love Him." <u>For to us God revealed them through the Spirit; for the Spirit searches all things, even the depths of God.</u> For who among men knows the thoughts of a man except the spirit of the man which is in him? Even so <u>the thoughts of God no one knows except the Spirit of God.</u> Now <u>we have received</u>, not the spirit of the world, but <u>the Spirit who is from God, so that we may know the things freely given to us by God</u>, which things we also speak, not in words taught by human wisdom, but in those <u>taught by the</u>*

Spirit, combining spiritual thoughts with spiritual words. But a natural man does not accept the things of the Spirit of God, for they are foolishness to him; and he cannot understand them, because they are spiritually appraised. But he who is spiritual appraises all things, yet he himself is appraised by no one. For who has known the mind of the Lord, that he will instruct Him? But we have the mind of Christ. (1 Corinthians 2:9-16)

It is clear from this passage of Scripture that once we are indwelt with the Holy Spirit, God reveals to us, through His Spirit, all things in the spiritual realm. It is through the Spirit that we learn of God and gain wisdom, knowledge, and understanding of the person and work of Jesus Christ, even to the point that we have the mind of Christ. Wow! Now that is an amazing truth. It's because we have the mind of Christ in us via the Holy Spirit that everything begins to change. The Spirit of God within us continually draws us toward God because *the Spirit Himself testifies with our spirit that we are children of God* (Romans 8:16). As we are drawn closer to God through the revelation of Truth by His Spirit, we begin to walk in righteousness and in alignment with His will.

Before I was born again, there really wasn't any truth of the gospel of Jesus Christ that resonated within me or testified of Him. After I was born again, the Spirit went right to work and a shift began to take place. The eyes of my heart were opened and God's Word awakened within me a strong desire to know Him more and to order my life in such a way as to live out the truth of His Word. The Spirit was continually leading me deeper and deeper into Truth. Everything began to change—my thoughts, my ambitions, my goals, my desires, and my wants. A change of heart was taking place; the mind of Christ was working within me. My will began aligning with God's will and His plan for my life. The Bible tells us in Psalm 37:4: *Delight yourself in the Lord; and He will give you the desires of your heart.* When we become born again, our new nature—the nature and character of Christ who resides within us—develops a hunger and thirst for God. Therefore, our desires change. As the Spirit of God leads us into Truth, God gives us the desires of our hearts because our desires start lining up with His will.

5. The Holy Spirit will glorify Me (John 16:14).

"He will glorify Me, for He will take of Mine and will disclose it to you" (John 16:14). The word *glorify* in the Greek is *doxazō*. It means to extol, magnify, celebrate, make renowned; to cause the dignity and worth of some person or thing to become manifest and acknowledged (Strong's G1392). To glorify someone is to magnify and make known who they are by giving an accurate estimate of that person's dignity and worth. Jesus tells us that the Holy Spirit will glorify Him; the Holy Spirit will make Jesus known by giving a correct estimate of His true nature. The role of the Holy Spirit is to shine the spotlight on Jesus, exalting Him and focusing all attention on the person and work of Jesus Christ. To illustrate this concept, consider the idea of floodlights. If you wanted to highlight a nativity scene, you would place floodlights so that viewers would not see the floodlights themselves, but rather the nativity. The focus of the viewers is that which the floodlights shine upon. This illustrates the role of the Holy Spirit in glorifying Jesus. The Holy Spirit is always pointing us to Christ. The Spirit is the "floodlight" that directs our attention and focus upon Him. This causes us to live our lives in such a way that makes Jesus known to others by giving a correct estimate of His dignity and worth. In this way, we express His nature and character to those around us. The Spirit—the "floodlight" within us—not only points us to Christ, but allows Christ to be revealed to others by how we live our lives.

The remainder of John 16:14 says, *...for He will take of Mine and will disclose it to you*. This states that the Holy Spirit will take what belongs to Jesus and disclose it to believers. All that is of Jesus Christ, who He is, His redeeming work, and His Truth, will be disclosed—revealed—to the believer by the Holy Spirit.

The Empowering Source of The Holy Spirit

Now that we have looked at the role of the Holy Spirit found in the Gospel of John, let's focus our attention on the process of change. As noted earlier, the Holy Spirit is the agent of change. He is our power source and the one who causes change to occur. We see in Acts 1 that just before Jesus ascended into heaven, He gathered His disciples together and commanded them not to leave Jerusalem. They were to wait for what the Father had promised. He told them they would soon be baptized with the Holy Spirit (Acts 1:4-5). In Acts 1:8, Jesus said to them, *"...you will receive power when the Holy Spirit has come upon you; and you shall be My witnesses both in Jerusalem, and in all Judea and Samaria, and even to the remotest part of the earth."* The disciples were instructed to wait because they needed to receive the necessary power to carry forth Christ's message to the world. In Matthew 28:19-20, Jesus had said to them, *"Go therefore and make disciples of all the nations, baptizing them in the name of the Father and the Son and the Holy Spirit, teaching them to observe all that I commanded you; and lo, I am with you always, even to the end of the age."* Before they were to begin their mission of proclaiming Christ to every nation, they needed to have the empowering source of the Holy Spirit. In Acts 1:8, the word *power* in the Greek is *dynamis*. It's where we get our English word dynamite. It means strength, power, ability, might; inherent power (Strong's G1411). Inherent within the Holy Spirit, there is power, strength, ability, and might. It is because of these attributes that Spirit-filled believers have the ability to change.

The Change Process

Thus far we have learned that once a person is born again, the Holy Spirit, who is the agent of change in the life of a Christian, begins to move in our lives. Without the Holy Spirit residing within us, a changed life with a heart for the things of God would not be possible. Before we delve into the change process, I want to provide a quick synopsis of the concept of change in the context of the Christian life as a whole.

Justification, Sanctification, and Glorification

The Christian life can be viewed in three stages: Justification, Sanctification, and Glorification. Justification is the word used to describe the change that occurs from being a non-believer to being a believer. Justification is a legal term that signifies acquittal. The word *justify* in the Greek is *dikaioō*. It means to declare or pronounce, one to be just, righteous, or such as he ought to be (Strong's G1344). Vine's states: Justification is the legal and formal acquittal from guilt by God as Judge; it is the pronouncement of the sinner as righteous, who believes on the Lord Jesus Christ (Vine's Expository Dictionary). When we repent of our sins and put our faith in Christ, it is in that very moment we are deemed justified. Our debt for breaking God's Law has been paid and we now have a right-standing before our righteous Judge. Our sins are forgiven and removed (Psalm 103:12). The sin-corrupted spirit within us is made anew (born again) and we are imputed with the righteousness of Jesus Christ (2 Corinthians 5:21). It is because of Jesus's sacrifice on the cross in taking the penalty for our sin, and His victory over death, that we can be legally declared righteous by God.

> *...but for our sake also, to whom it will be credited, as those who believe in Him* (God the Father) *who raised Jesus our Lord from the dead, He* (Jesus) *who was delivered over because of our transgressions, and was raised because of our justification.* (Romans 4:24-25)

A phrase widely used in Christian circles to explain justification is "just as if I'd never sinned." We look at it that way because that's the change that takes place. Our sins—past, present, and future— are removed and Christ's righteousness is imputed to us. There is an exchange in the nature of who are. Therefore, when we describe justification as "just as if I'd never sinned," it's an accurate statement. When God looks upon believers, He sees Christ's righteousness in us, not our sin; we have a clean slate—a right-standing before God.

The second stage of the Christian life is known as sanctification. Sanctification is the change process that occurs in the life of someone who has been born again. The word *sanctification* in the Greek is *hagiasmos*. It means consecration, purification (Strong's G38). Vine's States: It is translated as holiness and signifies separation to God and the resultant state; the conduct befitting those so separated. Sanctification is thus the state predetermined by God for believers, into which in grace He calls them, and in which they begin their Christian course and so pursue it (Vine's Expository Dictionary). Once we are born again, sanctification is the process in which we are separated unto God, and begin pursuing our calling of bearing the image of His Son, Jesus Christ.

The third stage of the Christian life is known as glorification. Though the word glorification is not found in either the Old or New Testament, the idea of glorification can be found in the Greek word *doxazō*, translated *glorify*. It means to extol, magnify, celebrate, make renowned; to cause the dignity and worth of some person or thing to become manifest and acknowledged (Strong's G1392). Glorification can be seen as the final culmination of sanctification. Glorification, in all but one passage of Scripture (Romans 8:30), places itself as a future event (Colossians 1:27; 2 Thessalonians 2:14; 2 Timothy 2:10; 1 Peter 5:1). It is a time in the future that takes place with the resurrection of believers and Jesus's second coming (1 Corinthians 15:43; Ephesians 5:27; Philippians 3:20-21; 2 Thessalonians 1:10). Also, it is an eternal state (2 Timothy 2:10; 1 Peter 5:10) for the saints. The term *saints* in the New Testament is a reference to believers who have put their faith in Jesus Christ. Glorification is that coming day when *in a moment, in the twinkling of an eye, at the last trumpet; for the trumpet will sound, and the dead will be raised imperishable, and we will be changed. For this perishable must put on the imperishable, and this mortal must put on immortality* (1 Corinthians 15:52-53). At the time of glorification, believers will have reached the highest level of sanctification—a time in which we will be perfectly conformed to the image of Christ. We will no longer be in a human body that is corrupt from sin and decay. We will be in a glorified, sinless body (Philippians 3:21; 1 John 3:2). It is a time in which both our bodies and our spirits will be totally free from the intrusive influence of the sin nature. Amen!

Let's now shift our focus back to the second stage of the Christian life—sanctification. Sanctification is often referred to as progressive sanctification. This is because change is a process that occurs over time; it doesn't happen overnight. From the moment we are born again, sanctification begins and progresses toward a life that reflects more of Christ's image. It continues until the day we die physically, at which point our spirits depart from our bodies of flesh and we are then in the presence of our Lord. Paul describes this process in Ephesians 4. In verse 13, he says, *"...until we all attain to the unity of the faith, and of the knowledge of the Son of God, to a mature man, to the measure of the stature which belongs to the fullness of Christ."* Essentially, Paul is saying from the moment we are born again until the moment we die, our goal as men and women of God is to become mature, "full-grown" image-bearers of Christ.

What the Change Process Entails

We learn in 2 Thessalonians 2:13 that the Holy Spirit is the one who sanctifies us. This is yet another role of the Holy Spirit in the life of a Christian. It is the Spirit who separates believers unto God and gives us the power to walk in righteousness. This causes change. We begin to change because the most important relationship in our lives has changed; we are no longer hostile toward God. I'll explain. Romans 8:6-7 states: *For the mind set on the flesh is death, but <u>the mind set on the Spirit is life and peace</u>, because <u>the mind set on the flesh is hostile toward God</u>; for it does not subject itself to the law of God, for it is not even able to do so.* Once we are reconciled to God, our hostility toward Him is removed. We become indwelt with the Holy Spirit and the Spirit goes right to work; the mind of Christ begins working within us (1 Corinthians 2:16). The desire within us changes from wanting to live independently from God, to loving Him above all else and desiring to live a life that pleases Him.

Put Off/Put On

There are two aspects to the process of sanctification: a "putting off" and a "putting on." After we have been born again, we "put off" our old lifestyles and behaviors and we "put on" the new lifestyles and behaviors. The old behaviors are those things we did when we were governed by our fleshly desires; we were slaves to the sin nature. The new behaviors are those things we do that arise from being governed by the Holy Spirit. Before we take a closer look at the "put off/put on" process in terms of our sanctification, it is important to note that this process has already occurred in terms of our justification.

Regarding Justification

All who have been justified and declared righteous by God have a right-standing with Him. Therefore, with regard to our spiritual condition in the eyes of God, we have positional righteousness. Our position of being *in Christ* is a settled matter. This is what grants us eternal life with our Lord and Savior. Let's look at this further.

For those who have been born again, the old nature of our sin-corrupted spirit has already been "put off." That happened the moment we repented of our sins and put our faith in Christ. The old sin-nature corrupted spirit died, and our new Christ-natured spirit was born.

> *Therefore if anyone is in Christ, he is a new creature; the old things passed away; behold, new things have come.* (2 Corinthians 5:17)

Our sin-corrupted spirit died at the cross when we made Jesus Christ our Lord and Savior. Additionally, our new sin-free nature of Jesus Christ has already been "put on;" we are now clothed in Christ's righteousness.

> *For all of you who were baptized into Christ have clothed*
> *yourselves with Christ.* (Galatians 3:27)

The baptism into Christ spoken of in Galatians 3:27 is not speaking of water baptism. It is speaking of Baptism of the Holy Spirit. Jesus told His disciples in Acts 1:5, *"...for John baptized with water, but you will be baptized with the Holy Spirit not many days from now."* In this verse, Jesus made a distinction between being baptized with water and being baptized with the Holy Spirit.

In both Galatians 3:27 and Acts 1:5, the word *baptized* in the Greek is *baptizō*. It means to immerse, to submerge (Strong's G907). While the concepts of water baptism and Baptism of the Holy Spirit are the same— an immersing—water baptism differs in that it is something believers do as an act of obedience to Christ's command (Matthew 28:19). After we have been born of the Spirit, water baptism is the act in which we publically declare that we are identifying with Christ. As we submerge ourselves under the water, we are dying to our old sin nature and burying it. As we rise out of the water, we are resurrecting to our new nature in Christ. Baptism of the Holy Spirit happens the moment we repent of our sins and put our faith in Christ. We are thus immersed with the Spirit of God. Therefore, once our spirits have been born again, the old sin nature has been put off and Christ's nature has been put on. Our born-again spiritual condition is what gives us positional righteousness, and thus, a right-standing before God.

Regarding Sanctification

Let's now turn our attention to what the "put off/put on" process means in terms of the sanctification process. Given that we still live in bodies of flesh, the old sin nature within us (that is, within our flesh, but not our born-again spirit—Romans 7:17-18) continues to wreak havoc on our minds, our will, and emotions. Though our bodies are still subject to the influences of the sin nature, our spiritual condition has been made new through being spiritually born again. Therefore, our practice of the new nature needs to reflect what God has now declared us to be—righteous. Our spiritual birth unites us with Christ in His death, burial, and resurrection, and our walk is to reflect our identification in Him (Romans 6:4).

When it comes to the concept of sanctification, I like to draw the analogy of clothing. Our old self wears "fleshly apparel" and our new self wears "Christian apparel." Once we are born again, we lay aside the old clothes—those behaviors governed by the flesh. After we are born again, we put on our new clothes—those behaviors that reflect the nature and character of the One residing within us, the Lord Jesus Christ. In essence, we put on Christ; *But put on the Lord Jesus Christ, and make no provision for the flesh in regard to its lusts* (Romans 13:14).

It's worth noting that the Bible has several ways of referring to the old nature and the new nature. Usage of the terms 'old self,' 'old nature,' 'old man,' or 'natural man,' all refer to who we were before our spiritual birth, in which we acted upon the influences of the sin nature. Usage of the terms 'new self,' 'new nature,' and 'new man,' refer to who we are once we are born again. Our new nature reflects the nature and character of Christ.

Ephesians 4:22-24 is a notable passage that speaks to the practice of putting off and putting on. It lays it out for us in a way that's easy to see the process. This passage gives us the prescription for change and we'll discuss it verse-by-verse.

> *22 In reference to your former manner of life,*
> *you <u>lay aside the old self</u>,*
> *which is being corrupted in accordance with the lusts of deceit,*
> *23 and that you <u>be renewed in the spirit of your mind</u>,*

24 and put on the new self,
which in the likeness of God has been created
in righteousness and holiness of the truth.
(Ephesians 4:22-24)

Before we dive into the process of change, it's important to have a clear understanding of the word *lust*. Given that most people often associate the word *lust* with sexual lust, a biblical definition is essential. The word *lust* in the Greek is *epithymia*. It means desire, craving, longing, desire for what is forbidden (Strong's G1939). Vine's states: It denotes a strong desire of any kind. Lusts of the flesh is a phrase that describes the emotions of the soul, the natural tendency towards things evil. Such lusts are not necessarily base and immoral, they may be refined in character, but are evil if inconsistent with the will of God (Vine's Expository Dictionary). We see from both the Greek and Vine's Expository definitions that lusts are those strong desires within us that motivate our behavior and become evil in nature when they are inconsistent with the will of God. That begs the question, if the lusts we have are not always evil, how do we determine when our lusts become evil, and therefore, inconsistent with the will of God? It is when our lusts/desires become demands, and we'll either sin to get what we want or sin when we don't get what we want. Let me give you an example. We all have within us a strong desire to be loved. The desire to be loved is not in and of itself evil. It's when our desire to be loved turns into a demand that it becomes a lust that is evil in nature. In other words, it becomes an idol of the heart. If we are willing to sin to get someone to behave lovingly toward us, or because they aren't behaving lovingly toward us, at that point, our desire for love has become a lust that is inconsistent with the will of God. In this example, our desire for love is a craving that motivates us to sin rather than be obedient to God. With that in mind, lust can simply be defined as any desire that cannot be fulfilled in the righteousness of God.

Put Off

Let's now take a look at the change process in Ephesians 4:22-24. *In reference to your former manner of life, you lay aside the old self, which is being corrupted in accordance with the lusts of deceit* (v. 22). The first thing we are to do is lay aside the old self—those behaviors motivated by corrupt sin nature, described here as *lusts of deceit.* The Apostle Paul, the author of the Book of Ephesians, tells us that the lusts of our old nature are deceitful. Why is that? It's because the strong desires that stem from the sin nature give a false impression that if we obtain what we crave, we will be satisfied. When we have strong desires that motivate us to sin, those lusts will never "deliver" that which we crave; they will never fill the void that's in our hearts. They may satisfy for a moment, but you'll never truly have what you desire if it's not freely given to you. There is always a cost. Our lusts that stem from the old nature deceive us into thinking we are going to get what we want. Therefore, Paul says that for all who have been born again, we are to put off the behaviors motivated by the sin nature because they are inconsistent with God's will. Put simply, we are to put off anything that causes us to sin.

Put On

Let's now skip ahead to verse 24, and then we'll tackle verse 23. Verse 24 says, *...and put on the new self, which in the likeness of God has been created in righteousness and holiness of the truth.* The words *put on* are represented by one word in the Greek, *endyō.* It means to sink into (clothing) (Strong's G1746). It is in the middle voice, indicating that the subject initiates the action and participates in the results. "To sink into" conveys more the idea of settling into or surrendering ourselves to, our new nature. Because our new nature desires to please God, we actively participate in putting on that which reflects His righteousness and holiness. Therefore, after we put off the "old clothes" of the old sin nature,

Paul tells us we are to clothe ourselves in the likeness of God, putting on the "new clothes" that represent Christ, both in character and nature.

As you can see, the process of change is a putting off of the old self, the old sin nature, and a putting on of the new self, the new nature of Jesus Christ. Sounds simple, right? Well, it can be. But more often than not, Christians can struggle with this. The change process requires effort, responsibility, and a level of commitment on our part. If we are not wholly committed to living our lives for Christ, we will find that the greater the disparity in our behavior between our old nature and our new nature, the greater our challenges. The Bible tells us that *He* (God) *who began a good work in you will perfect it until the day of Christ Jesus* (Philippians 1:6). But that doesn't mean we sit back and wait for the Lord to do all the work. We are to *grow in the grace and knowledge of our Lord and Savior Jesus Christ* (2 Peter 3:18). Our lack of growth in these areas is why so much has been written on the topic of change regarding the Christian walk, and it is the basis of Biblical Counseling. We must keep in mind that old habits don't disappear by themselves. They need to be replaced with new habits. This is why we are not instructed to simply "put off" the old nature and leave it at that. We are also instructed to "put on" the new nature. Once we have been born again, we need to understand we are no longer slaves to the sin nature; *…our old self was crucified with Him, in order that our body of sin might be done away with, so that we would no longer be slaves to sin* (Romans 6:6). We have been set free from the bondage of sin in our lives because the Holy Spirit is now ruling, *…and having been freed from sin, [we] became slaves of righteousness* (Romans 6:18). This means we wholly give ourselves over in service to righteous living. Oh yes, sin still makes its demands and will continue to do so this side of heaven because we live in a body of flesh. But our relationship to sin has changed because we are now united with Christ.

While many Christians can struggle with laying aside the behaviors of the old nature, Christians can also experience great victories of the Holy Spirit over our old ways. The Spirit in the life of the Christian has the strength to overcome the influence of the flesh. If we choose to abide in Christ and remain in close fellowship with Him, many of the habits and behaviors of the old sin nature seem to simply fall away. The degree of ease or difficulty we experience in putting off the old nature and putting on our new nature is in direct proportion to how connected we are to Christ and our commitment to rightly bearing His image. We are going to look more closely at the relationship between the believer and Christ in the following chapter. But for now, let's see what God's Word tells us about what enables us to lay aside our "fleshly apparel" and put on our "Christian apparel."

Be Renewed in The Spirit of Your Mind

Ephesians 4:23 gives us the answer as to how we make this transition. Verse 23 states, *...and that you be renewed in the spirit of your mind.* Our ability to put off our old behaviors and put on our new behaviors is through the renewing of our minds. The words *that you be renewed* are represented as one word in the Greek, *ananeoō*. It means to renew (in the mind) (Strong's G365). Vine's states: The "renewal" mentioned here is not that of the mind itself in its natural powers of memory, judgment, and perception, but "the spirit of the mind," which, under the controlling power of the indwelling Holy Spirit, directs its bent and energies Godward in the enjoyment of "fellowship with the Father and with His Son, Jesus Christ," and of the fulfillment of the will of God (Vine's Expository Dictionary). The influence of the Holy Spirit upon the spirit of our minds is what enables us to "sink into" our new nature in Christ. We are told in Titus 3:5 that it is the Holy Spirit who renews our minds. The Spirit directs our bent and energies toward God with a desire to please Him. However, we must understand that though it is the Holy Spirit who renews our minds, it doesn't mean we don't bear any responsibility for change.

The words *that you be renewed* in verse 23 are in the present passive form. This means it's a continuous action in which the subject is acted upon. The idea is of progress and growth. It is the Holy Spirit who continually renews our minds, but it is our openness and willingness to heed the voice of the Spirit and follow His lead, that will stir up our spirit to have a heart for the things of God and for living a life of holiness. If we resist or are indifferent to the Spirit's promptings of our hearts, then change and growth toward living a life of holiness will be thwarted. We must actively be open to the leading of the Spirit to allow Him to work in our hearts and minds and bring about continued renewal. Let's look at a couple of verses that speak to this concept of renewing our minds.

> *And do not be conformed to this world, but be transformed by the renewing of your mind, so that you may prove what the will of God is, that which is good and acceptable and perfect.* (Romans 12:2)

> *Set your mind on the things above, not on the things that are on earth.* (Colossians 3:2)

In Romans 12:2, we are told to not be conformed to this world, but to be transformed by the renewing of our minds. The word *transformed* in the Greek is *metamorphoō*. It means to change into another form (Strong's G3339). Vine's states: Said of believers, it is the obligation to undergo a complete change which, under the power of God, will find expression in character and conduct (Vine's Expository Dictionary). The verb *transformed* is in the present passive imperative form. This means it is a continuous action in which the subject is acted upon, and it is expressed as a command. We are commanded to be continually undergoing an inward change, a change which is produced by the Spirit, through the renewing of our minds. That change is a progression away from the world and what it offers, a world that is hostile toward God, and a progression towards God.

Colossians 3:2 tells us to set our minds on the things above. The words *set your mind* are represented as one word in the Greek, *phroneō*.

It means to direct one's mind to a thing, to seek, to strive for; to be of the same mind (Strong's G5426). The word *phroneō* is in the present active imperative form. This means it is a continuous action in which the subject produces the action, and it is expressed as a command. Believers are to continuously seek that which is above. What is meant by *the things above*? In Colossians 3:1, we read, *Therefore if you have been raised up with Christ, keep seeking the things above, where Christ is, seated at the right hand of God*. We are to continuously set our minds on seeking Christ. Keeping our minds on Christ will allow for greater renewal of our minds. The more our minds are renewed, the more our love for Christ deepens. It is out of our love for Him that the pathways that motivate us in our walk begin to open up, propelling us to walk more consistently in righteousness.

We see from the examples in Ephesians, Romans, and Colossians that there is an emphasis on the renewing of our minds. In each instance, the Apostle Paul, the writer of these three epistles, speaks of turning away from the world and/or our old nature and turning toward Christ, our new nature. This is because the continual renewing of our minds is that which will ultimately bring about an inward change. For there to be a genuine change in our outward behavior, not temporary or "forced" change, there needs to be an inward change—a change of heart, of mind, of our inner being. The Holy Spirit within us will effectively go to work to bring about renewal in our thinking, but we must actively and continually participate in it. As followers of Christ, it is imperative that we yield to the transforming influences of the Holy Spirit because how we think and what we believe determines how we behave. Therefore, our focus needs to be set on Christ and must remain on Him. If He is not our focus, then our natural tendency for succumbing to the influences of the sin nature will become the voice within us that gets louder and louder. Given that we still live in bodies of flesh, we must not take for granted that since we have been born again, we don't have to be vigilant about avoiding sin. Until we die physically, the influences of the sin nature over our minds, our will, and emotions will be in a continuous "tug-of-war" with our new nature in Christ (Romans 7:23). For the Spirit to gain victory over the flesh in the spiritual battle waging war within us, we must continually seek Christ and keep our minds focused on Him. So how do we stay focused on Christ?

Resources for Keeping Our Focus on Christ

Our best resource for keeping our minds focused on Christ is the Word of God. Christians need to be in the Word daily. The Bible is God's Good News. It's His redeeming love for the world and the revelation of His Son, Jesus Christ. It is in the Word that we learn about the true and living God, not the god of our imaginations. It is in the Word that we learn about our Lord and Savior, Jesus Christ. And it is in the Word that we learn about who we are in Him—our identity, our rich inheritance, and how we are to walk as His followers. Everything we need to know pertaining to life and godliness is found in the Word of God (2 Peter 1:3). Diligent study of God's Word is the lifeline of every believer. Yes, we can learn much about what God has to say in His Word by simply reading it, but it is the study of His Word that really brings His message alive. The study of Scripture is the one thing a person can do in this life and never regret it. It's one of the surest ways you will find the Holy Spirit speaking to you, guiding you, and renewing your mind.

Another resource for keeping our minds focused on Christ is to be in fellowship with other believers. It is so important in our spiritual walk to be around other brothers and sisters in Christ, especially when we are brand-new believers. Mature Christians can be a great resource for us in our own spiritual walk. They can also aid and support us in the areas in which we need accountability.

Worshipping together with our church family is also important. Christians can stay focused on Christ by *not forsaking our own assembling together...* (Hebrews 10:25). We are told in Scripture to devote ourselves to the teaching of God's Word, to fellowship, to partaking in Communion, and to prayer (Acts 2:42). One of the ways we do this is by corporately gathering together for the praise and worship of our Lord and listening to the sound teaching of biblical doctrine. Gathering together as the body of Christ is a time set aside to collectively give honor and praise to our God—the God who redeemed us and is worthy of praise.

As Christians, we are called to encourage and build one another up (1 Thessalonians 5:11). Regularly gathering together gives us many opportunities that we wouldn't have otherwise. It's a time to reach out to those who are hurting or are in need. It's a time to share in the blessings and joy of others. Being together with our church family is a wonderful way to build and strengthen our faith.

One of the roles of the pastor of a church is to equip the saints for the work of service in building up God's kingdom here on earth (Ephesians 4:12). This is accomplished through the sound teaching of biblical doctrine. There are many churches one can choose to attend here in America. I strongly recommend attending a solid Bible-teaching church. It's one of the surest ways to help keep our minds on Christ. When we gather together as one body, it's a set time in which we narrow our focus on God's Word. This will renew our minds, and thus, fuel our desire to walk in righteousness. If we aren't regularly hearing the Word of God being taught in church, our desire for Truth is likely to wane and we will be prone to stray.

The Outward Manifestation of Change

Now that we have looked at what the change process entails, let's turn our attention to what change looks like from a practical standpoint. What kind of changes would we see in someone who is born of the Spirit? Let's take a look at what Jesus told us.

> *"For there is no good tree which produces bad fruit, nor, on the other hand, a bad tree which produces good fruit. For each tree is known by its own fruit. For men do not gather*

figs from thorns, nor do they pick grapes from a briar bush.
The good man out of the treasure of his heart brings forth
what is good; and the evil man out of the evil treasure
brings forth what is evil; for his mouth speaks from that
which fills his heart." (Luke 6:43-45)

In this passage, Jesus makes an analogy between fruit and people's behavior. He tells us that each tree, analogous to each person, is known by the fruit—a person's outward behavior—it produces. The point is that people are known by the behaviors they exemplify. We also learn that what is in a person's heart is what he or she will manifest in his or her behavior.

We see this same analogy used in several New Testament Scriptures. John the Baptist used it when he was baptizing his Jewish brethren at the Jordan River as they confessed their sins. He instructed them to *"bear fruit in keeping with repentance"* (Matthew 3:8). As we recall from chapter three, to repent is to turn away from sin and toward God. John was telling his brethren that once they repented of their sins, their outward behavior should now reflect the change of their repentant hearts.

The Apostle Paul also used this analogy in a conversation he had with King Agrippa. He said, *"So, King Agrippa, I did not prove disobedient to the heavenly vision, but kept declaring both to those of Damascus first, and also at Jerusalem and then throughout all the region of Judea, and even to the Gentiles, that they should repent and turn to God, performing deeds appropriate to repentance"* (Acts 26:19-20). Paul used the word *deeds* instead of *fruit*, but given that fruit is the metaphor for outward behavior, the principle is the same as that which John the Baptist used. A Christian's spirit has been transformed and given a new nature. When God rescued us from the domain of darkness/Satan, and transferred us to the kingdom of Light/God's beloved Son (Acts 26:18; Colossians 1:13), He put a new spirit within us; He gave us a new heart (Ezekiel 36:26). Therefore, our behavior should match the inward change of our hearts. The "fruit" that each one of us produces comes from having

Christ's nature within us. The Holy Spirit will speak to our hearts and minds, initiating and driving change, as He turns our minds, our will, and our conscience into alignment with God. It is our responsibility to heed the promptings of the Spirit.

The changes in our behavior that are driven by the power of the Holy Spirit are often referred to in Scripture as *spiritual fruit*. This is because these behaviors stem from being born spiritually, and therefore, they reflect the nature and character of Jesus Christ. There are several characteristics of fruit that will help us better understand why these behaviors are referred to as fruit.

Characteristics of Fruit

Fruit is noticeable. If you see a tree that has apples on it, you will easily be able to identify the tree as an apple tree. Likewise, spiritual fruit is noticeable and will be evident to others. The new nature of Christ within the Christian will bear visible spiritual fruit.

Fruit isn't achieved by working. An apple tree doesn't have to work at producing apples. It occurs naturally because the seed that produces the apple tree is already "programmed" to bear apples. Likewise, spiritual fruit isn't achieved by working. Rather, it manifests as a natural outflow of being spiritually birthed. This is an important point. As Christians, we don't have to "muster up" goodness or self-control (two virtues/characteristics identified as fruit of the Spirit). It is Christ in us, through the power of His Spirit, that brings forth the fruit of His nature.

Fruit will mature and continue to be produced. A fruit tree will continue to bear fruit because the seed from which it came has the "DNA" within it to continually produce fruit. Fruit will mature as long as it is connected to the tree that gives it life. Likewise, spiritual fruit will continue to be reproduced because the Holy Spirit is the "seed" within us that has the "instructions" for development, maturity, and reproduction. Spiritual fruit will manifest and mature as long as it is connected to the Vine that gives it life. John 15:1 tells us that Jesus is the Vine. It is His life within us that allows us to continually produce spiritual fruit that matures.

Fruit is attractive. Jesus embodied the nine-fold fruit of the Spirit—love, joy, peace, patience, kindness, goodness, faithfulness, gentleness, and self-control (Galatians 5:22-23). Many people followed Him because they wanted to be near Him. Likewise, when Christians manifest spiritual fruit, others want to be around them.

Fruit nourishes. Fruit nourishes our bodies and sustains us. Likewise, spiritual fruit nourishes our lives and sustains us. The spiritual fruit of Christians also nourishes the lives of others. When Jesus was teaching in the Temple during the Feast of Booths, He said, *"He who believes in Me, as the Scripture said, 'From his innermost being will flow rivers of living water.'" But this He spoke of the Spirit, whom those who believed in Him were to receive* (John 7:38-39). The spiritual fruit in the lives of Christians will flow out of them and onto others, nourishing all like a river of living water.

It is important to keep in mind that both natural fruit and spiritual fruit need to be cultivated. Fruit-bearing trees can only bear fruit if they are fed and watered. For Christians to produce spiritual fruit, we too must be fed and watered. We do this through prayer, worship, and knowing our God through His Word.

Walk in a Manner Worthy of The Lord

As we further examine spiritual fruit, it will be helpful to understand some phrases found in Scripture in which we find a clear distinction between the lives of those who have been born again versus those who have not. Those who have not been born again are most often referred to as "being/living/walking in the flesh/darkness." Their walk or manner of lifestyle is that which is *against* Christ. Those who have the Holy Spirit living within them are referred to as "being/living/walking in the Spirit/Light." Their walk or manner of lifestyle is that which is *with* Christ. Given that the Christian's walk is to reflect the nature and character of Christ, let's focus on some of the passages in Scripture that exhort us to walk in this new manner and which speak to the changes one would expect to see in a Christian.

> *Therefore I, the prisoner of the Lord, implore you to* <u>*walk in a manner worthy of the calling with which you*</u> <u>*have been called,*</u> *with all humility and gentleness, with patience, showing tolerance for one another in love, being diligent to preserve the unity of the Spirit in the bond of peace.* (Ephesians 4:1-3)

> *For this reason also, since the day we heard of it, we have not ceased to pray for you and to ask that you may be filled with the knowledge of His will in all spiritual wisdom and understanding, so that you will* <u>*walk in a manner*</u> <u>*worthy of the Lord,*</u> *to please Him in all respects, bearing fruit in every good work and increasing in the knowledge of God; strengthened with all power, according to His glorious might, for the attaining of all steadfastness and patience; joyously giving thanks to the Father, who has qualified us to share in the inheritance of the saints in Light.* (Colossians 1:9-12)

> *Only* <u>*conduct yourselves in a manner worthy of the gospel*</u> <u>*of Christ,*</u> *so that whether I come and see you or remain absent, I will hear of you that you are standing firm in one spirit, with one mind striving together for the faith of the gospel.* (Philippians 1:27)

> *Just as you know how we were exhorting and encouraging and imploring each one of you as a father would his own children, so that you would* <u>*walk in a manner worthy of*</u>

the God who calls you into His own kingdom and glory.
(1 Thessalonians 2:11-12)

Once we have been born again, we are called to walk in a manner worthy of the gospel of Jesus Christ. We are to live a life that reflects the inward change of our hearts—hearts that have been cleansed by the blood of Jesus and desire to be pleasing to God. We do this by handing the reins of rulership over our lives to the Lord. As we do so, it is imperative that we begin heeding the promptings of the Holy Spirit, allowing Him to lead, guide, and direct our steps.

Let's take a look at one of the most notable passages of Scripture in which the old nature and new nature are contrasted. It first describes for us the old "fruit" we are to put off—those behaviors which stem from the sin nature. It then describes the new "fruit" we are to put on—those behaviors which are now possible given our spiritual birth.

But I say, walk by the Spirit, and you will not carry out the desire of the flesh. For the flesh sets its desire against the Spirit, and the Spirit against the flesh; for these are in opposition to one another, so that you may not do the things that you please. But if you are led by the Spirit, you are not under the Law. Now the deeds of the flesh are evident, which are: immorality, impurity, sensuality, idolatry, sorcery, enmities, strife, jealousy, outbursts of anger, disputes, dissensions, factions, envying, drunkenness, carousing, and things like these, of which I forewarn you, just as I have forewarned you, that those who practice such things will not inherit the kingdom of God. But the fruit of the Spirit is love, joy, peace, patience, kindness, goodness, faithfulness, gentleness, self-control; against such things there is no law. Now those who belong to Christ Jesus have crucified the flesh with its passions and desires. If we live by the Spirit, let us also walk by the Spirit. Let us not become boastful, challenging one another, envying one another. (Galatians 5:16-26)

We learn in this passage that if we allow the Spirit to lead us in our walk, we will not carry out the sinful habits of our old nature. Walking by the Spirit and walking by the flesh are two opposing forces. Given that we still live in bodies of flesh, we must yield ourselves to the inner promptings of the Holy Spirit so that we are Spirit-led. Our old nature was crucified with Christ (Romans 6:6; Galatians 2:20), and our new nature has risen with Christ (Colossians 3:1). Therefore, our manner of walk in this life must reflect this change.

The Fruit of The Spirit

In Galatians 5:22, the word *fruit* is in its singular form. This means there is one *fruit of the Spirit*, comprised of nine virtues. The evidence of the Holy Spirit operating in the lives of Christians manifests itself by these nine virtues. These virtues exemplify the very nature and character of Jesus Christ. This nine-fold fruit is the outward manifestation of the change that has taken place in the heart of a believer. It's the evidence of a life surrendered to the leading of the Holy Spirit.

Let's take a closer look at these nine outward signs that are evidence of a changed life. The fruit of the Spirit is love, joy, peace, patience, kindness, goodness, faithfulness, gentleness, and self-control (Galatians 5:22-23). Traditionally, these nine characteristics of the Spirit have been divided into three categories: 1) personal fruit/virtues that join us to God: love, joy & peace, 2) outreaching fruit/virtues that connect us to other people: patience, kindness & goodness, 3) inner character fruit/virtues that describe who we are on the inside: faithfulness, gentleness & self-control. These nine virtues are all part of one fruit, all of which are supplied by the Spirit. They cover our complete responsibility toward God and others. In essence, the fruit of the Spirit encompasses the entire Law of God; it reflects the two greatest commandments that Jesus gave us:

> *And He said to him, "'You shall love the Lord your God with all your heart, and with all your soul, and with all your mind.' This is the great and foremost commandment. The second is like it, 'You shall love your neighbor as yourself.' On these two commandments depend the whole Law and the Prophets."* (Matthew 22:37-40)

It is the fruit of the Spirit that makes it possible for us to be obedient to, and thus fulfill, the two greatest commandments; *...if you are led by the Spirit, you are not under the Law* (Galatians 5:18). If we allow ourselves to be led by the transforming power of the Holy Spirit, we are not bound by the Law. When we walk according to the Spirit, we are fulfilling the Law.

There's an abundance of Scripture that speaks to the type of change that occurs in the life of a Christian. But every type of behavior that one can expect to see from a Christian is encompassed by the fruit of the Spirit. For example, Colossians 3:12 states: *So, as those who have been chosen of God, holy and beloved, put on a heart of compassion, kindness, humility, gentleness and patience.* Two additional character traits seen here are a heart of compassion and humility. It is out of our love (fruit of the Spirit) for God and others that we are going to have a heart of compassion toward others and put their needs above our own. Also, because of the peace (fruit of the Spirit) that Christians have that comes from being reconciled to God, from that will flow a humble disposition. The various behavioral traits found in Scripture that one can expect to see in a Christian all come back to the fruit of the Spirit.

Without the indwelling Holy Spirit, a changed life that produces the fruit of the Spirit is not possible. While most of us have seen non-believers who can at times, display different aspects of the fruit of the Spirit, only the Spirit will produce *genuine* fruit. When this nine-fold fruit of the Spirit is manifested in a believer's life, God gets the glory. God's will and His kingdom agenda will be furthered, not the individual's. Below is an example of how people can, in appearance only, display the fruit of the Spirit.

One of the twelve disciples of Jesus was Judas Iscariot. This was a man who spent much time with Jesus. As Judas interacted with the other disciples, his behavior must have given the impression that he was a true follower of Christ. When Jesus mentioned that one of the twelve would betray Him, each one of them asked, "Lord, is it I?" (Matthew 26:22, NKJV). Apparently, Judas did not stand out as the one who was "most likely" to do such a thing. He must have displayed those types of behaviors one would expect to see in a Christian. However, his objective was not to further God's kingdom. He was ready and willing to betray Jesus for thirty pieces of silver (Matthew 26:15-16). He was never a true follower of Christ (John 17:12).

The Christian Walk

Now that we have discussed the change that occurs in the life of a Christian, I want to turn our attention to the Book of 1 John. Let's take a look at what the Apostle John had to say about the Christian walk.

> *This is the message we have heard from Him and announce to you, that God is Light, and in Him there is no darkness at all. If we say that we have fellowship with Him and yet walk in the darkness, we lie and do not practice the truth; but if we walk in the Light as He Himself is in the Light, we have fellowship with one another, and the blood of Jesus His Son cleanses us from all sin.* (1 John 1:5-7)

John tells us that God is Light. This speaks of His nature and His essence. God is perfectly righteous and holy, and in Him, there is no sin, nor darkness. Light and darkness are incompatible. If we walk in darkness—according to the sin nature—then we are not walking in the Light.

The Greek word for *truth* in this passage is the same word that is used in 1 John 1:8 which we covered in chapter two. It is God's objective Truth with respect to who He is, and all that He has purposed through His Son, Jesus Christ. The Greek word for *fellowship* is *koinonia*. It means community, communion, intimacy; joint participation (Strong's G2842). If we say we have fellowship with God—communion with Him—yet we walk in darkness, we lie and do not practice the truth. John is saying that our walk, or our manner of life, must demonstrate the spiritual fruit within us. If we walk in the Light as Christ is in the Light, then we not only have fellowship with God, we also have fellowship with one another.

Most of us have probably heard professing Christians make statements such as, "me and God...we're good," or "me and the big man upstairs have an understanding." I'm someone who considered myself to be "good with God" based purely on the reasoning of my imagination. It certainly wasn't a conclusion I came to based on the Word of God. But statements like these are revealing, especially when accompanied by a lifestyle that is inconsistent with the will of God. We may claim to have fellowship with God, but if the fruit of our lives doesn't bear that out, we lie and do not practice the truth. John's message in these verses is clear. We only have fellowship with God and one another if we walk in the Light. What we say or claim about our relationship with God is not what determines whether or not we are Christians. What does determine whether we are Christians is our manner of walk in this life. Have we had true repentance and fully placed our faith in Christ? Have we put off the sinful habits of our old nature? Is there spiritual fruit in our lives that reflects the nature and character of Christ? Are we growing in our faith and our Christian walk? Our answer to these questions will reveal whether or not we are walking in the Light.

We must remember that the Christian walk will not be perfect. But a Christian's walk should have an openness to it that can be easily seen by others. Though Christians will sin, there should never be a need to hide or walk in shame. Yes, Christians will feel ashamed of a sin they have committed, but an immediate response of confessing our sins to God is all that is needed for Him to cleanse us from all unrighteousness. Bear in mind, we no longer need to be cleansed from the penalty of sin. That was taken care of at the cross. We already have positional righteousness. We have been forgiven by God as Judge and declared righteous. However, we do need to be continually cleansed from the power and presence of sin. Unconfessed sin will always hinder our fellowship with God. Therefore, a believer's life is to be marked by an ongoing pattern of confession of our sins for the violation of God's Law. This is for our sanctification. We ask for forgiveness by God, not as Judge, but as Father. It is paternal forgiveness. And if we confess our sins, He is faithful and righteous to forgive us our sins (1 John 1:9). With that response, a Christian need not walk in shame nor feel condemned. Romans 8:1 tells us, *Therefore there is now no condemnation for those who are in Christ Jesus.* All our sin—past, present, and future—has already been removed. But we are called to be holy, even as He is holy (1 Peter 1:15-16). Therefore, we must confess our sins to God. With genuine confession, God cleanses us from our sins, and our fellowship with Him is easily restored. And by the power of the Holy Spirit, we will continue to walk in the Light.

If you find yourself struggling in your Christian walk, don't lose heart. The power of the Holy Spirit within you will enable you to grow and change, even if it's "baby steps." We do not all grow spiritually at the same pace. When Jesus was telling the Parable of the Sower to the crowd of people standing on the beach, He said, *"And others fell on the good soil and yielded a crop, some a hundredfold, some sixty, and some thirty"* (Matthew 13:8). The 'others' in this verse refers to the seed spoken of in the parable, which is representative of the Word of God (Matthew 13:19). Jesus said that those whose hearts are penetrated by His Word become born of God, and all yield a crop—some a hundredfold, some sixty, and some thirty. All true followers of Christ will yield spiritual fruit. We will not all yield the same amount to the same degree, but Jesus said we will all yield a crop of spiritual fruit. However, if you have no desire nor power to walk in the Light (in righteousness), regardless of what you claim or believe, according to 1 John 1:5-7, you are not born of God. You cannot walk in darkness and maintain fellowship with God.

Once you are born again, your life will be extremely different. This is not to say that a new Christian's behavior will necessarily appear extremely different, because not every new Christian was once living their life in such a way that was visibly against God's righteousness. But for everyone who becomes a true follower of Christ, the change is radical. It's as stark a contrast as being dead or alive. Ephesians 2:1-5 demonstrates this contrast:

> *And you were dead in your trespasses and sins, in which you formerly walked according to the course of this world, according to the prince of the power of the air, of the spirit that is now working in the sons of disobedience. Among them we too all formerly lived in the lusts of our flesh, indulging the desires of the flesh and of the mind, and were by nature children of wrath, even as the rest. But God, being rich in mercy, because of His great love with which He loved us, even when we were dead in our transgressions, made us alive together with Christ (by grace you have been saved).*

We learn from this passage that until we are born again by the Spirit of God, we are basically "dead men walking;" we are condemned to eternal death. In that condition, we live our lives based solely on our own ideas, ethical standards, needs, desires, and wants. We filter everything that comes at us in terms of how it relates to us personally, often responding in such a way as to make our lives more comfortable, easy, or happy. But once the Holy Spirit of God convicts us of our sin and we respond to God with genuine repentance and faith in His Son, we are made alive together with Christ. And to that, I say, "Amen!" As true followers of the Lord Jesus Christ, the Holy Spirit within us changes everything. Now we filter all that comes at us through a completely different lens. We no longer look at what comes our way in terms of how it relates to us personally. Rather, we deal with it from an eternal perspective. We think in terms of what God is doing in our lives, and how He is using circumstances and situations that He sets before us to mold and shape us into the image of His Son. We think in terms of living our lives in ways that bring Him glory and advance His kingdom. Life is no longer about our own ease, comfort, or happiness. For the Christian, our first and foremost goal is to love God above all else and to live a life that pleases Him (2 Corinthians 5:9). It is because of our faith in Christ and our obedience to Him that we have peace, comfort, strength, and joy. These are by-products of our obedience to God, who called us out of darkness and into the Light.

Jesus said, *"for where your treasure is, there your heart will be also"* (Matthew 6:21). If we have fully surrendered our lives over to Christ, our treasure—that which we hold dear—will be in heaven. We will have a heavenly mindset and will develop and cultivate a heart for the things of God. We will hold an eternal perspective in all things and walk accordingly.

Summary

The Holy Spirit of God indwells everyone who has come to repentance and faith in the Lord Jesus Christ. Once indwelt, the Holy Spirit immediately goes to work and begins aligning our wants and desires with God's will for our lives. This change, from being spiritually dead to spiritually alive, will always yield spiritual fruit. Believers will vary in the amount of spiritual fruit we produce, but there will always be evidence of a changed life. The manifestation of this evidence stems from Christians being connected to the Vine, Jesus Christ (John 15:5). As a result, Christians will progressively grow in faith and righteousness.

Chapter 7

AN ABIDING IN CHRIST

W E LEARNED IN CHAPTER SIX THAT ONE OF the hallmarks of a Christian is a changed life. This change is the direct result of being indwelt with the Holy Spirit. For all of us who are Christians, the Holy Spirit is our connection to God the Father and the Son, the Lord Jesus Christ. In this chapter, we are going to explore what it means to be connected to God the Father and the Son. In other words, we are going to learn what it means to abide in Christ.

The word used in Scripture to denote the connection between Christ and man is *abide*. The Greek word for *abide* is *menō*. It means to stay, continue, dwell, endure, remain, not to depart, to continue to be present (Strong's G3306). With this definition in mind, let's take a look at a beautiful passage of Scripture that illustrates what it means to abide in Christ. To get the context of this passage, a little background will be helpful. It was the night of the Jewish Passover, in which Jesus was soon to be handed over to His enemies. Jesus and His disciples had just finished the Passover meal in the upper room. Judas had already left the upper room with his plan to betray Jesus. Only the remaining eleven disciples were with Him. As they were making their way to the Garden of Gethsemane, Jesus spoke to His disciples, saying,

> 1 *"I am the true vine, and My Father is the vinedresser.*
> *2 Every branch in Me that does not bear fruit, He takes*
> *away; and every branch that bears fruit, He prunes it*
> *so that it may bear more fruit. 3 You are already clean*
> *because of the word which I have spoken to you. 4 Abide*
> *in Me, and I in you. As the branch cannot bear fruit of*
> *itself unless it abides in the vine, so neither can you unless*
> *you abide in Me. 5 I am the vine, you are the branches; he*
> *who abides in Me and I in him, he bears much fruit, for*
> *apart from Me you can do nothing. 6 If anyone does not*
> *abide in Me, he is thrown away as a branch and dries up;*
> *and they gather them, and cast them into the fire and they*
> *are burned. 7 If you abide in Me, and My words abide*
> *in you, ask whatever you wish, and it will be done for you.*
> *8 My Father is glorified by this, that you bear much fruit,*
> *and so prove to be My disciples. 9 Just as the Father has*
> *loved Me, I have also loved you; abide in My love. 10 If*
> *you keep My commandments, you will abide in My love;*
> *just as I have kept My Father's commandments and abide*
> *in His love. 11 These things I have spoken to you so that*
> *My joy may be in you, and that your joy may be made*
> *full."* (John 15:1-11)

Jesus began this discourse by saying that He is the true vine and His Father is the vinedresser. A vinedresser is a gardener or tiller of the soil. It's someone who attends to and lovingly cares for a garden to make sure that what he plants will produce the most bountiful harvest. As Jesus used the metaphor of a vine to convey His message, this would be very familiar to the disciples as the prophets of the Old Testament Scriptures also used this metaphor to describe the relationship between

God and the nation of Israel. In the Old Testament, it is Israel which is pictured as the vine or vineyard of God. *For the vineyard of the Lord of hosts is the house of Israel* (Isaiah 5:7). There are a number of Scriptures that speak to this, and they are found in Psalm 80, Isaiah 5, Jeremiah 2, Ezekiel 15 & 19, and Hosea 10. But of all those noted, the most illustrious is found in Isaiah 5:1-7. In these verses, Isaiah sings a song concerning God's vineyard, Israel. He sings of God having a vineyard on a fertile hill. God dug all around, removed its stones, and planted it with the choicest vine. God expected His vineyard to produce good grapes, but it only produced worthless ones. Since God cultivated it with care and yet it only produced worthless grapes, He had to take action. God's righteousness always demands justice. Therefore, God said He would remove its hedge, break down its wall, and lay it waste. This spoke of God's discipline towards the nation of Israel. They were in a degenerative state and God had to deal with their sin. The Jewish people had long since understood that the vineyard and vine were representative of their nation, Israel. Let's now go through John 15:1-11 and look at each statement made by Jesus.

Jesus, The True Vine

The first thing Jesus said to His disciples was that *He* is the true vine. With this statement, the vine as symbolic to the nation of Israel was now obsolete. Jesus stated the fact that He is the fulfillment of the symbolism of the vine in relationship to the vinedresser. This was a new concept to the Jews. Before Christ came, the Jewish people believed they were saved because they were/are God's chosen people. But now that their Messiah had come, the symbolism of their nation as the vine of God, as spoken by their prophets of old, was no more. Jesus was the fulfillment of those prophetic utterances. Christ's arrival into the world ushered in a new dispensation, a new covenant. We must now be rooted in Him, the only true connection to God the Father, our heavenly vinedresser. The word *true* in this verse in the Greek is *alēthinos*. It means that which has not only the name and resemblance but the real nature corresponding to the name, in every respect; real, true, genuine (Strong's G228). This makes it clear that Jesus is *the Vine*, both in name and in nature.

Though the Jewish people had understood themselves to be the vine of God's vineyard, their vineyard was never rightly connected to God due to their sin. But Jesus, who has no sin, is the true vine. He is rightly connected to God and God to Him. Jesus told His disciples they had to be connected to Him because their Jewish lineage alone was not enough to save them. This is true for all peoples and nations. Our connection to God comes only through His Son. It does not come from an affiliation with a group or a nation, nor any religious ceremonial connection such as Baptism, nor faithful church attendance. It reminds me of what John the Baptist said to the Pharisees and Sadducees as they were coming for baptism.

> *"Therefore bear fruit in keeping with repentance; and do not suppose that you can say to yourselves, 'We have Abraham for our father'; for I say to you that from these stones God is able to raise up children to Abraham. The axe is already laid at the root of the trees; therefore every tree that does not bear good fruit is cut down and thrown into the fire."* (Matthew 3:8-10)

John the Baptist was telling His Jewish brethren that God could easily raise up children of Abraham from stones! He wanted them to know that simply being a descendant of Abraham was not enough.

The words Jesus spoke to His disciples revealed the truth of the New Covenant. They must have an intimate and personal relationship with Him to be rightly connected to God. The same is true today. Jesus told us in John 14:6, *"I am the way, and the truth, and the life; no one comes to the Father but through Me."* This one statement made by Jesus nullified all other beliefs regarding how humanity must come to God the Father. It is also probably one of the hardest things to accept by many professing Christians. Remember, Jesus said you are either with Him or against Him (Matthew 12:30). A Christian cannot sit on the fence, nor go along to get along. A true follower of Christ is an adherent of all that Jesus said and recognizes and submits to His rulership and authority over his or her life. With that said, Christ's statement that He is the only way to God the Father is either true or it's not. If one professes to be a follower of Christ, then the notion that "all roads lead to heaven," cannot be true. To be rightly connected to God, we must be connected to Christ (1 Timothy 2:5; 1 John 2:23). It is only by the forgiveness of our sins through the shed blood of Jesus Christ and our faith in Him, that we are made right with God. Jesus is the One and only true Vine that connects us to God the Father.

Two Kinds of Branches

Let's now look at verse 2 of John 15. *"Every branch in Me that does not bear fruit, He takes away; and every branch that bears fruit, He prunes it so that it may bear more fruit."* There are two kinds of branches on the vine: those that produce fruit and those that don't. Jesus tells us in verse 5 that His followers are the branches. Christians receive nourishment and sustenance from being connected to Christ and will manifest Jesus in our lives as spiritual fruit. Those who claim to follow Christ, yet are not connected to Him, will not produce any fruit. Jesus stated that the branches that do not bear fruit, His Father takes away. The words *takes away* are comprised of one word in the Greek, *airō*. It means to bear away what has been raised, carry off: to take off or away; to rend away, cut off (Strong's G142). Vine's states: It is used in the Lord's statement, "Every branch in Me that beareth not fruit, He taketh it away." This does not contemplate members of the "body" of Christ, but those who (just as a graft which being inserted, does not "abide" or "strike") are merely professed followers, giving only the appearance of being joined to the parent stem (Vine's Expository Dictionary).

Given the definition of the words *takes away*, it is important to mention there is some controversy over what is meant by this verse. There are two main schools of thought regarding the branches that don't bear fruit. Some believe that Jesus is only speaking to true believers in this passage because He said, *"Every branch in Me...."* This is a strong statement that would cause one to come to this conclusion because only true believers are *in Christ*. Under this interpretation, the non-fruit-bearing branches that are taken away are viewed as being lifted up by the vinedresser to allow more sunshine and air to reach them so they can begin bearing fruit. Then there is another school of thought which views the non-fruit-bearing branches as simply being professed followers, but not true followers. They claim to believe in Christ, yet are not truly *in Christ*. Because they are only professing followers, they are removed from the vine. The Vine's Expository Dictionary definition supports this interpretation, indicating that the branches that are taken away refer to followers who only give the appearance of being joined to the parent stem. I lean toward this interpretation for a number of reasons. First, Jesus described what occurs with the branches that don't bear fruit—they are cast into the fire and burned (v. 6). Fire typically speaks of judgment. *Cast into the fire* can also mean a refining process. But Jesus said those branches are burned, not refined. Another reason I lean toward this interpretation is that Jesus said not everyone who calls Him 'Lord' will enter the kingdom of heaven (Matthew 7:21). He made it clear that the mere profession of Him as Lord is not what determines whether we are truly connected to Him.

> *"Many will say to Me on that day, 'Lord, Lord, did we not prophesy in Your name, and in Your name cast out demons, and in Your name perform many miracles?' "And then I will declare to them, 'I never knew you; depart from Me, you who practice lawlessness.' "* (Matthew 7:22-23)

There is also the Parable of the Sower which we find in Matthew 13:3-9, Mark 4:3-20, and Luke 8:5-15. Jesus taught His disciples that only some of the people who heard the Word of God allowed it to pierce their hearts. Those who heard the Word and accepted it were the ones who bore fruit (Mark 4:20). In each illustration, we see that not everyone who professes to be a Christian is a true follower of Christ. We saw an example of this in the previous chapter concerning Judas Iscariot. Judas spent approximately three years with Jesus and was numbered among the twelve. He was "attached" to Jesus—the true Vine—yet did not bear spiritual fruit. So while one can interpret this passage of Scripture to refer only to true believers in Christ, I lean toward it referring to both groups: those who profess to be in Christ and those who truly are in Christ. But whichever school of thought you subscribe to, Jesus said only those who abide in Him can bear fruit.

In the second part of verse 2, we see that every branch that does bear fruit is pruned by God so that it can bear more fruit. Most of us are familiar with the pruning process. It is something that is done to keep a tree healthy so that it will bear more fruit. The word *prune* in the Greek is *kathairō*. It's where we get our English word *catharsis*. It means to cleanse, of filth, impurity, etc.; to prune trees and vines from useless shoots; metaphorically, to cleanse from guilt (Strong's G2508). Pruning is a cleansing to remove impurities. Again, we find there are two main schools of thought on what this particular pruning means. Some view this as simply a cleansing of the believer through the Word of God. In this way, it's seen as a washing and renewing of the mind as we abide in God's Word, thus allowing His Word to transform our hearts as the Spirit speaks to us. It's not difficult to come to this conclusion given the very next verse. In verse 3, Jesus said to His disciples, *"You are already clean because of the word which I have spoken to you."* However, there is another school of thought. Many Bible scholars see this as God cutting away those things in a believer's life that are not in line with God's will so that they can continue to produce more fruit. When we look at it this way, we find that it can encompass a whole host of circumstances that might be unwanted or uncomfortable. In this scenario, God will use any circumstances required in order to strengthen our faith and get us back into alignment with His will. My first read-through of this Scripture brought me to the idea that to be pruned is to be cut back. If we are "cut back" in order to produce more fruit, then, of course, there will often be pain. God in His sovereignty will sometimes use adverse circumstances to bring us back into alignment with His will. This is in keeping with Hebrews 12:6 which states, *For those whom the Lord loves He disciplines....* Personally, I can see how this could easily be either. God is not limited in how He chooses to prune us so that we become more fruitful. But what is clear, is that regardless of how He does it, He does it. God cleanses us of our impurities—those things in our lives that are in opposition to His holiness. He does this through the sanctification process so that we may become more fruitful in living a life that is in alignment with His will and rightly bears the image of His Son.

Though some see the pruning process as something God does that doesn't seem appealing, God as our heavenly vinedresser, who lovingly cares for His vineyard, is actually a beautiful picture of what He does in our lives. We see Him here as the vineyard owner who truly cares about what He has planted. His goal—a harvest that yields the peaceful fruit of righteousness (Hebrews 12:11). A gardener who prunes is never closer to the plant than when his hands are right there on it, removing dead branches and carefully pruning back fruitful ones. God knows each one of us intimately and therefore, knows exactly what we need to produce a more bountiful harvest, which ultimately brings Him glory (John 15:8).

God's Word Cleanses Us

John 15:3 states: *"You are already clean because of the word which I have spoken to you."* Jesus told His disciples that it was by His very words—the truth He had spoken since they had been with Him—that they had already been made clean. The word *clean* in the Greek is very similar to the word *prune*. It is *katharos*. It means clean, pure; physically, like a vine cleansed by pruning and so fitted to bear fruit; ethically, free from corrupt desire, from sin and guilt; blameless, innocent; unstained with the guilt of anything (Strong's G2513). Jesus's words have a cleansing effect on us. He told His disciples they were already pure and free from sin and guilt because they had personally been abiding with Him for the past three-and-a-half years. Their faith and belief in Him as their Savior (Matthew 16:16) had them rightly connected to God the Father.

The cleansing effect of Jesus's words greatly increases the importance of studying Scripture. Let's take a look at Psalm 119:9-16. The writer of this psalm is unknown, however, many Bible scholars believe it was most likely written by David. Psalm 119 is the longest chapter in the Bible, containing one-hundred and seventy-six verses. This is a psalm that glorifies and exalts God's written word. All throughout this psalm, there are references to the written Word of God—His laws, His statutes, His commandments, His ordinances, His precepts, His judgments, and His testimonies. The psalmist declares his joy and peace that come from living a life of obedience to God's Word, even in the midst of adversity. The psalmist has a strong desire to know, understand, and hold tightly to the Word of God so that he may stand firm in times of distress and remain in fellowship with God.

> *"How can a young man keep his way pure?*
> *By keeping it according to Your word.*
> *With all my heart I have sought You;*
> *Do not let me wander from Your commandments.*
> *Your word I have treasured in my heart,*
> *That I may not sin against You.*
> *Blessed are You, O Lord;*
> *Teach me Your statutes.*
> *With my lips I have told of*
> *All the ordinances of Your mouth.*
> *I have rejoiced in the way of Your testimonies,*

As much as in all riches.
I will meditate on Your precepts
And regard Your ways.
I shall delight in Your statutes;
I shall not forget Your word." (Psalm 119:9-16)

The writer of this psalm asks the question, "how can a young man keep his way pure?" The word 'way' is a reference to the psalmist's way of life—his lifestyle. He then answers his own question by stating that we keep our way pure according to God's Word. It is that plain and simple. It is through God's written Word, the Holy Scriptures of the Bible, that we learn what it means to live a godly life. We learn who God truly is and what He expects of His children. The psalmist emphasizes the importance of all that God has said and that we are not to wander from it. We are to treasure His Word in our hearts. We are to learn it, rejoice in it, meditate on it, delight in it, and never forget it. The more we treasure and learn God's Word, the greater the cleansing effect it has on us.

For me personally, it was through studying the Word of God that I became saved. As I dug deeper and deeper into the Word of God, Truth was continually being revealed to me by His Spirit. Hebrews 4:12 tells us, *For the word of God is living and active and sharper than any two-edged sword, and piercing as far as the division of soul and spirit, of both joints and marrow, and able to judge the thoughts and intentions of the heart.* Without a doubt, this is an undeniable truth. God's Word is razor-sharp and pierces the heart as nothing else can. It reveals to us who we are apart from Him and how desperately we need Him. Once that truth grabs a hold of us, there is no turning back. The Holy Spirit does His job as He shines the spotlight on our need for Jesus with a force and clarity that brings us to our knees in repentance. After we repent and put our faith in Christ, abiding—remaining—in His Word is what deepens and strengthens our connection to Him. God's Word will continually reveal those things in our lives that we need to put off so that we can accurately bear the image of Christ. Let's see why this is so important as we turn our attention back to the next statements made by Jesus in John 15:4-6.

Abide In Christ

> 4 "*Abide in Me, and I in you. As the branch cannot bear fruit of itself unless it abides in the vine, so neither can you unless you abide in Me. 5 I am the vine, you are the branches; he who abides in Me and I in him, he bears much fruit, for apart from Me you can do nothing. 6 If anyone does not abide in Me, he is thrown away as a branch and dries up; and they gather them, and cast them into the fire and they are burned.*" (John 15:4-6)

We already noted that to abide means to stay, to remain. Jesus instructs us to remain in Him; we remain in Him, He remains in us. He also states that just like branches on the vine, we must remain connected to Him in order to bear fruit. Why? Because apart from Him we can do nothing! So this begs the question, how exactly do we remain; how do we abide?

We Abide by Obeying

Jesus said, "*If you keep My commandments, you will abide in My love; just as I have kept My Father's commandments and abide in His love*" (John 15:10). To abide in Christ is to keep His commandments. To 'keep' His commandments means to obey His commandments. What are Jesus's commandments? They can be found in Matthew 22:37-40. A Pharisee asked Jesus which commandment of the Law was the greatest. Jesus responded,

> "*You shall love the Lord your God with all your heart, and with all your soul, and with all your mind. This is the*

great and foremost commandment. The second is like it,
You shall love your neighbor as yourself. On these two com-
mandments depend the whole Law and the Prophets."

Jesus expounded further on the type of love we are to have for others by saying, *"A new commandment I give to you, that you love one another, even as I have loved you, that you also love one another"* (John 13:34). Jesus commands us to not only love our neighbor as ourselves but to love others in such a way that mirrors His love for us. How did Christ love us? Selflessly; sacrificially. He loved us to the point of death. He selflessly laid down His life as the substitute sacrifice for the penalty of our sins, in order to bring about our highest good—eternal life. When we love God above all else and love others the way Christ loves us, a natural outflow of this love will bring forth obedience to Him and His Word. When we love as Christ commanded, we fulfill not only God's Ten Commandments given to us in the Book of Exodus but also everything that Christ taught.

Another key verse that speaks to abiding is found in 1 John 3:24. *The one who keeps His commandments abides in Him, and He in him. We know by this that He abides in us, by the Spirit whom He has given us.* We can know we are abiding in Christ by our obedience to His commandments. We also learn that we can know that Christ is abiding in us by the Spirit He has given to us.

We Abide by Obeying Jesus's Teachings

Anyone who goes too far (runs ahead; wanders away) *and does not abide in the teaching of Christ, does not have God; the one who abides in the teaching, he has both the Father and the Son* (2 John 9). The Apostle John states that for us to *have God*—that is, to be rightly connected to God—we must abide in the teachings of Christ. If we do so, we are truly connected to both God and Jesus. We see a similar verse in 1 John 2:24. *As for you, let that abide in you which you heard from the beginning.*

114

If what you heard from the beginning abides in you, you also will abide in the Son and in the Father. We can have confidence that if we abide in the teachings of Jesus, then we are abiding in both the Son and the Father.

We also learn in the Gospel of Luke that we are wise if we act on—obey—Jesus's words. Jesus was speaking to His disciples and the crowd of people who had come to hear Him. Jesus said,

> *"Why do you call Me, 'Lord, Lord,' and do not do what I say? Everyone who comes to Me and hears my words and acts on them, I will show you whom he is like: he is like a man building a house, who dug deep and laid a foundation on the rock; and when a flood occurred, the torrent burst against that house and could not shake it, because it had been well built. But the one who has heard and has not acted accordingly, is like a man who built a house on the ground without any foundation; and the torrent burst against it and immediately it collapsed, and the ruin of that house was great."* (Luke 6:46-49)

The first thing Jesus asked was why do we call Him 'Lord' if we do not obey Him? That's a good question and one we should ask ourselves. Many professing Christians will call Jesus their Lord and Savior, yet not obey Him. The word *Lord* in the Greek is *kyrios*. It means he to whom a person belongs; the possessor and disposer of a thing, the owner; one who has control of the person, the master (Strong's G2962). To call Jesus 'Lord' is to state that we obey Him as our owner/master. Jesus asked this question because He wanted the people to understand the difference between those who simply call Him Lord, as opposed to those who honor and submit to Him as Lord.

Jesus then used an analogy to make His point. He depicted those who merely claim He is Lord as those who build their house on the ground without a foundation. Of those who honor Him as Lord, He depicted them as those who build their house on a solid foundation. The houses may look the same above ground, but one of them only gives the appearance of being well-built. You won't be able to detect which one was built upon a solid foundation until the storms of life come. During a storm, it will become clear. The houses that withstand the storms are analogous to those who obey Jesus. They hear and wisely act upon His words. Their foundations are built upon Jesus Christ Himself. With Jesus as their foundation, they are given the strength to stand firm in the midst of adversity. Without a solid foundation, the ruin of a house will be great.

We see a similar passage in 2 Thessalonians 2:15. *So then, brethren, stand firm and hold to the traditions which you were taught, whether by word of mouth or by letter from us.* The word *traditions* in the Greek is *paradosis*. It means a giving over which is done by word of mouth or in writing, i.e. tradition by instruction, narrative, precept, etc. (Strong's G3862). Paul, the author of 2 Thessalonians, is not referring simply to the traditions of men. The context of Paul's letter refers to the traditions that he and other disciples taught the believers in Thessalonica regarding the gospel of Jesus Christ. We are instructed to stand firm upon the solid foundation of the gospel of Jesus Christ.

All these verses show us that we abide in Christ by being obedient to Him and all that He taught. If we are to be obedient to all that He taught, we need to know what He taught. We learn and come to know what Jesus taught through reading the Scriptures. Being in the Scriptures daily is of utmost importance.

Jesus Himself told us how important it is that we obey the words He taught us.

> "*If anyone loves Me, he will keep My word; and My Father will love him, and We will come to him and make Our abode with him.* He who does not love Me does not keep My words; and the word which you hear is not Mine, but the Father's who sent Me." (John 14:23-24)

God the Father and the Son abide in us when we keep Jesus's words. It's a two-way street; we abide in Christ through obedience to Him and His Word, and He abides in us. It is through our obedience, birthed out of our love for Christ and a desire to please Him, that we abide in Him.

We Abide by Living Like Jesus

Another way we abide in Christ is by living like Christ. First John 2:6 states, ...*the one who says he abides in Him ought himself to walk in the same manner as He walked*. This verse begins as a claim one might make about him- or herself as being someone who abides in Christ. If you claim you abide in Christ, the Apostle John says your walk, or manner of behavior, ought to be in the same manner as Jesus walked. Our lives should bear fruit that proves we are followers of Christ. Of course, that begs the question, what was the manner in which Jesus walked?

As we study the life of Jesus, the manner in which He walked this earth is quite evident. This will not be an exhaustive account of everything we learn about Jesus, but we will take a broad look at some of His character traits as we examine the life He lived while on this earth.

Once again, let's look at Galatians 5:22-23. *But the fruit of the Spirit is love, joy, peace, patience, kindness, goodness, faithfulness, gentleness, self-control; against such things there is no law.* All these attributes are found in Jesus Christ. And as noted earlier, once we are born again, we too, take on these same attributes. They all describe Jesus's nature and character. With that in mind, as we take a look at the manner in which Jesus walked, everything He said and did stem from these nine virtues.

Love

As I've studied the life of Jesus, the most prominent character trait that comes across is His incredible love for all mankind. He has a deep, abiding love for humanity that is unmistakable. As we see His life on display throughout the gospels, He didn't just love a few choice men and women, He loved everyone. This included those who mistreated Him as well as those whom He confronted and chastised. Jesus loved unconditionally and sacrificially. This means He put others' needs above His own without regard to any gain for Himself. We see this primarily played out on the cross. Jesus said, *"Greater love has no one than this, that one lay down his life for his friends"* (John 15:13). Jesus chose to come to this earth for the very purpose of sacrificing Himself on our behalf. We are told in Philippians 2:6-8, that Jesus, *who, although He existed in the form of God, did not regard equality with God a thing to be grasped, but emptied Himself, taking the form of a bond-servant, and being made in the likeness of men. Being found in appearance as a man, He humbled Himself by becoming obedient to the point of death, even death on a cross.* Jesus emptied Himself. This means He willingly laid aside His equality with God the Father to become a man. He took on the form of a bond-servant—one who serves willingly by giving himself up to another. He humbled Himself, becoming obedient to the point of death on a cross. Out of His love for us, Jesus *chose* to become a man and die on the cross. This is not to say the human side of Him didn't struggle with knowing what awaited Him. He had full knowledge of the reason He came to this earth and He agonized over it. In Luke 12:50, Jesus said, *"But I have a baptism to undergo, and how distressed I am until it is accomplished!"* Previously, we learned that the word *baptism* means 'an immersion.' Jesus was fully immersed in the agony that was set before Him. He felt much pressure in anticipation of that moment in which victory over sin and death would be accomplished.

The distress Jesus felt over what He was about to endure also comes across when we see Him praying to the Father in the Garden of Gethsemane. Three times He asked His Father, "if it is possible, let this cup pass from Me" (Matthew 26:39, 42, 44). His flesh didn't want to be crucified. But the power of His Spirit was greater than that of His flesh, and therefore, He submitted to the Father's will. Each time He asked that the cup pass from Him, He immediately followed it up with, *"yet not as I will, but as You will."* The 'cup' was a reference to His awaiting crucifixion, in which God's wrath would be poured out on Him. He was willing to take the punishment for our sin, the punishment that we all deserve. We recall Jesus's words in John 14:6, saying, *"I am the way, and the truth, and the life; no one comes to the Father but through Me."* This is why God did not allow the cup to pass from His Son. Christ dying for our sins was, and still is, the *only* way for sinful man to be reconciled to a holy God.

As we bring to mind Jesus's prayer in the garden as well as Philippians 2:6-8, we see that Jesus *chose* to come to earth to redeem us. The word *redeem* means to liberate by payment of ransom (Strong's G3084). Jesus chose to come to earth to buy us back from the slave market of sin; He came to set us free from sin's bondage. Jesus came willingly, despite what it would cost Him. He did this out of His great love for us so that we can have eternal life with Him and the Father. That is a level of love I will never fully understand, at least not this side of heaven. Knowing what awaited Him and what it would accomplish, is enough to show me that He loves unconditionally and sacrificially—a love beyond measure. He sacrificed His own life for my sake and the sake of all humanity.

Loving sacrificially and unconditionally is exactly what our love for others should look like. Love is an action, not a feeling. We are commanded by God to love others whether we feel like it or not. It is an intentional act toward someone with a desire for their highest good. Their needs are to be placed before our own, and we are to love whether we believe people are deserving of it or not. Paul wrote in Romans 5:8, *But God demonstrates His own love toward us, in that while we were yet sinners, Christ died for us.* God didn't ask us to prove we were worthy of His love. He sent His only Son to die for us while we were still at enmity with Him. This is a great example of how we are to love others. We are to love without pre-condition, and we are to sacrifice our own needs and wants for the sake of another's highest good.

Compassion

Jesus's love for others brought forth compassion, mercy, and a willingness to help those in need. One of my favorite things Jesus said was, "I am willing." This was the response He gave when a leper came and bowed before Him and said, "Lord, if You are willing, You can make me clean." Jesus stretched out His hand and touched him, saying, "I am willing." The man was then healed of his leprosy (Matthew 8:2-3; Luke 5:12-13). Those words from our Lord touch me deeply. Jesus, who is God in human flesh and more awesome and great beyond anything we can imagine, is so moved by our need, however great or small, that He says, "I am willing." It is so humbling and moves me to tears. That's the heart of Jesus's compassion and mercy seen throughout the four gospels. Jesus had such compassion for others that it compelled Him to help and heal. He made peoples' needs a priority, always putting their needs above man-made traditions and rules. We see this played out a number of times in the gospels. The Pharisees would question Jesus about healing, which they viewed as "working," on the Sabbath. Jesus acted when He saw a need. His compassion had no bounds. He fed the hungry. He healed those who were physically or mentally sick. He raised the dead. He spread His message of salvation to the lost and sent out His disciples to do the same. He had compassion for the downtrodden, the blind, the lame, and infirm. Jesus had such mercy and compassion for others—a great example of how we should live our lives. We too must show compassion toward the mental, physical, and spiritual needs of others and should always be ready to respond to human sorrow, pain, and suffering.

Prayer/Intercession

All four gospels note that Jesus would often go away by Himself to pray. He desired time alone with the Father. Sometimes I think to myself, of all the people in this world who wouldn't need to pray, it would be Jesus. But no, Jesus needed that one-on-one time with the Father as it allowed

Him to remain intimately connected to Him. Remaining connected to the Father through prayer keeps us in communion with Him and helps us discern God's will for our lives. It was after an entire night of prayer that we see Jesus choosing His twelve disciples (Luke 6:12-13). What a great example when we are faced with making decisions. Spending time in prayer produces an atmosphere in which we are more receptive to the promptings of the Holy Spirit. When we lean on God for His wisdom, He will provide us with the direction and guidance we need in all areas of our lives.

We also see Jesus praying for believers in John 17. He prayed for all who would hear His message and respond to it by repentance and faith. Though my name doesn't appear in the Bible, I am most definitely included! Jesus, through this specific prayer, interceded on my behalf. *"I do not ask on behalf of these alone* (the eleven remaining disciples)*, but for those also who believe in Me through their word"* (John 17:20). Every single one of us who has come to a saving faith in the Lord Jesus Christ is found in these words. We are the *those also* who come to believe in Him through the teaching of God's Word from those who have come before us. Jesus goes on to say in verse 21, *"that they* (again, a reference to all who have come to faith in Christ throughout the ages) *may all be one; even as You, Father, are in Me and I in You, that they also may be in Us, so that the world may believe that You sent Me."* As believers, we are all one in Christ. We are in Him and He is in us (John 15:5). How wonderful and comforting it is to know that Jesus had me in mind when He prayed this prayer to the Father. What does this tell me? I matter to Him.

Jesus is our great intercessor. Hebrews 7:25 tells us, *Jesus is able also to save forever those who draw near to God through Him, since He* (Jesus) *always lives to make intercession for them.* The most important way Jesus interceded for us was in the way we all need most—as our sacrificial Lamb who reconciles sinful man to a holy God (2 Corinthians 5:18, 21). His current ministry includes continual intercession for the saints. We also learn that Jesus is our Advocate, the One who pleads our case before the Father when we come to God in confession (1 John 2:1-2). We learn from

Jesus's example that we are to remain connected to the Father through prayer, and we are to be intercessors for others. When we spend time alone with God our Father, pouring out our hearts to Him, listening to His voice through the promptings of the Holy Spirit, and interceding for others who need prayer, we are following Christ's example.

Obedience to God's Will

Jesus always did the will of the Father (John 5:30; 8:29). From the moment He entered this world until the time He left it, Jesus was obedient to the Father, even to the point of death (Philippians 2:8). In order for us to be obedient to the Father, we have to know the Father's will. If we do not spend time in prayer, nor in God's Word, nor listen to sound biblical teaching, how will we know the will of the Father? We won't. We must be intimately connected to God. Our connection to the Father is what will fuel our desire to know and be obedient to His will.

Several verses in the Bible make a direct reference to God's will for us. For example, the Apostle Paul tells us in 1 Thessalonians 5:18, *...in everything give thanks; for this is God's will for you in Christ Jesus.* And in 1 Thessalonians 4:3, we find, *For this*—walking in a manner that pleases God (v.1)—*is the will of God, your sanctification....* The word *will* in the Greek is *thelēma*. It means: of what God wishes or has determined shall be done by us: commands, precepts (Strong's G2307). Given this definition, the will of God can be summed up in one statement—obedience to Him and His Word. That means yielding to, trusting in, believing in, and acting upon all that God asks of us.

God's desire for our obedience to Him is clearly seen in 1 Samuel 15. God gave Saul, the king of Israel, a specific command. When the prophet Samuel later questioned Saul about carrying out God's command, Saul told Samuel he had obeyed what God asked of him (1 Samuel 15:20). But he had not. The evidence was all around them. The sounds of bleating sheep and lowing oxen contradicted Saul's statement. God had given Saul a direct command, and Saul disobeyed. Saul said he had obeyed because, for the most part, he had done what God asked of him. But partially obeying God—picking and choosing for ourselves which commands of God we decide to obey—is direct disobedience.

God was not pleased with Saul, and therefore, rejected him as king. God's position regarding disobedience to Him and His rejection of Saul, was spoken through the prophet Samuel:

> *"For rebellion is as the sin of divination, and insubordination is as iniquity and idolatry. Because you have rejected the word of the Lord, He has also rejected you from being king."* (1 Samuel 15:23)

God wants obedience, not just some semblance of it.

> *"Has the Lord as much delight in burnt offerings and sacrifices as in obeying the voice of the Lord? Behold, <u>to obey is better than sacrifice</u>."* (1 Samuel 15:22)

God doesn't want anything we have to offer Him if we give it to Him from a place of disobedience. God wasn't interested in Saul's sacrifices or burnt offerings; He wanted obedience. The same is true for us. God doesn't want us to offer up prayers or make personal sacrifices if they are not done from a heart that desires to please Him and remain obedient to Him. Doing the will of the Father is to be obedient to all that the Father asks of us. Jesus is our great example. He always did the will of the Father. Though we may fall short from time to time, the Father's will must always be our aim.

Proclamation of the Gospel

The gospel message encompasses Jesus's death, burial, and resurrection. It is what Jesus accomplished for us on the cross so that we might be saved. During His earthly ministry, His death, burial, and resurrection had not yet occurred. Therefore, what we see Jesus proclaiming is the kingdom of heaven (Matthew 4:17) or the kingdom of God (Luke 4:43), both of which are the same thing—a system or government comprised of the power, strength, rule, and authority of God. We learn in Matthew 28:18 that all authority has been given to Jesus in heaven and on earth. Colossians 1:13 tells us that God *rescued us from the domain of darkness, and transferred us to the <u>kingdom of His beloved Son</u>*. Therefore, Jesus, His rulership, power, strength, and authority *is* the Kingdom. Though there is a difference in the way the authors of the gospels note this kingdom, there is no difference in their meaning. So why the difference in writing, noting one as the kingdom of heaven and the other as the kingdom of God?

Matthew wrote his gospel primarily to a Jewish audience who were familiar with the writings of the prophets. While the Old Testament doesn't use the specific phrase *kingdom of heaven* or *kingdom of God*, the idea of God's Kingdom is there, such as we see in Daniel 2. In Daniel 2:34-35, the stone, cut without hands, crushes the statue, and thus becomes a great mountain and fills the whole earth. The stone is representative of Jesus. When He returns to rule and reign on earth, He will establish His Kingdom which will fill the whole earth. In addition to their knowledge of the Scriptures, the Jewish people revered the name of God to the point of never uttering His name aloud. They also left out the vowels of His name when they noted it in writing. They simply wrote, "YHWH," so as not to dishonor God. Luke, on the other hand, was writing to a Gentile audience in which this level of reverence did not exist. The Gentiles were not familiar with the God of Israel. Given that Luke was writing to a different audience, he used *the kingdom of God* rather than *the kingdom of heaven*.

Jesus told us in Matthew 3:2, *"Repent, for the kingdom of heaven is at hand."* Jesus said the kingdom of heaven *is at hand* because the kingdom of heaven was now living among them. When Jesus was questioned by the Pharisees as to when the kingdom of God was coming, the last part of His response to their question was that the kingdom of God was in their midst (Luke 17:21). Jesus was clearly referring to Himself. If there is a kingdom, then it follows that there is a king who rules and reigns over that kingdom. As noted above, God rescued us from the domain of darkness and transferred us to the kingdom of His beloved Son, and Jesus is the King (John 18:36; Revelation 19:16).

We learn in the Gospel of Luke that while Jesus was in the synagogue, He read from the book of the prophet Isaiah. Jesus read out loud from where it was written:

> "*The Spirit of the Lord is upon Me, because He anointed Me to preach the gospel to the poor. He has sent Me to proclaim release to the captives, and recovery of sight to the blind, to set free those who are oppressed, to proclaim the favorable year of the Lord.*" (Luke 4:18-19)

Jesus closed the book, gave it back to the attendant, and sat down. He then said, *"Today this Scripture has been fulfilled in your hearing"* (Luke 4:21). Jesus *is* the gospel, the kingdom of heaven, which had come to earth and was now living among them. It was He who would release the captives—those in bondage to sin. It was He who would open the eyes of the unbelieving so that they could see Him as their Messiah. And it was He who would set free those who were oppressed by the weight of sin.

In Luke 4:43, Jesus said, *"I must preach the kingdom of God to the other cities also, for I was sent for this purpose."* Jesus's ministry was to preach Himself, as the Messiah, to the Jewish nation. Jesus told us that He came to seek and to save that which was lost (Matthew 18:11; Luke 19:10). Jesus came to preach that He is the only way to the Father. He would become the propitiation for the sin of mankind, that whosoever believed in Him would have eternal life (John 3:16). Anyone who would place his or her faith in Him would be set free—free from the bondage of sin and free from eternal death.

What does Jesus's proclamation of the gospel mean for us? It is the same message we are to preach and share with the world. Jesus said to His disciples,

> *"Go therefore and make disciples of all the nations, baptizing them in the name of the Father and the Son and the Holy Spirit, teaching them to observe all that I commanded you; and lo, I am with you always, even to the end of the age."* (Matthew 28:19-20)

As followers of Christ, we are to proclaim the gospel message, making disciples of all who are within our sphere of influence, teaching them all that Jesus commanded.

Reliance Upon God's Word

Another prominent aspect of Jesus's ministry was His reliance upon God's written word. We will see the significance of this more thoroughly in a later chapter, but it's important to note here Jesus's high view of Scripture. He quoted Old Testament Scripture often, thus validating it as the written Word of God. Jesus knew the Scriptures thoroughly and He used them often. For example, we see His use of Scripture when He combated temptation (Matthew 4:1-11; Mark 1:12-13; Luke 4:1-13). This shows us the importance of knowing the Word of God. The Word of God is Truth (John 17:17). Knowing God's Word helps us discern between God's Truth and everything else (Psalm 119:105; Ephesians 4:14). When we have His Word in our hearts and minds, we are at-the-ready to combat anything that comes our way, including temptation.

We are told: *Put on the full armor of God, so that you will be able to stand firm against the schemes of the devil* (Ephesians 6:11). In Ephesians 6:14-17, the Apostle Paul tells us what that armor consists of and how we are to use it. Of all the "weapons" of armor we are to employ, all are defensive except one. The only offensive "weapon" in our armor is the sword of the Spirit, which is the Word of God (Ephesians 6:17). When we know Truth, we can stand firm on the solid foundation of Jesus Christ, and not be moved, swayed, or carried away by the things of the world. We must be rooted and grounded in God's Word. Jesus quoted Scripture often, applying it as needed. This is a great example for us. Let us follow His example by relying upon, and applying, the Word of God as needed.

A Servant's Heart

We also see Jesus as the one who *did not come to be served, but to serve, and to give His life a ransom for many* (Matthew 20:28). Some Scriptures specifically refer to Jesus as God's Servant (Isaiah 42:1-4; Philippians 2:7), but Jesus's own life reflected a servant's heart, attitude, and actions. Jesus taught that humility and servanthood stem from the attitude of the heart and the two are linked together.

> *"You know that those who are recognized as rulers of the Gentiles lord it over them; and their great men exercise authority over them. But it is not this way among you, but whoever wishes to become great among you shall be your servant; and whoever wishes to be first among you shall be slave of all."* (Mark 10:42-44)

Jesus stated that rulers and officials like to flaunt their authority over the people they rule. But He taught His disciples that it would be different among them. Whoever wanted to become great or be placed in a position of authority, must be a servant of the people. Our attitude and actions toward others are to be such that we humble ourselves in service to them.

A servant is someone who recognizes the needs of others and has a heart for meeting those needs. Jesus saw and met the needs of those around Him. He met our greatest need—forgiveness of sin—when He gave up His life for us, allowing all who come to Him in repentance and faith to have everlasting life. Jesus not only met our greatest need, but we see throughout the gospels how He met the needs of those around Him. He healed, fed multitudes, brought the dead to life, and even washed others' feet. Washing the feet of others was a duty relegated to the lowliest servant of the master's house. Jesus, during His final Passover meal with His disciples, washed their feet and said,

> *"You call Me Teacher and Lord; and you are right, for so I am. If I then, the Lord and the Teacher, washed your feet, you also ought to wash one another's feet. For I gave you an example that you also should do as I did to you. Truly, truly, I say to you, a slave is not greater than his master, nor is the one who is sent greater than the one who sent him. If you know these things, you are blessed if you do them."* (John 13:13-17)

It is amazing to me that Jesus served His disciples by washing their feet. Jesus is the One by whom *all things were created, both in the heavens and on earth, visible and invisible, whether thrones or dominions or rulers or authorities – all things have been created through Him and for Him* (Colossians 1:16). The Creator of the heavens and the earth, and the One to whom all authority belongs, humbled Himself and became a servant. There is no greater example of servanthood than this. No matter our status in life, whether it is one of authority and power, or one of great reliance upon others for help, or anything in between, at our core, we should have a humble spirit with a desire for meeting the needs of others.

Standing for Righteousness/Confronting Evil

Lastly, as we look at how Jesus lived out His life, we see that He stood for righteousness and did not allow unrighteousness to go unchallenged.

He never shied away from confronting hypocrisy and evil. We see this played out a number of times throughout the gospels. Jesus often confronted the religious leaders of His day to expose their sin. He would do so either by addressing their behavior directly or by speaking in parables. I feel a caveat is needed here when it comes to confronting such atrocities. Everything Jesus did stemmed from a position of love, compassion, and mercy. When He confronted the hypocrisy and evil of others, it was to expose their sin so that they would recognize their need for forgiveness, and thus, their need for a Savior. In other words, it was done so that they would recognize their need for Him. Jesus didn't come to condemn, He came to save (John 3:17). As we confront hypocrisy and evil, we must do so from a position of love, without judgment or condemnation. Though we may be accused of judging or condemning, if we confront from a position of genuine love, we are following Christ's example. The Apostle Paul tells us in Ephesians 5:11, *"Do not participate in the unfruitful deeds of darkness, but instead even expose them."* Like Christ, as we confront and expose deeds of unrighteousness, we must not participate in sin. Our goal in exposing sin should always be to bring others to godly sorrow that brings about repentance.

> *I now rejoice, not that you were made sorrowful, but that you were made sorrowful to the point of repentance;... For sorrow that is according to the will of God produces a repentance without regret, leading to salvation, but the sorrow of the world produces death.* (2 Corinthians 7:9-10)

When we confront evil, our actions must reflect those of Christ. Our goal should always be to bring others to a place of repentance—repentance that leads to their salvation or brings them back into fellowship with God and in alignment with His will.

As we sum up how Jesus lived His life, we see that it was a way of living that went beyond the status quo. It's an "upside-down" type of living. Jesus taught us that our lives are to reflect this new way of living. We are to love our enemies and pray for those who persecute us (Matthew 5:43-44). If anyone wants to sue us and take our shirt, we are to let him have our coat also. Whoever forces us to go one mile, we are to go with him two (Matthew 5:40-41). And when someone is weighed down with burdens, we are to help bear those burdens (Galatians 6:2).

In addition to living life beyond the status quo, Jesus raised the standard of what constitutes being guilty before a holy God. He said that hating someone makes us guilty of murder, and lusting after someone causes us to commit adultery in our hearts (Matthew 5:22, 28). As followers of Christ, we are held to a high standard of behavior, a standard that Jesus Himself set for us. If our lives reflect this higher standard, then we are truly abiding in Christ (1 John 2:6).

We Abide by Being in The Word

Another way in which we abide in Christ is by remaining in His Word. Let's look at a passage of Scripture in the Gospel of John.

> *As He spoke these things, many came to believe in Him.*
> *So Jesus was saying to those Jews who had believed Him,*
> *"If you continue in My word, then you are truly disciples*
> *of Mine; and you will know the truth, and the truth will*
> *make you free." (John 8:30-32)*

Jesus was speaking to two groups of people: those who had come to believe *in* Him (v. 30), and those who believed the words spoken by Him (v. 31). There is a difference between the two. Some believed *in* Him. They put their faith in Him and submitted to Him as Lord and Savior. Others believed Him, acknowledging that what He said was true. To address the difference, Jesus made a point of saying that if they continued in His Word, only then would they be His true disciples. The word for *continue* in this verse is the same word in the Greek for *abide*, it is *menō* (Strong's G3306). If we profess to be a Christian, yet do not abide in the Word of God, Jesus makes it clear that we are not His true disciples.

Genuine followers of Christ are those who are committed to remaining in God's Word. If we never read nor study the Word of God, how will we know if we are living a life that resembles Christ's? We are told in Colossians 3:16 to let the Word of Christ richly dwell within us. That means we should be in the Word of God to the degree that it is the primary influence in our lives. It is by being in the Word that we hear God's voice, learn of His nature and character, get His direction and guidance, and come to know Truth. Remaining in the Word reveals our commitment to Truth. Our goal isn't simply to gain more knowledge regarding biblical "information." We remain in God's Word because we are fully committed to knowing Truth. Jesus said, *"and you will know the truth, and the truth will make you free"* (John 8:32). Initially, when we repent and put our faith in Christ, we are set free from the penalty of sin. Then as we remain in the Word, the Holy Spirit convicts our hearts to the truth of God's Word. Thus, we begin living a life that reflects His Truth. With the Holy Spirit residing within us, not only are we free from the penalty of sin, but we are also free from the power of sin. God's Truth gets a hold of us and we are liberated. There is freedom in Jesus Christ, and it can only be found by abiding in His Word.

Jesus said, *"It is written, 'Man shall not live on bread alone, but on every word that proceeds out of the mouth of God"* (Matthew 4:4). This was His response when He was being tempted by Satan in the wilderness shortly before He began His earthly ministry. Jesus was quoting Deuteronomy 8:3. In Deuteronomy 8, God told Moses that he and the nation of Israel must remember all He had done for them during their wanderings in the wilderness. He wanted them to understand that their sustenance during that time was not just the physical food He provided, but that their true sustenance came from their obedience to His Word. We not only have God telling us we are to live by every word that proceeds out of His mouth, but we also have Jesus confirming God's exact words. There are 32,102 verses in the Bible, comprised of 783,137 words.

I'd say we have an ample supply of words we need to know! We cannot live by that which we do not know.

On one of the occasions in which Jesus was confronting the hypocrisy of the Pharisees, He said, *"You hypocrites, rightly did Isaiah prophesy of you: 'This people honors Me with their lips, but their heart is far away from Me. But in vain do they worship Me, teaching as doctrines the precepts of men.'"* (Matthew 15:7-9). If we are not regularly feeding and nourishing ourselves on the Word of God, then we are subject to being easily swayed by the false doctrines of men (Ephesians 4:14). This will ultimately take us down a path that leads to destruction. We may think we are "right with God" because we give the appearance of having a form of godliness. We may go to church, do good deeds, and adhere to teachings based on the traditions of men. But if we are not wholly submitted to Jesus Christ, learning of Him and desiring to obey and honor Him, then no matter what we say or do, our hearts are far from Him. Jesus unequivocally stated we are only true disciples of His if we remain in His Word.

For us to obey all that Jesus taught and to live lives that reflect His, we must be in the Word. The Word of God provides everything we need to live out the Christian life (2 Peter 1:3). It is through the Word of God that we come to know and learn of Jesus. It's in the Word that we discover Truth and become convicted in our hearts of our need for Him. It's in the Word that we see the depth of His love for us and come to value the importance of being solely dependent on Him. And it is in the Word where our love for Him deepens. As our love for Him deepens, our hearts desire to live according to all that He taught.

Branches That Abide in The Vine Bear Fruit

We have learned that to abide in Christ is to obey Christ and His teachings, to walk in the same manner He walked, and to remain in His Word. Let's now shift our focus back to our passage in John 15, reviewing verses 4-6.

> 4 *"Abide in Me, and I in you. As the branch cannot bear fruit of itself unless it abides in the vine, so neither can you unless you abide in Me. 5 I am the vine, you are the branches; he who abides in Me and I in him, he bears much fruit, for apart from Me you can do nothing. 6 If anyone does not abide in Me, he is thrown away as a branch and dries up; and they gather them, and cast them into the fire and they are burned."*

The second sentence in verse 4 is where we'll begin. *"As the branch cannot bear fruit of itself unless it abides in the vine, so neither can you unless you abide in Me."* Jesus tells us that as branches—His followers—on the vine, we cannot bear fruit unless we abide in Him. To reiterate from an earlier explanation, we can certainly do things that give the appearance of bearing fruit, but the difference will be found in our motivation. The Spirit changes the motivation of our hearts, giving rise to the desire within us to further God's kingdom. Genuine fruit of the Spirit only comes from having the Holy Spirit within. God's nature begins to manifest within us, which brings forth the fruit of His Spirit.

"I am the vine, you are the branches; he who abides in Me and I in him, he bears much fruit, for apart from Me you can do nothing" (v. 5). Jesus mentions again that He is the vine. When He first said He was the vine (v. 1), He followed it up with who His Father is in relationship to Him. This time He follows it up with who His followers are in relationship to Him. All our sustenance comes from Jesus. As long as we abide in Christ, we will bear much fruit; without Him, we can do nothing. If we are not rightly connected to Christ, all our righteous deeds are like a filthy garment (Isaiah 64:6). We may give the appearance of being "connected" to Christ, but if we are not truly connected to Him, it amounts to nothing. Only those who are truly connected to Christ produce the fruit of the Spirit.

Branches That Do Not Abide in The Vine Are Burned

Now let's look at verse 6. Jesus said, *"If anyone does not abide in Me, he is thrown away as a branch and dries up; and they gather them, and cast them into the fire and they are burned."* We already know that we, His followers, are the branches in this metaphor. Jesus stated that anyone who does not abide in Him dries up on the vine. The branches that dry up are then gathered and burned in the fire. A vine branch that does not produce fruit is pretty much useless. The dead branches of grapevines are not useful for creating things, nor are they good for keeping a fire burning; at best, dead branches may serve as kindling to start a fire. Therefore, they need to be removed so they don't drain the plant's strength and energy, nor breed disease among the connected branches that bear fruit. God—our heavenly Vinedresser—removes all branches that are not abiding in the Vine of His Son. We see a progression: thrown away, dried up, gathered together, cast into the fire, and burned. All non-fruit-bearing branches will be forever separated from the Vine and the Vinedresser; their destiny—burned by fire. Burned by fire is the ultimate consequence for failing to abide in Christ.

There are four primary schools of thought regarding the meaning of verse 6. However, I believe they can easily be broken down into two. The position you take as you begin with this passage in John 15 will determine where you end up in verse 6. If you see this passage of Scripture as Jesus speaking only to those who are His true followers, then it would follow that in this verse, Jesus was speaking of either being cast out from fellowship with Him or possibly a loss of eternal rewards at the Judgment Seat of Christ. All believers will appear before the Judgment Seat of Christ in which he or she will be recompensed for his or her deeds (2 Corinthians 5:10). However, if you subscribe to the school of thought in which the branches that do not produce fruit refer to either professing followers or true followers who become apostates, then it would follow that this verse speaks of judgment regarding the unsaved. As stated earlier, I believe that in this passage of Scripture, Jesus is referring to both professing followers and true followers. Therefore, I believe that the dead branches, represented as those who do not abide in Christ, are those who merely profess to be Christians. Some may have made a profession of faith at some point or had an emotional experience in which they heard the Word of God and believed it. But if they never truly repented and wholly surrendered their lives to Christ, they are not true Christians. We see this same distinction in some similar teachings by Jesus.

As we learn from the Parable of the Sower, only some of those who hear the Word of God and accept it become saved and thus, produce fruit (Mark 4:3-8; 20). This parable is consistent with Jesus's teaching that narrow is the way that leads to life, and there are few who find it (Matthew 7:14). "Followers" who do not abide in the Vine—the unsaved—lack the Holy Spirit. The Spirit is the One who enables Christians to bear fruit, and He serves as our guide to lead us into Truth. *...if anyone does not have the Spirit of Christ, he does not belong to Him* (Romans 8:9). Therefore, anyone who does not belong to Christ is not saved and is eternally condemned. This is the fate of the dead branches. The unsaved will be judged at the Great White Throne and thrown into the Lake of Fire (Revelation 20:11-15), *where their worm does not die, and the fire is not quenched* (Mark 9:44, 48).

Let's look a little closer at the dead branches that are burned. Again, they represent those who do not abide in Christ. The word *burned* is in the present tense, indicative mood, and in the passive voice (Strong's G2545). The present tense indicates a continuous action. The indicative mood is used to declare a statement of fact as something that is true. And the passive voice indicates that the subject is acted upon. Given the tense, mood, and voice of the word *burned*, it seems clear to me that Jesus is speaking of judgment. We see in John 15:6, that *burned by fire* lines up with what takes place for all who never come to a saving faith in Jesus Christ. In Mark 9, when Jesus was speaking about being cast into hell, His description of hell was noted as an unquenchable fire where the person's worm never dies and the fire is never quenched (Mark 9:43-44).

This indicates a continuous action (present tense). Jesus was speaking the truth regarding the reality of hell (indicative mood), in which God in His judgment, takes action upon the non-believer (passive voice).

This should serve as a very sobering reality for all professing Christians who are unsure about their salvation. If you are a true follower of the Lord Jesus Christ, there should be no doubt about your salvation. John wrote in his epistle, *These things I have written to you who believe in the name of the Son of God, so that you may know that you have eternal life* (1 John 5:13). If you have any doubt about your salvation, you would be wise to examine yourself to see if you are truly in the faith (2 Corinthians 13:5). There is nothing that brings more peace of mind than knowing beyond a shadow of a doubt, that your eternal destination is heaven, where you will live eternally in the presence of our Lord and Savior, Jesus Christ.

If you are someone who sees this analogy differently and you don't view being *cast into the fire and burned* as God's judgment upon the unbeliever, there isn't an interpretation of this that would favor a desirable outcome. Severed fellowship with Christ can only lead to heartache as you navigate through life, and a loss of rewards at the Judgment Seat of Christ will never matter more to you than the moment you find you are without.

A Promise of Answered Prayer

Let's now look at the remaining verses in our passage in John 15. *"If you abide in Me, and My words abide in you, ask whatever you wish, and it will be done for you"* (v. 7). I must say, after what Jesus just told us in verse 6, this is mighty refreshing! Jesus says if we remain in Him, and His words remain in us, we can ask whatever we wish and it will be done for us. This is a wonderful promise and blessing of God. I realize there will be many who will read this and disagree based on the fact that they asked God for something and did not receive it. With that in mind, let's examine this further to see what we can learn.

There is no doubt that the more we abide in Christ, the more we will see our prayers being answered. Why is that? All our nourishment, in the form of wisdom, knowledge, and understanding of God's Word, comes from being connected to Christ. The greater that connection, the more we will follow the Spirit's leading, and thus, ask for things according to God's will. Our desires will fall more in line with God's desires. We'll find that our own will decreases, and our desire for God's will increases. In other words, we are going to start asking God for the right things—the things He desires for us.

We learn from Scripture that there are prerequisites to effective prayer. Jesus begins verse 7 with the word *if*. This means it is a conditional statement. We will experience the blessings of answered prayers when we abide in Christ. Otherwise, there is no promise from God to answer our prayers.

Another prerequisite to prayer can be found in John 14:13. *"Whatever you ask in My name, that will I do, so that the Father may be glorified in the Son."* To ask for something in the name of someone is to ask for something by the authority of, or in the power of, that person. When we pray to the Father, we are to pray in the name of God's Son, Jesus (see also John 15:16, 16:23). When God grants a prayer request made in the name of His Son, it brings glory to the Father. It gives an accurate estimate of the love and willingness of the Father to bring about our requests.

There are more prerequisites to effective prayer and they are found in 1 John. John writes:

> *Beloved, if our heart does not condemn us, we have confidence before God; and whatever we ask we receive from Him, because we keep His commandments and do the things that are pleasing in His sight.* (1 John 3:21-22)

There are three things in these verses that shed light on asking and receiving. One, our hearts must not condemn us. This means we need to be free from any guilt in our hearts and have a clear conscience. This comes only through repentance. Our hearts will condemn us if there is any sin in us that we have not confessed before God. Two, we receive whatever we ask because we keep His commandments. This means obedience to Him and His Word. Three, we do the things that are pleasing to God. This means we are bearing spiritual fruit and living in such a way that reflects the image of His Son. Remember, sanctification is a continuous process in which we progressively become more like Jesus Christ. The more we become like Him, the more we desire what He desires. Therefore, the more we see our prayers being answered.

Bearing Fruit Glorifies The Father

Now let's look at John 15:8. Jesus said, *"My Father is glorified by this, that you bear much fruit, and so prove to be My disciples."* Let's review what is meant by the word *glorify*. It means to extol, magnify, celebrate, make renowned; to cause the dignity and worth of some person or thing to become manifest and acknowledged (Strong's G3192). Essentially, Jesus is saying His Father is honored and made known to others when we bear much fruit. Bearing much fruit reveals that we belong to His Son. Remember, the fruit of the Spirit is God's manifestation of His nature and character within us that arises as a result of our spiritual birth. When we bear much fruit, our example allows the world to see Christ in us, and this brings honor and glory to the Father.

Notice the progression of fruit-bearing in John 15:1-8. The branches that are connected to the Vine bear fruit (v. 2). They are then pruned so that they bear *more* fruit (v. 2). As we abide in Christ, we bear *much* fruit (vv. 5 & 8); fruit, more fruit, much fruit. Bearing much fruit implies an abundant harvest. Our heavenly Vinedresser, who lovingly tends His garden with His Son, supplies His branches with all the nutrients, strength, and energy needed for a fruitful harvest. It is then that God is accurately represented to the world.

Verse 8 also tells us how we can know for sure that we are true disciples of Jesus. Only true disciples bear fruit. We are not followers of Christ by mere profession. The evidence that we belong to Christ is found in our connectedness to Him. Being rightly connected to Christ will generate an outward display of a spirit-filled life. Jesus said that the fruit of the Spirit manifested in our lives is what proves we are His disciples.

Abiding in His Love

Now let's look at verses 9 and 10. *"Just as the Father has loved Me, I have also loved you; abide in My love. If you keep My commandments, you will abide in My love; just as I have kept My Father's commandments and abide in His love."* Jesus told His disciples that He has loved them in the same manner that the Father has loved Him. Remember, Jesus said, "I always do the things that are pleasing to Him" (John 8:29). Jesus's love for us is equal to the Father's love for Him. That is extraordinary love. Jesus loved all people unconditionally and sacrificially. His love was a choice made by His will that sought the highest good of others. It is this kind of love in which we are to remain. In verse 10, He goes on to say how we are to abide in His love—by keeping His commandments. The bottom line is this, if we remain in Jesus's love for us by being obedient to His commandments, His love will flow through us and out of us. That will be the evidence that we are indeed abiding in His love.

Our Joy Made Full in Christ

The last verse of our passage in John 15 states, *"These things I have spoken to you so that My joy may be in you, and that your joy may be made full"* (v. 11). Jesus explained to His disciples there is a reward, so to speak, for abiding in Him. That reward is His joy.

We all long for joy in this life. Many seek after it, but not all find it. Oftentimes, our level of joy or happiness is based on circumstances. The more ideal the circumstances, the greater our level of happiness. But the joy of Christ—His joy—is different. It is not dependent upon circumstances. For the Christian, joy is a by-product of our obedience to Christ and His Word. Therefore, the circumstances, whether ideal or less than ideal, do not rob a Christian of joy. Our joy comes from being able to rest in the fact that we live our lives under the profound love (John 3:16), protection (Psalm 121:7), guidance (Psalm 48:14), and care of our heavenly Father (1 Peter 5:7). We rest in the fact that we have the assurance of eternal salvation (Hebrews 5:9; 1 John 5:13) and the hope of one day soon, meeting our Savior face-to-face (Titus 2:13). When we abide in the love of Christ, resting in these truths and obeying our Lord is what gives us the joy of Christ.

Christians Know The Voice of Jesus and Follow Him

As I bring this chapter to a close, I take us now to John 10. Here we find Jesus teaching about the Good Shepherd. Jesus makes a distinction between a good shepherd and the false shepherds of Israel. He uses the analogy of a shepherd and his sheep to depict His relationship with His followers. In verse 14, Jesus tells us that He is the good shepherd, and He knows His own and His own know Him. In verse 3, He says the good shepherd calls his own sheep by name and leads them. In verse 4, He says the sheep follow him because they know His voice. In verse 5, He tells us the sheep will not follow a stranger because they do not know the voice of a stranger. This exemplifies the relationship between Christ and His followers. If Jesus, the Good Shepherd, knows His sheep by name and they know His voice and follow Him, this speaks of a personal connection—a relationship—He has with His followers. As followers of Christ, we can discern between His voice and everyone else's. If you are someone who professes to be a Christian, yet you never read nor study the Word of God, how do you know whose voice you are listening to? Knowing the voice of Jesus only comes from an intimate relationship with Him—a relationship that is cultivated by abiding in Him.

Summary

A Christian is someone who is connected to Christ and desires to remain connected to Christ. Jesus said apart from Him, we can do nothing. Therefore, only those who are connected to Him will bear spiritual fruit. He also said the branches that do not abide in Him dry up and are burned. If we profess to be a Christian, yet do not abide in Christ, Jesus Himself tells us that we are not connected to Him, the true Vine. If we are not connected to Christ, it is not possible to be a Christian.

Chapter 8

A LOVE FOR OTHERS

"**A** BIDE IN MY LOVE.**" THIS IS WHAT JESUS TOLD US** in John 15:9. To abide in His love means to remain in His love and not depart from it. We also recall Jesus said the two greatest commandments are: *"You shall <u>love the Lord your God with all your heart, and with all your soul, and with all your mind,</u>"* and *"You shall <u>love your neighbor as yourself</u>"* (Matthew 22:37, 39). Later, Jesus spoke of the kind of love we are to have for our neighbor and said,

> *"A new commandment I give to you, that you <u>love one another,</u> even <u>as I have loved you,</u> that you also love one another. By this <u>all men will know that you are My disciples, if you have love for one another</u>."* (John 13:34-35)

Though Jesus was speaking directly to His disciples, His love for them was the same love He showed to every person He encountered. It is the love of Jesus that we are to have for one another.

Of everything we have discussed thus far regarding the Christian life, love is at the top of the list. Love is what should define us as followers of Christ. Jesus said love is the one thing that *all men*, meaning all humanity, will be able to observe as evidence that we belong to Him (John 13:35). Even those who do not know God personally should be able to see there is something different about the way Christians love. The Bible tells us that God is love (1 John 4:16). This means that love is the essence of who He is. Therefore, the very essence of Jesus, who is God in human flesh (John 1:14; Colossians 2:9), is also love. Given the commandment by Jesus to love one another as He has loved us, all followers of Christ should have an unmistakable love for others.

We discussed the kind of love Jesus had for others in the chapter titled, An Abiding in Christ. As a quick review, Jesus loved selflessly and sacrificially, without precondition, even to the point of death. Jesus lived a sinless life, yet He died a criminal's death on a cross. Except for His love for us, He had no reason to be our substitute sacrifice. He died the death that we all deserve. But Jesus had our highest good in mind as He made His way to Calvary and willingly laid down His life. He chose to endure the cross, making a way for sinners to come into a right relationship with their Creator. Jesus said, *"Greater love has no one than this, that one lay down his life for his friends"* (John 15:13).

Agape Love

Let's examine this great love that Jesus had for the world. We'll begin by looking at the type of love referred to in John 15:13 in the original Greek language. The word for *love* in this verse is *agapē*. It's the same word for *love* that we are going to explore in 1 Corinthians 13:4-8a. It is defined as affection, goodwill, benevolence, charity (Strong's G26). The word charity in this definition is not used the same way we commonly refer to it today. When we think of charity in today's terms, we think of such things as alms-giving, in which we donate time, money, or goods to those who are in need. But charity in this sense is a benevolent disposition in the hearts and minds of Christians towards God, our fellow brothers & sisters in Christ, and all humanity. At its core, agape love is centered on bringing about another's highest good.

Unlike the English language, the Greek language has four separate words for the word *love*. They are Eros, Storge, Philio, and Agape. Eros refers to erotic love which has a romantic and sexual component. Storge refers to familial love, such as a love between brothers and sisters and parents and children. Philio refers to brotherly love, a love between friends that is affectionate, kind, and welcoming. Then there is agape. Agape love is the highest form of love. It's a love that seeks another's highest good, without regard to "cost." Jesus embodied and displayed this kind of love. Agape love gives without condition; it gives even when the giving of that love is not warranted by the receiver and/or the receiver is hostile or rejects it. It is self-sacrificing; it's a love that puts another's needs above our own. It is selfless; it doesn't demand anything in exchange for what is given. Agape love builds others up and lets them know, beyond a shadow of a doubt, they are loved.

The Apostle Paul describes the visible manifestation of agape love in his first letter to the Corinthians. He writes:

> *Love is patient, love is kind and is not jealous; love does not brag and is not arrogant, does not act unbecomingly; it does not seek its own, is not provoked, does not take into account a wrong suffered, does not rejoice in unrighteousness, but rejoices with the truth; bears all things, believes all things, hopes all things, endures all things. Love never fails… .* (1 Corinthians 13:4-8a)

As you can see from this list, love is an act of will. It is not a feeling. Indeed, we can certainly feel the effects of love, but in and of itself, love is not simply a feeling. Jesus's choice to go to the cross was an act of will and nothing less. I can't imagine anyone would ever *feel* like dying a death on a cross that he or she didn't deserve, not even Jesus. We saw from a previous chapter how Jesus agonized over knowing what awaited

Him. But as He said in His prayer to the Father, "not My will, but Yours be done" (Luke 22:42). This great act of love, to be our sin-bearer, was an act of volition.

Love, The Primary Component of The Christian Walk

Paul tells us in his letter to the Corinthians that love is the primary component of the Christian walk. Without it, our Christianity is futile.

> *If I speak with the tongues of men and of angels, but do not have love, I have become a noisy gong or a clanging cymbal. If I have the gift of prophecy, and know all mysteries and all knowledge; and if I have all faith, so as to remove mountains, but do not have love, I am nothing. And if I give all my possessions to feed the poor, and if I surrender my body to be burned, but do not have love, it profits me nothing.* (1 Corinthians 13:1-3)

Ultimately, love is what defines us as Christians. As Paul said, without it, we are nothing more than a clanging cymbal, mere noise-makers. Anything we do in the name of Christianity, whether it's diligently studying God's Word, serving faithfully in some ministry, or even preaching the gospel, it profits us nothing if we do not have love.

True Love

It is important to note that while agape love is giving, selfless, unconditional, and self-sacrificing, it doesn't mean it's a love that accepts all, approves all, and allows all. It's a love that operates within the boundaries of God's Truth.

> *And this I pray, that your love may abound still more and more in real knowledge and all discernment, so*

that you may approve the things that are excellent, in
order to be sincere and blameless until the day of Christ;
having been filled with the fruit of righteousness which
comes through Jesus Christ, to the glory and praise of God.
(Philippians 1:9-11)

We learn from these verses that true love must operate within the boundaries of real knowledge and discernment. Agape love has boundaries that stem from God's righteousness. These boundaries keep love pure and undefiled.

Let's look at this same passage in the Amplified version of the Bible. This version adds a level of clarity to what Paul is trying to convey.

And this I pray, that your love may abound more and
more [displaying itself in greater depth] in real knowledge
and in practical insight, so that you may learn to recog-
nize and treasure what is excellent [identifying the best,
and distinguishing moral differences], and that you may
be pure and blameless until the day of Christ [actually
living lives that lead others away from sin]; filled with the
fruit of righteousness which comes through Jesus Christ, to
the glory and praise of God [so that His glory may be both
revealed and recognized]. (Philippians 1:9-11, AMP)

The two words *real knowledge* are represented by one word in the Greek, *epignōsis*. It means precise and correct knowledge, used in the New Testament of things ethical and divine (Strong's G1922). The Amplified version of these verses sheds a little more light on how our love should manifest. When we combine the Strong's definition with the Amplified version, real knowledge and discernment are an integral part of agape love in that both give us the ability to recognize what is excellent. They help us to identify the best in ethical & divine knowledge, and they allow us to distinguish moral differences. Also, we are to love in such a way that how we live leads others away from sin. If love did not have the boundaries of real knowledge and discernment, our love for others would not be able to do this. Rather, it would be a permissiveness of all things. Righteousness and permissiveness are mutually exclusive. If we are to be filled with the fruit of righteousness that comes through Christ, then permissiveness of sin and allowances of injustice are not possible. We can only truly love others when we love within the boundaries of real knowledge and discernment.

The Reason Christians Love

Let's now look at why we love. For starters, Christians love because we are commanded by God to do so. Jesus told us we are to love God with all our heart, soul, and mind and to love our neighbor as ourselves (Matthew 22:37, 39). Jesus said, *"On these two commandments depend the whole Law and the Prophets"* (Matthew 22:40). That means the sum total of the entire Law of God is love. In 1 John 4:19, we are given the reason behind the command: *We love, because He first loved us.* God is the initiator of love, we are the responders. Without His love for us, we would not know nor recognize true agape love. Why is this? We can find the answer in Luke 7:36-50.

Jesus was invited to the home of a Pharisee. While He was there reclining at the table, a woman, who is noted in the text as a sinner, heard that Jesus was there. She brought with her an alabaster vial of perfume. She was weeping and began to wet Jesus's feet with her tears. She was wiping His feet with her hair while kissing and anointing them with the perfume. The Pharisee, Simon, was thinking to himself that if Jesus truly was a prophet, He would know what sort of person this woman was whom He was allowing to touch Him. Jesus answered Simon's thoughts by telling him a story about a moneylender who had two debtors. One owed him five hundred denarii and the other fifty. When they were both unable to repay, the lender graciously forgave them both. Jesus then asked Simon which of the two debtors would love him more. Simon answered he supposed the one whom he forgave more. Jesus told him he had judged correctly. Jesus then compared the woman's actions to Simon's actions with regard to how they were treating Him as a guest of honor. Simon had done nothing for Jesus, while this woman had washed His feet with her tears and anointed them with perfume. Jesus then said, *"For this reason I say to you, her sins, which are many, have been forgiven, for she loved much; but he who is forgiven little, loves little"* (Luke 7:47). This is the reason Christians love. It's because we have been graciously forgiven by God Almighty, and our sins have been removed as far as the east is from the west (Psalm 103:12). We've placed our faith in God's Son, the Lord Jesus Christ, who gave His life to pay a debt that we owed, yet could never pay. Our sins have been wiped clean by the blood of Jesus Christ. As a result, we are able to express God's agape love *because the love of God has been poured out within our hearts through the Holy Spirit who was given to us* (Romans 5:5). And since we have the power of the Holy Spirit within, we are to *be imitators of God, as beloved children; and walk in love, just as Christ also loved [us] and gave Himself up for us, an offering and a sacrifice to God as a fragrant aroma* (Ephesians 5:1-2). We love because we are so incredibly loved by the very One who created us. God made a way for us to be reconciled to Himself, by sending His only Son to die on a cross and take upon Himself the punishment for our sin. We love much because we have been forgiven much.

Love—The Benchmark For Spiritual Maturity

As we saw in a previous chapter, love is the first virtue of the nine-fold *fruit of the Spirit* found in Galatians 5:22. It is listed first because for Christians, everything we do hinges on it. In the Book of Colossians, Paul tells us about the new "Christian apparel" we are to put on. Out of everything he noted, love is at the top of the list (Colossians 3:14). Paul reiterates that message in 1 Corinthians 13:13, *"But now faith, hope and love, abide in these three; but the greatest of these is love."*

Before we take a closer look at what our lives should look like when we choose to love others as Christ loved, let's remind ourselves of something. We must not mistake Christians for "perfect" people who always love others exactly the way Christ did. Though we are called by Christ to be perfect as our heavenly Father is perfect (Matthew 5:48), we still live in bodies of sinful flesh, and sanctification is a progressive process. Christians are forgiven people who have placed our faith in Jesus Christ. The Holy Spirit within us serves as our "GPS"—our internal guide—who gives us the power, ability, and desire to love as Christ loved. So while we may not love flawlessly at all times, there will be evidence of Christ's love in all who belong to Him because His Spirit living within us compels us to love.

As already noted, love is an act of will. This is why the Apostle Paul, in 1 Corinthians 13:4-8a, describes love in terms of action—that which can be seen as a visible demonstration of the love that is within us. Paul describes love in these terms knowing people will irritate one another and behave inappropriately at times. Paul is concerned with the Christian's response to such irritants. When Paul wrote this letter, he was addressing specific issues within the Church at Corinth. The chapters that lead up to this portion of Scripture speak to these issues. They were dealing with such things as divisiveness, sexual immorality, lawsuits, and heresy about the resurrection, just to name a few. Based on that, he "hits the nail on the head," of what love should and should not look like when dealing with the behaviors people exhibit as they interact with one another. They had been emphasizing their spiritual gifts as the benchmark for spiritual maturity. But Paul's corrective response let them know there is a more excellent way, and that way is love. Love is the benchmark for spiritual maturity.

The Attributes of Love

We will take a brief look at each attribute of love that Paul notes in 1 Corinthians 13:4-8a. We'll then follow up with what the Apostle John tells us in the Book of 1 John regarding our love for God and others.

Love is Patient

The word *patient* in the Greek is *makrothymeō*. It means to persevere patiently and bravely in enduring troubles and in bearing the offenses and injuries of others; to be mild and slow in avenging, to be long-suffering, slow to anger, slow to punish (Strong's G3114). Patience is a passive action. Therefore, it is identified as a behavior in which we use restraint and exercise self-control in circumstances that would otherwise stir up a sinful, knee-jerk reaction.

We learn from several passages of Scripture that God is patient. One of my favorites is found in Peter's second epistle.

> *The Lord is not slow about His promise, as some count slowness, but is patient toward you, not wishing for any to perish but for all to come to repentance.* (2 Peter 3:9)

We see from this verse that what we may perceive as God acting slowly, is actually His patience toward us. He waits for each one of us to come to repentance so that we can live with Him for eternity. Talk about having your patience tried! Not only is God patient with every one of us today, but we see all throughout the Old Testament how the Israelites, God's chosen people, "tried His patience." I'm so grateful that God is patient. I shudder to think of my destiny had I either died or the Rapture (see 1 Thessalonians 4:13-18) had occurred before I came to a saving faith in Christ. Love is patient. In the same way our Father is patient with us, we too must exercise patience with one another.

Love is Kind

The word *kind* in the Greek is *chrēsteuomai*. It means to show one's self mild or useful, to use kindness, to act benevolently (Strong's G5541). Kindness is an active action. It is expressed as a behavior that does something. For example, it can be expressed as being helpful to someone, saying something edifying, or wanting to give in a way that is useful or beneficial for another's needs. Ephesians 4:32 tells us, *be kind to one another [and] tender-hearted, forgiving each other, just as God in Christ has also forgiven [us]*. The condition of our heart—our attitude—will determine our behavior. A soft heart tends to lend itself to kindness and forgiveness, both of which reflect our Father's heart. The Bible tells us it is God's kindness that leads us to repentance (Romans 2:4). We've all heard the phrase, "you'll catch more flies with honey than with vinegar." As Christians, we are more likely to win souls to Christ by the kindness of God being expressed through our behavior.

Love is Not Jealous

The next eight attributes tell us what love is not. The word *jealous* in the Greek is *zēloō*. It means to burn with zeal; to be heated or to boil with envy, hatred, or anger; to desire earnestly or pursue; to envy (Strong's G2206). To be jealous is to want something someone else has. It's a mindset and issue of the heart that can have damaging and lasting effects on relationships. Rather than rejoicing over the blessings of another, jealousy can fuel our hearts with all kinds of feelings that are in opposition to love. If left unchecked, these feelings will often lead us into sin in order to satisfy or justify our feelings. We are told in 1 Corinthians 3:3 that when we behave jealously, we are like mere men, walking in the flesh. This is the opposite of walking by the Spirit. When others have something we want, whether it's something tangible or intangible, if there is any kind of envy or jealousy in our hearts, it's almost impossible for us to be happy for them or to rejoice at their blessings. The Apostle Paul said he had learned to be content no matter his circumstances (Philippians 4:11). That is an excellent goal for every one of us. Being content in all circumstances helps take our focus off of ourselves and what we might lack, and allows us the freedom to delight in the blessings of others.

Love Does Not Brag

The word *brag* in the Greek is *perpereuomai*. It means to boast of one's self; a self-display, employing rhetorical embellishments in extolling one's self excessively (Strong's G4068). To brag is to talk one-self up. It's a characteristic based on an inflated sense of self. Pride is at the root of bragging. It's a pride in our own achievements and character traits with a need to make sure that others believe them to be true as much as we profess them to be true. In contrast, love does not bring attention to self. Love is others-oriented. Loving actions need no embellishing nor do loving actions need to be in the limelight.

> *Thus says the Lord, "Let not a wise man boast of his wisdom, and let not the mighty man boast of his might, let not a rich man boast of his riches; but let him who boasts boast of this, that he understands and knows Me, that I am the Lord who exercises lovingkindness, justice and righteousness on earth; for I delight in these things," declares the Lord. (Jeremiah 9:23-24)*

No matter the measure in which God has blessed us in gifts, attributes, and talents, if we are going to boast, let us boast only in Him, the One through whom we have been so graciously endowed.

Love is Not Arrogant

The word *arrogant* in the Greek is *physioō*. It means to inflate, to be puffed up, to bear one's self loftily, be proud (Strong's G5448). Arrogance is also rooted in pride. It is a focus on self due to an inflated sense of self-importance. It is a belief that our own level of understanding and knowledge, or our gifts and talents, exceeds that of others, and we proudly put our superior abilities, gifts, and talents on display. We learn in 1 Corinthians 8:1 that knowledge makes one arrogant, but love edifies. I like the New Living Translation of this verse. It reads: *But while knowledge makes us feel important, it is love that strengthens the church*. This is an excellent truth for keeping our own measure of self-importance in check. No matter how well-versed we are on a given topic, or how well-gifted in some area, it is God who has blessed us with the ability to learn, retain information, and hone our skills. Forgetting where our gifts and talents come from tends to lend itself to feelings of self-importance. This can often have the effect of tearing others down. Once again, love is not self-centered. Love strengthens, it does not tear down. There is nothing about love that has at its roots, a need or desire to behave arrogantly.

Love Does Not Act Unbecomingly

The word *unbecomingly* in the Greek is *aschēmoneō*. It means to behave (one's) self uncomely, behave (one's) self unseemly (Strong's G807). In other words, it means to behave rudely. Behaving rudely can be seen as being insensitive, ill-mannered, or disrespectful to others. Love does not behave this way. Love behaves graciously, gently, politely. *A gentle answer turns away wrath, but a harsh word stirs up anger* (Proverbs 15:1). If one claims to be a Christian, yet behaves rudely, it is a sure-fire way to deter others from wanting to know more about the God we serve.

Love Does Not Seek Its Own

The word for *seek* in the Greek is *zēteō*. It means to seek in order to find; to require; to crave, demand something from someone (Strong's G2212). To seek its own is a reference to being self-minded, self-centered, and self-consumed. It's a demanding position of one's own way. Those who seek their own self-interests often have few friends. There is nothing wrong with pursuing our goals and dreams in life. But we are called to seek first God's kingdom and His righteousness (Matthew 6:33). When we don't, our own needs, desires, and wants become top priority. Any time we make what we want more important than what God asks of us, we lose focus on the needs of others. We tend to behave in hurtful ways, often towards those who matter to us most. *Let no one seek his own good, but that of his neighbor* (1 Corinthians 10:24). Like Jesus, our love should be others-centered. He always sought the highest good for others, and that is exactly how our love for others should always be expressed.

Love is Not Provoked

The word *provoked* in the Greek is *paroxynō*. It means to irritate, arouse to anger; to exasperate, to burn with anger (Strong's G3947). This speaks to what a person can tolerate, endure or withstand. Many things can make us angry. We all have our "buttons" that people push. Love doesn't succumb to those advances. We will never win souls to Christ by losing our tempers or becoming exasperated with others. Allowing ourselves to become provoked can lead to some pretty unfavorable consequences.

When the Israelites were grumbling in the desert for a lack of drinking water, in response, Moses failed to obey God's command to 'speak' to the rock to bring forth water. Rather, he became provoked by their grumbling and struck the rock with his rod. This outburst is the reason God kept Moses from entering the promised land (Numbers

20:9-13). While it may seem like a harsh consequence, it had much deeper implications. Moses was chosen by God to be the mediator between God and His people. By behaving as he did, Moses completely misrepresented the heart of God. He did not treat God as holy in the sight of the sons of Israel (Numbers 20:12). As Christians, we are to accurately represent the God we serve. When we don't, we may ruin our witness for Christ. Now some of you may be thinking, "wait...the Bible tells us that Christians can be angry at the same things that anger God." That is completely true, but we must always be careful how we display righteous anger. The Bible tells us, *be angry, and yet do not sin* (Ephesians 4:26). If we experience righteous anger, that anger should never go unchecked to the point that it causes us to sin. Rather, it should propel us to stand for God's Truth, pointing others to Christ.

Love Does Not Take Into Account a Wrong Suffered

There are a couple of words we need to look up for this one. The single Greek word for *take into account* is *logizomai*. This is an accounting term in which a ledger entry is made and counted so that it will not be forgotten. It means to reckon, count, calculate; to deliberate; to take an inventory (Strong's G3049). The three words *a wrong suffered* in the Greek is *kakos*. It means: not as it ought to be; base, wrong, or wicked; injurious, destructive (Strong's G2556). Taking into account a wrong suffered refers to what we think about a situation. The New King James Version renders it simply—love thinks no evil. To take into account a wrong suffered is essentially to keep a mental record of wrongs committed against us. As Christians, we are commanded to forgive those who have wronged us. This doesn't assume that when we forgive we become "doormats" for another's injustices toward us, nor does it assume that the pain they caused us isn't real. It means we no longer hold their actions toward us or someone we love against them. We may not always forget what occurred because we can't always control the thoughts that enter our minds. But we can control whether or not we decide to entertain those thoughts. We can choose instead to think about what is true, honorable, right, lovely, pure, of good repute, and worthy of praise (Philippians 4:8).

When Peter asked Jesus how often he should forgive his brother of a sin committed against him, he asked if he should forgive up to seven times. Jesus replied, *"I do not say to you, up to seven times, but up to seventy times seven"* (Matthew 18:21-22). Love does not keep an inventory of acts of unrighteousness committed against us. For all who belong to Christ, all of our debts—our sins committed against a holy God—have been canceled and nailed to the cross; there is no longer a ledger of hostile decrees against us (Colossians 2:14). Once God forgives us, He no longer takes into account our sins (Jeremiah 31:34). Given how much grace God has extended to us, we too must extend that same grace to others.

Love Does Not Rejoice in Unrighteousness, But Rejoices With The Truth

The Greek word for *unrighteousness* is *adikia*. It means injustice; a deed violating law and justice (Strong's G93). Let's begin by looking at the first part of this statement. To rejoice in unrighteousness is akin to being happy when we learn of someone else's hurts, failures, shortcomings, or misfortune. Love does not take pleasure in any kind of wrong. I would imagine that many of us have experienced a sense of delight, whether openly or to ourselves, after hearing about an unfavorable situation for someone, especially if it's something we had thought, "he had it coming!" Christian love is grieved when we hear of the misfortune of others, regardless of whether or not it was self-inflicted. When others have been victims of someone else's sin, or they are caught up in their own sin, our goal for them should always be restoration (Galatians 6:1). Remember, love seeks to bring about another's highest good. It has no interest in tearing someone down.

The second part of this statement, which gives us a contrast, tells us that love rejoices with the truth. The word for *rejoice* in the Greek is *chairō*. It means to be glad; to rejoice exceedingly (Strong's G5463). As followers of Christ, we stand on the truth of God's Word and should always want the truth, in any situation, to prevail. Given that we live in a day and age in which we have 24-hour news outlets, it's so easy to see how truth can get twisted. No matter how you "slice the cake," there is only one truth to every situation and only one Truth upon which Christians stand. We are to rejoice when truth prevails. When we see lives being changed as the truth of the gospel of Jesus Christ penetrates the hearts and minds of others, we are to delight and rejoice in that.

Now that we have seen what love is not, Paul takes us back to what love does. The next four attributes of love have one thing in common— the phrase *all things*. *Love bears all things, believes all things, hopes all things, endures all things* (1 Corinthians 13:7). That little word *all* in the Greek means the exact same thing in English—all! Love doesn't bear only some things, or believe certain things, or hopes what it can, or endures only what it feels like. No. God's love is different and therefore, as followers of Christ, ours must be too. Love bears, believes, hopes, and endures *all things*.

Before we look at each of these, let's remind ourselves again of the backdrop against which everything on this list of love was given to us. It is precisely because we are dealing with imperfect people, ourselves included, that Paul gave us this list in the first place. People don't always put their best foot forward or behave just the way we think they ought to. People will often disappoint us in how they behave. Therefore, it is up to us to love them through *all things* despite what we view as their shortcomings or grating personalities.

Love Bears All Things

The word *bear* in the Greek is *stegō*. It means to cover, conceal the errors and faults of others; to bear up against, and so endure (Strong's G4722). Given our backdrop of dealing with what we view as the imperfections of others, bearing all things can be summed up in this truth: *Above all, keep fervent in your love for one another, because love covers a multitude of sins* (1 Peter 4:8). People will sin against us. But rather than pointing out someone's flaws, Christian love will cover or conceal the faults and flaws of others. This of course assumes that in those moments, the boundaries of love and God's righteousness do not demand justice. Bearing all things means we are going to love others through the jabs, quirks, and shortcomings. As Christians, we are called to bear up against the insults and injuries spewed out against us. Jesus is our perfect example of what it looks like to bear up against insults and injuries for the sake of others.

Love Believes All Things

The word for *believes* in the Greek is *pisteuō*. It means to think to be true, to be persuaded of, and place confidence in, of the thing believed (Strong's G4100). Let's begin by noting what this is not stating. This is not saying that Christians are to believe lies. Christians aren't called to be gullible (Proverbs 14:15). Rather, Christians are to give the benefit of the doubt and believe well of others, especially when there is no evidence to the contrary. We don't immediately assume guilt in someone without having all the facts. We are not to assess a person's behavior with immediate skepticism or judgment of their motives. We are to believe the best. Romans 4:8 states: *"Blessed is the man whose sin the Lord will not take into account."* When God deals with us, if we have been justified by the blood of His Son, then He does not take into account our sin. Oh, make no mistake, we'll continue to sin to one degree or another because we still live in bodies of flesh. But God doesn't see us through the lens of our mistakes. He sees us as we will be—in our glorified, sinless state. God sees us through the lens of His perfect Son. Therefore, we too are to see the best in others. People naturally seek to live up to others' standards when they know we see the best in them. It's what we often see in children who desire to please their parents.

Love Hopes All Things

The word for *hopes* in the Greek is *elpizō*. It means to hopefully trust in (Strong's G1679). Love places confidence in a good or better outcome in the future. If someone disappoints us, we are called to have hope that their best is yet to come. As long as someone has breath, there is always hope. There is hope for their salvation, hope for their future, and hope for their best to be who God has called them to be. Though Jesus knew Peter would deny Him three times (Matthew 26:34), Jesus had hope for his future. Jesus told Peter to tend His sheep (John 21:17), an instruction He knew Peter would soon carry out. No life is hopeless. Therefore, we are to encourage and edify others as we hope for their highest good.

Love Endures All Things

The word for *endures* in the Greek is *hypomenō*. It means to remain; to abide, not recede or flee, to persevere under misfortunes and trials, holding fast to one's faith in Christ; to bear, bravely and calmly, ill-treatments (Strong's G5278). Love perseveres through trials, insults, injuries, and disappointments. This is not enduring just for the sake of enduring itself. Rather, it's an enduring with the hope of bringing about a change in someone based on our ability to persevere through the hurts they spew out on us. We are to endure all things for the sake of Christ Himself, who endured so much for us. Jesus endured His trial, scourging, insults, and the cross, to bring about reconciliation between God and man for all who come to Him in repentance and faith. True love will not be deterred, nor recede, under opposition and will hold steady its course. Love endures for the sake of bringing about another's highest good.

Love Never Fails

Let's look at verse 8 in its entirety to get the proper context.

Love never fails; but if there are gifts of prophecy, they will
be done away; if there are tongues, they will cease; if there
is knowledge, it will be done away. (1 Corinthians 13:8)

Paul makes a distinction between the temporal nature of the gifts of
the Holy Spirit and the eternal nature of love. Paul let the Corinthians
know that the gifts of the Holy Spirit are temporary; they will not last
into eternity. They are only for the time of the church age to edify the
Church. He then contrasted that to the eternal nature of love itself. Paul
made the point that there is no end to love; love never fails. First John
4:8 states that God is love. Since God is eternal (Isaiah 40:28), then love
itself is eternal and will last forever.

Our love for others must reflect the eternal nature of love. This
means our love should have staying power. We will face many adverse
circumstances in this life, many of which will involve others who are not
operating at a level with our highest good at heart. Therefore, love must
always be the driving force that propels us into action as we respond.
Love is a choice, an act of will. Our decision to love is to never cease.

Our Call to Love Others

As we reflect on this passage in 1 Corinthians 13:4-8a, a great way
to gain a greater understanding of what is being said is to replace the
word *love* with the name *Jesus*. Jesus is patient, Jesus is kind, Jesus is not
jealous, and so on. When we do that, it's easy to grasp these truths as we
see the expression of agape love played out in the life of Christ. A test of
our own level of spiritual maturity can then be measured by replacing
the word *love* with our own name. When we do that, does it ring true,
or is it pretty far from it? Jesus said,

"If you love those who love you, what credit is that to you?
For even sinners love those who love them. If you do good
to those who do good to you, what credit is that to you? For

161

even sinners do the same. If you lend to those from whom you expect to receive, what credit is that to you? Even sinners lend to sinners in order to receive back the same amount. But love your enemies, and do good, and lend, expecting nothing in return; and your reward will be great, and you will be sons of the Most High; for He Himself is kind to ungrateful and evil men." (Luke 6:32-35)

Our call to love others, even those who interact with us with the most ungrateful and spiteful hearts, is what Jesus commands Christians to do. How we respond to others in less-than-favorable encounters is a good gauge of our level of spiritual maturity. It is our response in these situations that demonstrates to the world there is something different about the way Christians love. It's a love that proves, even to unbelievers, that we belong to Christ. *"By this all men will know that you are My disciples, if you have love for one another"* (John 13:35).

Loving the unlovable can sure seem like a tall order. But let's keep something in mind. When God sent His Son to die for us, taking upon Himself the penalty for our sin, He didn't do so because we are such deserving, wonderful, loving people—just the opposite. God demonstrated His own love toward us, in that while we were yet sinners, Christ died for us (Romans 5:8). God extended His grace toward us while we were still hostile toward Him (Romans 8:7)—stubborn and unrepentant, storing up wrath for ourselves that God's righteousness must judge (Romans 2:5). Though the sin is ours and we deserve the just punishment for it, God's love for us is so great that He Himself paid the penalty. That is love! If that kind of love can be freely given to us, then that's the kind of love we are to freely give others. This is not an impossible task. The Holy Spirit living within us is our Helper and He embodies all the characteristics of Jesus Christ Himself. That means we have the power and ability to love as He loved. When God gives us a command, He always provides the means for us to carry it out.

Our Love For God

We have looked at why love is so important in the Christian walk, addressing the type of love God has for us, the reason we love, and what love is and is not. Let's now turn our attention to the Book of 1 John. The Apostle John speaks to the relationship between the love we have for others and our love for God. John's writings never disappoint. True to form, he breaks down Truth for us in such a way that there is no room for *if's, and's,* or *but's.*

> If someone says, "I love God," and hates his brother, he is a liar; for the one who does not love his brother whom he has seen, cannot love God whom he has not seen. (1 John 4:20)

As you may recall from a prior chapter, this isn't the first time we've seen the Apostle John boldly tell us we are liars if we claim something to be true, but it doesn't line up with the Word of God. That's always hard to hear because most of us aren't particularly fond of being confronted with Truth when it exposes a flaw in our thinking. But just because something is difficult to hear, it should never steer us away from knowing and understanding Truth. We are told that merely saying we love God is not what determines whether or not that is true. The evidence that we love God is seen in our actions. Do our actions demonstrate that we love others the same way Christ loves us?

When we take into account the proper context in which the Book of 1 John was written, we find that John wrote this letter to Christians. His use of the word *brother* is a reference to a fellow believer in Christ. At a bare minimum, he's saying we are to love our brothers and sisters in Christ. That is the true test of our love for God. If we are at odds with other believers and have hate in our hearts for them, John makes it clear that we do not love God, regardless of what we might claim. He flat out tells us that we cannot love God, whether we believe we do or not, if we don't love our very own brothers and sisters in Christ. We are to love our fellow believers. Jesus broadens that scope for us, stating that we are to love our neighbor as ourselves. Who is our neighbor? It's everyone—those who belong to Christ and those who do not.

John also states:

> We know that we have passed out of death into life, because we love the brethren. He who does not love abides in death. (1 John 3:14)

When John speaks of passing from death into life, he is referring to our spiritual state. Once we are born again, we are spiritually alive in Christ, and from that moment forward we have eternal life. Our death here on this earth is merely the gateway from life on earth to life in the presence of our Lord and Savior. The second part of this verse tells us that those who do not love, abide in death. We learned in the last chapter that the word *abide* means to remain. We can therefore conclude, those who do not love remain spiritually dead.

Summary

The primary characteristic of God that is to be manifested by the believer is love. Love is the essential component of the Christian walk. Without it, all our efforts, no matter how sincere, profit us nothing. Christians will not love perfectly, but Christians will demonstrate evidence of God's love within them as experienced and witnessed by those around them.

Chapter 9

A HEART FOR THE LOST

Seeing the people, He felt compassion for them, because they were distressed and dispirited like sheep without a shepherd. Then He said to His disciples, "The harvest is plentiful, but the workers are few. Therefore, beseech the Lord of the harvest to send out workers into His harvest." (Matthew 9:36-38)

T HESE VERSES IN MATTHEW 9 WERE SPOKEN by Jesus as He was going through all the cities and villages in the Galilee region. He was teaching in the synagogues, proclaiming the gospel of the kingdom and healing every kind of disease and sickness (Matthew 9:35). The first time I read through these verses it broke my heart. I could picture Jesus in my mind's eye as He looked out at a sea of humanity in all their brokenness of sin. They were sheep without a shepherd, in need of the good news of the kingdom of heaven. I felt a heaviness in my own heart at the weight of what Jesus must have been feeling as He looked upon the multitude of lost souls—so many lost, so few to reach them.

As we take a closer look at these verses, we see that several analogies are drawn regarding the multitudes of people and Jesus's disciples. The analogies regarding the multitudes of people are made in two ways. First, they are likened to sheep. Sheep are not known for their intelligence, and without a shepherd to keep them in the fold, they easily stray from the flock. Second, Jesus likened the people to a harvest that is ready and ripe for picking.

Jesus then likened His disciples to shepherds. A shepherd's job is to lovingly tend to, protect, and care for his sheep. Jesus inferred that His disciples were to be the workers who would be sent out into the harvest of humanity to shepherd the people. They were to work the fields to bring in the harvest of souls.

We then see Jesus telling His disciples to earnestly pray to the Lord of the harvest to send out workers into His harvest. This begs several questions. Why was it necessary for workers to go into God's harvest? Why did it matter and to what end? Upon "gathering" the harvest, what were they to then do with that harvest? These are the questions we will be answering as we look at another hallmark of the Christian—a heart for the lost.

All of Us Like Sheep Have Gone Astray

Let's begin by defining what is meant by the word *lost*. In simplified terms, it means someone who isn't saved. A lost soul is someone who has not been born again; he or she is spiritually dead and is currently destined to spend eternity separated from God. I use the word *currently* because, until our last breath, we all have the opportunity to repent and place our faith in Jesus Christ. But until we do, we are lost. A lost soul does not recognize, nor submit to, the Lordship of Jesus Christ. As such, the lost, like sheep, are prone to wander and stray away from God.

All of us like sheep have gone astray, each of us has turned to his own way; but the Lord has caused the iniquity of us all to fall on Him. (Isaiah 53:6)

Sheep wander when they are not being led by their shepherd. Without the shepherd to care for and protect them, their chances of survival are slim. Their natural inclination to stray can cause them to get into situations they can't get out of on their own; their destiny—"lunch" for a predator that seeks to devour them!

Jesus, The Good Shepherd

John 10:1-18 is where we see the relationship between a good shepherd and his sheep. Jesus Himself describes this relationship for us. These verses are included below so that you can easily reference them throughout this section of our study.

1 "Truly, truly, I say to you, he who does not enter by the door into the fold of the sheep, but climbs up some other way, he is a thief and a robber. 2 But he who enters by the door is a shepherd of the sheep. 3 To him the doorkeeper opens, and the sheep hear his voice, and he calls his own sheep by name and leads them out. 4 When he puts forth all his own, he goes ahead of them, and the sheep follow him because they know his voice. 5 A stranger they simply will not follow, but will flee from him, because they do not know the voice of strangers." 6 This figure of speech Jesus spoke to them, but they did not understand what those things were which He had been saying to them.

7 So Jesus said to them again, "Truly, truly, I say to you, I am the door of the sheep. 8 All who came before Me are thieves and robbers, but the sheep did not hear them. 9

I am the door; if anyone enters through Me, he will be saved, and will go in and out and find pasture. 10 The thief comes only to steal and kill and destroy; I came that they may have life, and have it abundantly.

11 "I am the good shepherd; the good shepherd lays down His life for the sheep. 12 He who is a hired hand, and not a shepherd, who is not the owner of the sheep, sees the wolf coming, and leaves the sheep and flees, and the wolf snatches them and scatters them. 13 He flees because he is a hired hand and is not concerned about the sheep. 14 I am the good shepherd, and I know My own and My own know Me, 15 even as the Father knows Me and I know the Father; and I lay down My life for the sheep. 16 I have other sheep, which are not of this fold; I must bring them also, and they will hear My voice; and they will become one flock with one shepherd. 17 For this reason the Father loves Me, because I lay down My life so that I may take it again. 18 No one has taken it away from Me, but I lay it down on My own initiative. I have authority to lay it down, and I have authority to take it up again. This commandment I received from My Father." (John 10:1-18)

In this passage, Jesus draws an analogy between Him and those who belong to Him. He also makes two "I am" statements; *"I am the door"* (v. 9), and *"I am the good shepherd"* (v. 11). When we come to a saving faith in Christ, we are gathered into Jesus's sheepfold, and we enter by way of Him, the door. *"I am the door; if anyone enters through Me, he will be saved, and will go in and out and find pasture"* (v. 9). Sheepfolds in ancient middle-eastern times were enclosures that had a narrow opening with no door. After the shepherd brought his sheep into the enclosure, he would then lie down and sleep in the narrow doorway; his body served as the door. This way the sheep could not leave without the shepherd's knowledge and any predators would have to pass over the shepherd to get to the sheep.

Once we are born again and brought into Jesus's sheepfold, He is our Good Shepherd. Psalm 23 gives us a beautiful picture of how well the Good Shepherd cares for His sheep. Though I don't include the psalm here, it is noted in the Epilogue where I highlight this illustration. But for now, let's look at the relationship between the Good Shepherd and His sheep as found in this passage in John 10.

The Good Shepherd and His Sheep

Christians are the "sheep" who belong to Jesus, the Good Shepherd. We follow Him because we know the sound of His voice (v. 4). He knows us and we know Him (v. 14), and He lays down His life for His own (v. 11). After Jesus made the statement that He is the Good Shepherd who lays down His life for His sheep, He then compared the good shepherd to a hired hand. He tells us that if the sheep are being cared for by a hired hand, the hired hand will leave the sheep and flee if he sees a wolf coming. He flees because he is not the owner of the sheep and is not concerned about them (vv. 12-13). The wolf then snatches the sheep and scatters them. This is a perfect description of our fate before we are brought into the sheepfold of Christ. The unsaved don't know the true Shepherd's voice and therefore, will blindly follow the voice of another—someone who is not concerned about them and who has no interest in bringing about their highest good. When a wolf comes and the hired hand flees, the scattered sheep are left unprotected and lost. Should they perish before they are found by the Good Shepherd, the Lord Jesus Christ, their fate is sealed.

Before we come to a saving faith in Christ, we are lost. We are lost "sheep" who have been scattered. The good news is that Jesus, our Good Shepherd, seeks the lost; *"For the Son of Man has come to seek and to save that which was lost"* (Luke 19:10).

This teaching in John 10 comes on the heels of the narrative found in John 9 in which Jesus healed a blind man. When this man was questioned by the Pharisees about how he had received his sight, he told them it was by Jesus. But the Pharisees didn't believe him. They even questioned the man's parents as to how their son, who was born blind, now had sight. His parents were afraid to answer because the Jews had stated that if anyone confessed Jesus to be the Christ, he was to be put out of the synagogue (John 9:1-22). Out of fear, the man's parents said their son could speak for himself. After questioning the man again and still not believing him, the Pharisees put him out of the synagogue. *Jesus heard that they had put him out, and finding him, He said, "Do you believe in the Son of Man?" He answered, "Who is He, Lord, that I may believe in Him?" Jesus said to him, You have both seen Him, and He is the one who is talking with you." And he said, "Lord, I believe." And he worshiped Him* (John 9:35-38).

We see in John 9:35 that Jesus *found* the man He had recently healed. The man had just been put out of the synagogue which meant he was no longer allowed to partake in Jewish worship. He had been kicked out of the "sheepfold of Judaism." But Jesus found him. And by his faith in Jesus as the Christ, this man was now brought into a new sheepfold, the sheepfold of our Lord and Savior, Jesus Christ.

As the narrative continues into John 10, not only did this previously blind Jewish man enter into Jesus's sheepfold, but Jesus said He had more "sheep" to bring into His fold.

> *"I have other sheep, which are not of this fold; I must bring them also, and they will hear My voice; and they will become one flock with one shepherd." (v. 16)*

The *other sheep* Jesus said He must bring into His fold is a reference to the Gentiles—people who are not Jews. It is my belief that the first sheepfold in this allegorical teaching, as depicted in verses 1-5, is a reference to Judaism. Until Christ came, the Jews had the Law of God to keep and preserve them as a nation; they were a people set apart unto God, a "sheepfold" separate from the world. But when Christ came, He broke down that barrier and by His blood, brought both Jew and Gentile together as one body—one sheepfold with one Shepherd.

> *Therefore remember that formerly you, the Gentiles in the flesh, who are called "Uncircumcision" by the so-called "Circumcision" (Jews), which is performed in the flesh by human hands — remember that you were at that time separate from Christ, excluded from the commonwealth of Israel, and strangers to the covenants of promise, having no hope and without God in the world. But now in Christ Jesus you who formerly were far off have been brought near by the blood of Christ. For He Himself is our peace, who made both groups into one and broke down the barrier of the dividing wall, by abolishing in His flesh the enmity, which is the Law of commandments contained in ordinances, so that in Himself He might make the two into one new man, thus establishing peace, and might reconcile them both in one body to God through the cross, by it having put to death the enmity.* (Ephesians 2:11-16)

Jesus revealed to us in John 10 that there is just one sheepfold, and it belongs to Him, the Good Shepherd, in which there are no distinctions. *There is neither Jew nor Greek* (a reference to Gentiles), *there is neither slave nor free man, there is neither male nor female; for you are all one in Christ Jesus* (Galatians 3:28). Anyone who repents and places his or her faith in Christ becomes a part of His sheepfold, and we are all one in Him.

Lost and Found

Let's now turn our attention to the Gospel of Luke. In Luke 15, we find Jesus telling three parables, all with a common theme—lost and found. This teaching by Jesus is in response to a comment made by the Pharisees and the Scribes in Luke 15:2. They were grumbling about His behavior and Jesus responded with a series of parables. Luke 15:1 gives us the setting; *Now all the tax collectors and the sinners were coming near Him to listen to Him.*

One thing we notice at the outset is that the crowds were attracted to Jesus. The people were coming to Jesus to be near Him and to listen to Him. The people in this setting are described as tax collectors and sinners. During Jesus's time, these folks were considered to be at the "bottom rung" of society. The Pharisees and Scribes thought themselves to be at the "top rung." They were the religious elite. They saw themselves as righteous and were appalled that Jesus, who was supposed to be a man of God, would dine with such people. Here we see Jesus's heart of compassion. He did not shy away from anyone, not even those considered the most abhorrent in society. *"I have not come to call the righteous but sinners to repentance"* (Luke 5:32). Jesus had a heart of compassion for the lost.

Luke 15:2 tells us what sparked this teaching. *Both the Pharisees and the scribes began to grumble, saying, "This man receives sinners and eats with them."* (Luke 15:2). Upon hearing their comment, Jesus launched into three parables. He used these parables to expose the hearts of the Pharisees and Scribes. As He spoke, their self-righteous attitudes became apparent. The heart of our heavenly Father also became apparant. Jesus then drove home the message of how unlike their hearts were compared to the Father's. We'll look at all three parables and then make some comparisons.

The Lost Sheep

3 So He told them this parable, saying, 4 "What man among you, if he has a hundred sheep and has lost one of them, does not leave the ninety-nine in the open pasture and go after the one which is lost until he finds it? 5 When he has found it, he lays it on his shoulders, rejoicing. 6 And when he comes home, he calls together his friends and his neighbors, saying to them, 'Rejoice with me, for I have found my sheep which was lost!' 7 I tell you that in the same way, there will be more joy in heaven over one sinner who repents than over ninety-nine righteous persons who need no repentance. (Luke 15:3-7)

The Lost Coin

8 "Or what woman, if she has ten silver coins and loses one coin, does not light a lamp and sweep the house and search carefully until she finds it? 9 When she has found it, she calls together her friends and neighbors, saying, 'Rejoice with me, for I have found the coin which I had lost!' 10 In the same way, I tell you, there is joy in the presence of the angels of God over one sinner who repents." (Luke 15:8-10)

The Lost Son (The Prodigal Son)

11 And He said, "A man had two sons. 12 The younger of them said to his father, 'Father, give me the share of the estate that falls to me.' So he divided his wealth between them. 13 And not many days later, the younger son gathered everything together and went on a journey into a distant country, and there he squandered his estate with loose living. 14 Now when he had spent everything, a severe famine occurred in that country, and he began to be impoverished. 15 So he went and hired himself out to one of the citizens of that country, and he sent him into his fields to feed swine. 16 And he would have gladly filled his stomach with the pods that the swine were eating, and no one was giving anything to him. 17 But when he came to his senses, he said, 'How many of my father's hired men have more than enough bread, but I am dying here with hunger! 18 I will get up and go to my father, and will say to him, "Father, I have sinned against heaven, and in your sight; 19 I am no longer worthy to be called your son; make me as one of your hired men."' 20 So he got up and came to his father. But while he was still a long way off, his father saw him and felt compassion for him, and ran and embraced him and kissed him. 21 And the son said to him, 'Father, I have sinned against heaven and in your sight; I am no longer worthy to be called your son.' 22 But the father said to his slaves, 'Quickly bring out the best robe and put it on him, and put a ring on his hand and sandals on his feet; 23 and bring the fattened calf, kill it, and let us eat and celebrate; 24 for this son of mine was dead and has come to life again; he was lost and has been found.' And they began to celebrate.

25 "Now his older son was in the field, and when he came and approached the house, he heard music and dancing. 26 And he summoned one of the servants and began inquiring what these things could be. 27 And he said to him, 'Your brother has come, and your father has killed the fattened calf because he has received him back safe and sound.' 28 But he became angry and was not willing to go in; and his father came out and began pleading with him. 29 But he answered and said to his father, 'Look! For so many years I have been serving you and I have never neglected a command of yours; and yet you have never given me a young goat, so that I might celebrate with my friends; 30 but when this son of yours came, who has devoured your wealth with prostitutes, you killed the fattened calf for him.' 31 And he said to him, 'Son, you have always been with me, and all that is mine is yours. 32 But we had to celebrate and rejoice, for this brother of yours was dead and has begun to live, and was lost and has been found.'" (Luke 15:11-32)

A Heart of Compassion For That Which is Lost

Let's begin by looking at the analogies that are drawn in these parables. The shepherd, the widow, and the father are all representative of God the Father. The sheep, the coin, and the son are all representative of that which was lost. The older brother in the third parable is representative of the Pharisees and Scribes. They are also implicitly represented in all three parables as those who did not rejoice over that which was found.

Now let's look at the heart of the shepherd, the widow, and the father. In the first two parables, the shepherd and the widow make concerted efforts to find what was lost. It's important to note that once a sheep has gone astray, it does not have the wherewithal to find its shepherd or its flock. It is helplessly lost and in need of its shepherd to bring it back into the fold. To find a sheep that has gone astray, a shepherd's search can sometimes be quite dangerous. We don't have to look much further than 1 Samuel 17:34-36 to get a picture of this. David told King Saul of several encounters in which he had to fight off lions and bears as he was tending his father's sheep. As he went after the predators, David was putting his own life in jeopardy. Yet he bravely fought them off, killing them for the sake of saving the life of the sheep. When shepherds searched for lost sheep, the potential dangers of doing so required uncompromising effort and self-sacrifice.

The widow's search for her lost coin required that she be diligent and thorough. Unlike a sheep that might bleat when it is lost, a coin can do nothing to give you clues regarding its whereabouts. An inanimate object is hopelessly lost. Without an exacting effort on the part of the seeker, it would not be found.

In the third parable, we don't see the father leaving his home to find his son. But the Scripture does tell us in verse 20 that while the son was still a long way off, his father saw him, felt compassion for him, and ran to embrace and kiss him. This is a son who had been willfully lost. He chose to sever his relationship with his father by walking away from all the blessings of being the son of a father who loved, cared for, and provided for him. The fact that the father had seen him from a long way off would indicate that the father was watching for him, patiently waiting for his son's return.

We learn from these three parables that the hearts of the shepherd, the widow, and the father are self-sacrificing, diligent, thorough, and patient. As they searched, we see a heart of compassion for that which was lost. This is the heart of God the Father as He seeks the lost. This is the heart of Jesus Christ. As noted earlier, Jesus said the following about Himself, *"For the Son of Man has come to seek and to save that which was lost"* (Luke 19:10). For those of us who belong to Christ, there dwells within us a heart that reflects our Father's heart—a heart for the lost.

The Attitude of The Heart

Let's now turn our attention to the heart of the Pharisees and Scribes. As Jesus told these parables in sequence, the difference between their hearts and the heart of God the Father became increasingly apparent. To see the difference, let's compare the attitudes of the shepherd, the widow, and the father, with the attitude of the Pharisees and Scribes.

When the shepherd, the widow, and the father found that which was lost, all three parables tell us they had great joy in finding what had been lost (vv. 5, 9, 24). They rejoiced and celebrated. Their joy was so great they invited their friends and neighbors to rejoice with them (vv. 6, 9, 24). This tells us that the joy in finding that which was lost extends beyond God the Father's joy. The friends of the shepherd, the widow, and the father all celebrated with them. There's even great rejoicing in heaven! *"I tell you that in the same way, there will be more joy in heaven over one sinner who repents than over ninety-nine righteous persons who need no repentance."* (v. 7). Verse 10 is similar: *"In the same way, I tell you, there is joy in the presence of the angels of God over one sinner who repents."* These verses make it clear that every time a person repents and puts his or her faith in Jesus Christ, not only does God rejoice, but all the angels in heaven do as well. Likewise, Christians, who are represented in these parables as the friends of the shepherd, the widow, and the father, experience an overwhelming desire to rejoice when even one sinner repents and puts his or her faith in Jesus Christ.

Now let's look at the attitude of the Pharisees and Scribes. They are represented by the older brother in the third parable and they are implicitly represented as those who did not rejoice with the one who had found that which was lost. As we look at the attitude of the older brother, we learn in verse 28 that he became angry after hearing the news about his brother's return and the celebration that was being held in his honor. His father even had to go out and plead with him to come in and join the celebration. The older brother had a self-righteous attitude, reminding his father that he had been serving him for many years and had never neglected his commands. Given all his years of serving his father, he felt that if anyone deserved a feast and a celebration with friends, it was him. He saw himself as more worthy of his father's blessings than his younger brother who had squandered his father's wealth with prostitutes and loose living.

Let's examine the reason the older brother chose not to rejoice with the father and join in the celebration of his brother's return. It is the same reason the Pharisees and Scribes were upset that Jesus would eat with tax collectors and sinners. The prodigal son told his father he had sinned against heaven and him, acknowledging he was no longer worthy to be his son. Similarly, tax collectors and sinners are pretty much aware of their depravity, making it easier for them to recognize their need for a savior. Just like the prodigal son, their sins are overt and "worn on their sleeve." But the Pharisees and Scribes, who were the religious leaders in the days of Jesus, and the older brother in the parable, didn't see themselves as sinners. The religious leaders prided themselves on keeping the letter of the Law. Likewise, the older brother told his father that he had never neglected any of his father's commands. These individuals believed they were righteous, trusting in themselves and viewing others with contempt (Luke 18:9). But Jesus knew their hearts as He spoke these parables. The true nature of their hearts is revealed to us in another section of Scripture. In Luke 11:39, Jesus said to the Pharisees, *"Now you Pharisees clean the outside of the cup and of the platter; but inside of you, you are full of robbery and wickedness."* Jesus could see right through them and even called them hypocrites (Matthew 23:25). They loved giving the appearance of being "clean on the outside" because it resonated with the image they so loved to project. They wanted others to see that they were not like "those sinners" on the "lower-rung" of society. But on the inside, their hearts were far from clean. Jesus knew better and called them out on it on several occasions. This is why the older brother did not rejoice with the father at the younger son's return. He believed himself to be the one worthy of a celebration. Likewise, the Pharisees and Scribes, who trusted in their own righteousness, also believed themselves worthy based on their own merit. After all, they kept the commands of the Law and they certainly weren't doing those blatantly sinful acts that the prodigal son, tax collectors, and sinners were doing. But like the Pharisees and Scribes during the times of Jesus, just because we might be disciplined enough to give the appearance that we are "keeping God's Law," doesn't mean we are righteous. *There is none righteous, not even one* (Romans 3:10). Unless we have the righteousness of Christ in us, our outward behaviors, no matter how impeccable, are like a filthy garment (Isaiah 64:6).

We now know the reason why the older son in the parable, as well as the Pharisees and Scribes, were not able to rejoice when that which was lost was found. They had not experienced the overwhelming joy of having mercy (a just punishment withheld) and grace (undeserved favor granted) extended to them. Since they did not see their need to repent of their sins, they did not know the joy of God's love for them in granting forgiveness of their sins. Only those who know what it means to be forgiven and set free from the bondage of sin will rejoice when another sinner repents and places his or her faith in Christ.

The joy of salvation is the reason Christians love to share their faith. We have experienced God's mercy and grace; His mercy, in that He has withheld spiritual death that is justly due us in an unrepentant state, and grace, in that He has given us the righteousness of Christ in exchange for our sin. Religious and/or self-righteous people, like the Pharisees and Scribes, trust in their own righteousness, believing they'll get to heaven based on their own merit. They don't become excited when sinners repent and surrender their lives to Christ because they don't understand it. They've not experienced what it means to be born again and therefore don't know the joy of it. Those who are merely religious believe that their works of righteousness, such as going to church, paying tithes, doing acts of charity, and so on, are what will ensure their entrance into heaven. Without a personal relationship with Jesus Christ, it is impossible to know and understand the joy of what it means to be saved.

Before I was saved, had I been told that a lost soul had been won for Christ, my best response might have been, "that's nice." And had I been witness to someone coming to a saving faith in Christ, I probably would have thought it odd, perhaps may have even questioned it as having anything to do with the Lord. That just wasn't something I ever saw or experienced in my circles. For me to grasp the weight of someone's decision to repent and place his or her faith in Christ, I would not only have had to first experience saving faith, but I would also have had to understand the gravity of the eternal consequences of sin. And that…I did not. So rejoice over it? No, it wouldn't have happened. Only friends of the Good Shepherd and the Father rejoice over a lost soul being saved.

Before my spiritual birth, I only knew *of* Christ. But I didn't truly know Him, and therefore, I did not understand what it means to belong to Him and to have His Holy Spirit living within me. Without the indwelling of the Holy Spirit, it is not possible to know the joy that rests in the love of our Father, who sought us out to bring us into the sheepfold of His Son. For it is the Spirit who does a work in our hearts, who turns our love and affections towards the things of Christ and gives us the joy and peace that only comes from being a child of God. We rest in knowing we will one day come into His presence for all eternity. Only those who belong to Christ rejoice when that which was lost is found.

Workers in God's Harvest

At the beginning of this chapter, we looked at Matthew 9:36-38. After discussing these verses, I posed some questions: Why was it necessary for workers to go into God's harvest? Why did it matter and to what end? Upon "gathering" the harvest, what were they to then do with that harvest? We'll now answer those questions.

We've already concluded that the harvest represents lost souls. This conclusion is supported by the fact that immediately following Jesus's words in Matthew 9:36-38, He summoned His twelve disciples (Matthew 10:1) to go out to the lost sheep of the house of Israel (Matthew 10:6) and preach the kingdom of heaven (Matthew 10:7). In addition, we learned in chapter six that though the Holy Spirit is the one who convicts us of our sin and shows us our need for a Savior, it is primarily through human instruments that this work of God is accomplished. Therefore, we see that workers are needed to go into God's harvest. God uses His children—men and women who are filled with His Spirit—to accomplish His purposes. This world is filled with lost souls and we, the human hands and feet of Christ, are commanded by Jesus to reach His lost sheep and preach the gospel message.

After Jesus had risen from the dead, He spent forty days presenting Himself alive to His apostles and others, speaking of things concerning the kingdom of God (Acts 1:3). During one of these times, He appeared to His disciples in Galilee.

> *And Jesus came up and spoke to them, saying, "All authority has been given to Me in heaven and on earth. Go therefore and make disciples of all the nations, baptizing them in the name of the Father and the Son and the Holy Spirit, teaching them to observe all that I commanded you; and lo, I am with you always, even to the end of the age." (Matthew 28:18-20)*

This command by Jesus to His "workers," to go into God's "harvest," is what is commonly referred to as the Great Commission. As followers of Christ, we are commissioned by Him to reach the lost. This means we are to share His message of salvation with the world. We are to tell others of the good news of Jesus Christ—that all who come to repentance and faith in Him, can be forgiven and set free from the bondage of sin and be granted eternal life with our Savior.

It is through our proclamation of the gospel message—God's workers going into the harvest—that God brings the increase and more souls are brought into the sheepfold of Jesus Christ. Once they are in the fold, we are instructed by Jesus what to do with God's harvest. We are commanded to baptize them in the name of the Father, Son, and the Holy Spirit, and teach them all that Jesus commanded. In order for us to teach all that Jesus commanded, we have to know what He commanded. This is why it is vitally important for Christians to know the Word of God. Our number one job as followers of Christ is to be His ambassadors—workers in the harvest. The job of an ambassador is to represent the interests of his king and country. As Christians, our citizenship is in heaven (Philippians 3:20), and Jesus is our King (Revelation 19:16). Since we are in the world but not of the world (John 17:16), it is our job to accurately represent our King while we are here on earth. Our King has given us the ministry of reconciliation—reconciling a broken and lost world to a righteous and holy God.

> *Now all these things are from <u>God</u>, who reconciled us to Himself through Christ and <u>gave us the ministry of reconciliation</u>, namely, that God was in Christ reconciling the world to Himself, not counting their trespasses against them, and He has committed to us the word of reconciliation.* (2 Corinthians 5:18-19)

For believers to fulfill the ministry of reconciliation, we need to know God's Word and be intimately connected to Christ. This will equip us to boldly proclaim, by the power of the Holy Spirit, His message of salvation to the world.

The Eternal Consequences of Sin

I noted earlier that before I was saved, in order for me to have rejoiced over one sinner who repented and placed his or her faith in Christ, I would have had to grasp the weight of that decision; first, by having experienced saving faith, and second, by understanding the gravity of the eternal consequences of sin. The latter is what we are going to look at now.

I've mentioned throughout this book that those who do not repent and place their faith in Christ will be eternally separated from God. However, I've only briefly alluded to the full implications of that statement. Stating that the unsaved will be eternally separated from God, as significant as that it is as a stand-alone statement, isn't an adequate representation of the entirety of God's Word. It doesn't accurately convey the full weight of that message. Therefore, a broader scope of what is meant by that statement is vital.

Eternal separation from God is the end result for all who reject the gospel of Jesus Christ. The word *gospel* in the Greek is *euangelion*. It means a reward for good things; the glad tidings of salvation through Christ; the proclamation of the grace of God manifest and pledged in Christ (Strong's G2098). Essentially, gospel means good news. The gospel message is good news because it's a message of the hope of salvation through Jesus Christ. So if that's the good news, does that mean there is bad news? Let's find out.

I noted in chapter six that being saved is synonymous with being born again. We are saved from the eternal consequences of sin, which is both physical and spiritual death. For those of us who have repented and placed our faith in Christ, it is our job to preach the *full* message of Christ. We are not only to tell others the good news, but also the consequences for rejecting the good news. The Apostle Peter said,

> *"And He* (Jesus) *ordered us to preach to the people, and solemnly to testify that this is the One who has been appointed by God as Judge of the living and the dead."* (Acts 10:42)

The *living and the dead* are references to the saved and unsaved. The saved are referred to as living because our spirits are alive. We have been born again. The unsaved are referred to as dead because their spirits are dead in the sense that they are corrupted by the sin nature. If left in that unregenerate condition, they will not inherit eternal life.

We learn from Acts 10:42 that our job as Christians is two-fold: to proclaim the gospel message and to testify that Jesus is our Judge, and judgment is coming. Let's also recall that all authority has been given to Jesus in heaven and on earth (Matthew 28:18). *For not even the Father judges anyone, but He has given all judgment to the Son* (John 5:22). Therefore, we must preach both the good news and the bad news, *because He* (God) *has fixed a day in which He will judge the world in righteousness through a Man* (Jesus) *whom He has appointed, having furnished proof to all men by raising Him from the dead* (Acts 17:31). Since there is a coming day in which Jesus will judge us in righteousness, we must have His righteousness in us to be granted eternal life. Eternal life is found only in Him (1 John 5:11). When judgment day comes, anyone who has rejected the good news of Jesus Christ will be judged according to the words that Jesus spoke.

> *"He who rejects Me and does not receive My sayings, has one who judges him; <u>the word I spoke is what will judge him at the last day</u>."* (John 12:48-50)

We must also keep in mind that God's Word is not only able to judge our deeds but also the thoughts and intentions of our hearts (Hebrews 4:12). Jesus, our righteous Judge, will deal out retribution to those who do not know God and do not obey the gospel of our Lord Jesus (2 Thessalonians 1:8). *These will pay the penalty of eternal destruction, away from the presence of the Lord and from the glory of His power* (2 Thessalonians 1:9). We learn from this verse that the consequences of sin and death are like two sides of the same coin—eternal separation from God; eternal destruction.

We all know that the bodies of flesh we currently live in are finite. But our spirit within us is not. Our spirits live eternally. The Bible is replete with verses that indicate an eternal state after physical death. When Jesus was teaching His disciples about end times and the final judgment, He ended with a reference to the destination of those who are the accursed ones (Matthew 25:41), the unsaved, and those who are blessed of His Father (Matthew 25:34), the saved. Jesus said, *"These will go away into eternal punishment, but the righteous into eternal life"* (Matthew 25:46). This verse indicates that our spirits will live eternally in one of two conditions, either in eternal punishment or eternal life.

Our eternal "address" is decided while we are alive on this earth. It is based on our rejection or acceptance of Jesus Christ as Lord and Savior. At the moment we die, our spiritual condition, whether spiritually alive (saved) or spiritually dead (lost), is sealed. Hebrews 9:27 tells us, ...*it is appointed for men to die once and after this comes judgment*. There are no second chances for our spiritual fate after we have breathed our last breath.

It also needs to be noted that our eternal spirit will not be without a body. Jesus Himself told us, *"Do not fear those who kill the body but are unable to kill the soul; but rather fear Him who is able to destroy both soul and body in hell"* (Matthew 10:28). Though this statement is a reference to the fate of those who are spiritually dead, it does indicate that our spiritual state will include a body. For those of us who die in Christ, we'll receive bodies that have been transformed to live eternally with Christ in a glorified state (Philippians 3:21). For those who die outside of Christ, they'll receive bodies that have been transformed to live in disgrace and everlasting contempt (Daniel 12:2). Our eternal state will include both body and spirit.

Let's take a closer look at the eternal state for those who reject Christ. Jesus Himself gives us some descriptions of the setting and the experience. We already saw that Jesus said, *"Do not fear those who kill the body but are unable to kill the soul; but rather fear Him who is able to destroy both soul and body in hell"* (Matthew 10:28). This tells us there is a place where God will destroy both soul and body, and that place is hell. It is a place of eternal fire that was prepared for the devil and his angels (Matthew 25:41). It is a place where there will be weeping and gnashing of teeth (Matthew 13:50), and it is a place of eternal punishment (Matthew 25:46). For those who are there, their worm never dies—they are continually fed upon—and the fire is not quenched (Mark 9:48). We also learn from other Scripture that it is a place of black darkness (Jude 1:13), and it is ultimately known as the Lake of Fire (Revelation 20:15). It is a lake that burns with fire and brimstone, which is the second death (Revelation 21:8). It is referred to as the second death because it is the destination for all who are both physically dead (first death) and spiritually dead (second death). As a reminder, we are born into this world spiritually dead as a result of sin entering the world through Adam. Unless our spirits are born again, we will die both a physical death and a spiritual death. Hence the saying, born once (physical birth), die twice (physically & spiritually), born twice (physically & spiritually), die once (physical death).

Given the descriptions of the Lake of Fire, I can't fully wrap my mind around what that experience would be like. The dire descriptions of the Lake of Fire are enough to let me know that I don't want a single soul to end up there. The thought of willfully choosing to reject a God who loves me more than I can fathom, in exchange for eternal punishment and destruction, is terrifying to me. I've known quite a few people in my life who have believed that life here on earth is hell. I even once believed it was a good probability given the amount of evil and suffering in the world. But the truth is, no matter how bad we have it here on earth, God's presence is still here (Psalm 139:7). As long as we are here, there is hope. It's only after an absolute rejection of the gospel of Jesus Christ that all hope is lost.

A Christian's Heart—For The Lost to Be Saved

People will often ask why it is that Christians "push" their faith on others. The simple answer is because that is what Christ commands us to do (Matthew 28:19-20). We are told to contend earnestly for the faith (Jude 1:3), conducting ourselves with wisdom toward unbelievers and making the most of every opportunity (Colossians 4:5). But it's more than our mere obedience to Christ's command. Once we have been born again, the Holy Spirit does a work in our hearts and it becomes our desire to see lost souls come to a saving faith in Jesus Christ. We know what it was like before we came to Christ and how we, like sheep, wandered away from God. We know what it means to be forgiven and set free from the bondage of sin. We know what it's like to have peace *with* God and the peace *of* God. We know the joy of following our Good Shepherd as He leads, cares, and provides for us. We know we have the assurance of salvation, and we know our hope in Christ is real; we will live eternally with our Lord and Savior. Lastly, we understand the consequences of rejecting Christ. So what may seem like "pushing" our faith as we share the good news of Jesus Christ, is actually our heart's desire to see lost souls saved. Our hearts and minds become set on going out into God's harvest and proclaiming the full message of Jesus Christ: the good news and the bad news. The Bible tells us, *...there is salvation in no one else; for there is no other name under heaven that has been given among men by which we must be saved* (Acts 4:12). Salvation and eternal life are only found in Christ. *And if anyone's name [is] not found written in the book of life, he [will be] thrown into the lake of fire* (Revelation 20:15).

I understand that for those who choose to reject Christ, it will perhaps always seem like Christians "push" their faith on them. For those of us who follow Christ, we are told that to those who are being saved from among the perishing, we are a Christ-like fragrance, a life-giving perfume. But to those who are perishing, we are a dreadful smell of death and doom (2 Corinthians 2:15-16, NLT).

When it comes to the plight of the unsaved, we truly see the heart of God in the three parables of Lost and Found. When we couple that with what we learn in 2 Peter 3:9, that the Lord is patient toward us, not wishing for any to perish but for all to come to repentance, it is very clear that God doesn't want a single human soul to perish, nor does He take pleasure in the death of the wicked (Ezekiel 33:11). That is why He Himself provided a way of redemption. He sent His Son, the Good Shepherd who seeks every lost soul, who laid down His own life for the sake of His sheep, so that we might be reconciled to God and raised to everlasting life.

Summary

Christians have a heart that reflects our Father's heart—a heart for the lost. Christians rejoice with the Good Shepherd when even one sinner repents and places his or her faith in Christ. We do so because we've experienced the overwhelming love of God through His forgiveness of our sins, and we understand the consequences of rejecting His Son, the One through whom forgiveness is made possible. It is a day to rejoice indeed when one more soul escapes eternal destruction, having been restored to the Father and brought into the sheepfold of Jesus Christ. If you are someone who claims to be a Christian, yet there isn't anything in you that either rejoices over sinners being saved or desires to reach the lost, I exhort you to examine yourself. See if you are in the faith.

Chapter 10

A HIGH VIEW
OF SCRIPTURE

FOR THOSE OF US WHO CLAIM TO FOLLOW
Jesus, it behooves us to ask, which Jesus are we following? That
may seem like a crazy question, but before I became a Christian, I just
assumed I was following the Jesus of the Bible. This notion isn't a far
stretch as the Apostle Paul brought up this same issue in his second
letter to the Corinthians. Paul wrote that just as Eve had been deceived
by the craftiness of the serpent, he was concerned that their minds
would be led astray from the simplicity and purity of devotion to
Christ. He pointed to the idea that there are false preachers who
might come and preach a different Jesus (2 Corinthians 11:3-4). A
different Jesus? Who would have thought?

It wasn't until I began to study the Word of God that I came
to realize, that for many years, I was not a follower of the Jesus of
the Bible. I believed that Jesus was God's Son and that He was God
in human flesh. Therefore, the Jesus in whom I believed was the
same God in whom I believed. But it's what I believed about God
that made the difference. I saw God primarily as a God

of love, grace, and mercy because those are His attributes that worked best with how I chose to live my life. This allowed me the freedom to live according to the constructs of my own thinking. I believed that God loved me unconditionally based on *my* definition of love. And I could follow that kind of "love." I liked this God; I could follow this Jesus. I liked the Jesus who was a sweet baby boy, born in a manger, who didn't require anything of me. I liked the Jesus who said, "Ask, and you shall receive." I liked the Jesus who was willing to lay down His life for me. But I didn't particularly care for the Jesus who held me to a higher standard. I didn't want to pay heed to the Jesus who said that lusting after someone was equivalent to committing adultery, or having hate in my heart toward someone was equivalent to murder. I didn't want to hear that I should love my enemies, and I certainly didn't like that Jesus knew the thoughts and intentions of my heart. I knew what was in my heart! Nope, I was not following the Jesus of the Bible. I was following a different Jesus.

If we claim to follow Jesus Christ—and there's only one—then we cannot follow the Jesus of our imaginations. If our knowledge of Jesus is limited to some memorized Scripture verses or listening to a 45-minute sermon every Sunday that may or may not include a teaching on the nature and character of Christ, then the less likely it is we know the true Jesus. To follow the Jesus of the Bible, it is imperative that we know who He is, what He said, and that we take Him at His word. The less we know about Him, the less likely we are His followers.

I would venture to say that it is impossible to truly follow anyone if we don't know much about them. At best, we may think highly of them or be a "fan." If we claim to be a Christian, yet don't believe that the Bible is the written Word of God, or only believe that certain parts of the Bible are true, then we do not hold the same view of Scripture that Jesus held. Jesus held the Scriptures in high regard and knew them to be the inerrant, infallible Word of God. If we don't believe what Jesus said is true about the Scriptures, how can we believe anything He said?

Jesus believed that God's Word is Truth—every single word of it, from Genesis to Revelation.

When Jesus was speaking to the Father about His followers, He said, *"Sanctify them in truth; Your word is truth"* (John 17:17). This is a clear indication that Jesus believed God's Word is Truth. Jesus also said that God Himself is true (John 8:26), and there is a Spirit of Truth (John 14:17). The Spirit of Truth testifies of Jesus (John 15:26; 1 John 5:6). We also see that Jesus only spoke the words the Father gave Him: *"for the words which You gave Me I have given to them"* (John 17:8). This is further expressed in a different passage of Scripture in which we find John the Baptist discussing Jesus with his disciples, saying, *"For He whom God has sent speaks the words of God..."* (John 3:34). We learn from John 3:34 and 17:8 that Jesus's words were the words of God Himself. All of these verses indicate the following: God's Word is Truth, the Spirit of God is Truth, and since Jesus speaks the words of God, it follows that His words are Truth. If Jesus spoke Truth and we claim to follow Him, then we will have the same view of the Bible He had. So what did Jesus think of the Bible? That's what we are going to look at in this chapter.

We'll begin with a passage of Scripture taken from Jesus's Sermon on the Mount. Jesus said,

> *17 "Do not think that I came to abolish the Law or the Prophets; I did not come to abolish but to fulfill. 18 For truly I say to you, until heaven and earth pass away, not the smallest letter or stroke shall pass from the Law until all is accomplished. 19 Whoever then annuls one of the least of these commandments, and teaches others to do the same, shall be called least in the kingdom of heaven; but whoever keeps and teaches them, he shall be called great in the kingdom of heaven."* (Matthew 5:17-19)

These few sentences speak volumes regarding Jesus's view of Scripture. We'll go through it carefully to make sure we get a clear understanding of His view of the Word of God.

Jesus Believed God's Word Bore Witness to Himself

"Do not think that I came to abolish the Law or the Prophets; I did not come to abolish but to fulfill" (v. 17). This statement by Jesus is a good indication that some in His audience probably insinuated or blatantly remarked that He opposed the Law of God. It seems their interpretation of the Law may have been different from what they were hearing Jesus say. Jesus often challenged their interpretations, especially regarding the Sabbath. Jesus let His audience know that He did not come to disregard or get rid of God's Law. He came to fulfill it. Jesus completely upheld God's Law through His perfect obedience to it.

Jesus equated Himself with being on the same plain of authority as the Law and the Prophets. This was expressed through His statement in which He said He came to fulfill the Law and the Prophets. As one who is the fulfillment, the implication is that all that was contained in the Old Testament Scriptures, was merely a shadow of the One who was to come in whom all the Law and the Prophets would be satisfied and made complete. Put simply, all of Scripture points to Jesus. The writers of the Old Testament wrote about the One to come who would uphold the entirety of the Law and come in the manner as foretold in the Scriptures.

Jesus expressed this same truth on other occasions. He told the Jews, *"You search the Scriptures because you think that in them you have eternal life; it is these that testify about Me"* (John 5:39). In other words, all the pages of Scripture were about Him, showing that through Him, eternal life was made possible. Then there was the occasion on the road to Emmaus. It had been three days since Jesus had been crucified, died, and buried. Two disciples were talking while on their way to the village of Emmaus. They were very discouraged regarding recent events surrounding Jesus as they had been hoping it was Jesus who was going to redeem Israel. While engaged in their discussion, Jesus approached the two and began traveling with them. Not recognizing Jesus, they told Him about what had happened that morning at the tomb, in which the women found it empty. They said the women had been told that Jesus was alive. But those who went to the tomb didn't see Him. Jesus then said,

> "O foolish men and slow of heart to believe in all that the prophets have spoken! Was it not necessary for the Christ to suffer these things and to enter into His glory?" Then beginning with Moses and with all the prophets, He explained to them the things concerning Himself in all the Scriptures. (Luke 24:25-27)

We learn from Jesus that in *all* the Scriptures, beginning with Moses and all the prophets—the entire Old Testament—are things concerning Jesus Himself. It is Jesus who fills the pages of all the Old Testament Scriptures in that they all spoke of the Messiah to come.

We see another time in which Jesus revealed He was the fulfillment of Scripture. It occurred at the beginning of His ministry.

> And He came to Nazareth, where He had been brought up; and as was His custom, He entered the synagogue on the Sabbath, and stood up to read. And the book of the prophet Isaiah was handed to Him. And He opened the book and found the place where it was written, "The Spirit of the Lord is upon Me, because He anointed Me to preach the gospel to the poor. He has sent Me to proclaim release to the captives, and recovery of sight to the blind, to set free those who are oppressed, to proclaim the favorable year of the Lord." And He closed the book, gave it back to the attendant and sat down; and the eyes of all

*in the synagogue were fixed on Him. And He began to say
to them, "Today this Scripture has been fulfilled in your
hearing."* (Luke 4:16-21)

Jesus claimed that this passage found in the Book of Isaiah, a book that
was written 700 years before He arrived on earth, was speaking of Him.

The Bible is unlike any other book of faith in that it contains fulfilled
prophecy. Jesus made it clear that He was not only the subject of the
Old Testament Scriptures but He was the fulfillment of those Scriptures.
Jesus fulfilled over 300 prophecies regarding His first coming. The Bible
contains 66 books, written at different times spanning 1500-1600 years.
It was written in three different languages by over forty different authors.
These authors came from diverse backgrounds during different times of
history and wrote from three different continents. The Bible displays a
reliable history and accurate transmission of the Scriptures over time.
It speaks on the most controversial topics, such as, "who is God?" and
the meaning and purpose of life. Yet despite the vast period of time over
which it was written and the diversity of authors, the writings of the
Bible contain a single unified message—One would come to redeem
the world. It is a message of salvation that is found in the person of Jesus
Christ. Jesus is center-stage in all the Scriptures.

Jesus Believed God's Word Has Authority

Once again we'll look at Matthew 5:17. *"Do not think that I came
to abolish the Law or the Prophets; I did not come to abolish but to fulfill."* Jesus recognized the two major divisions of the Old Testament
Scriptures: The Law and the Prophets. When the Bible speaks of the
Law, there are three commonly held views. The narrow view is a reference to only the Ten Commandments, the Decalogue, given by God
to Moses in the Book of Exodus. Then there is a broader view, held
by many Jews, often referred to as the Law of Moses and includes the
first five books of the Old Testament, known as the Torah. Lastly, there

is the view that refers to the entire body of Old Testament Scriptures, known as the Tanakh. The Prophets is a reference to those men found in Scripture who were chosen by God to speak to the nation of Israel as His appointed mouthpiece. When we see the Law and the Prophets referred to in the New Testament, it's the designation that encompasses all of the Old Testament Scriptures. Jesus also recognized the Psalms as part of the Scriptures.

> *Now He said to them, "These are My words which I spoke to you while I was still with you, that all things which are written about Me in the Law of Moses and the Prophets and the Psalms must be fulfilled."* (Luke 24:44)

As we see from verse 17 in our passage in Matthew, Jesus referred to the Law as *the* Law. The definite article *the* indicates that it is not some generic Law, but rather, *the* Law of God. Exodus 20 is the chapter where we see God giving Moses the Ten Commandments. It begins as follows, *Then God spoke all these words, saying....* When Jesus referred to the Law, it was *the* Law as given *by God*. And in John 10:35, when Jesus was responding to the charge of blasphemy by the Jews, contained within His reply, He said, *"and the Scripture cannot be broken."* Jesus held the view that the Scriptures were given by God and therefore, embodied God's authority as Creator and sovereign ruler of the world.

Jesus also indicated that His words are equal in authority to the words God gave to Moses. In John 5:46-47, Jesus said, *"For if you believed Moses, you would believe Me, for he wrote about Me. But if you do not believe his writings, how will you believe My words?"* Moses lived about 1500 years before Jesus. Moses wrote Genesis, Exodus, Leviticus, Numbers, and Deuteronomy, the first five books of the Bible. Yet despite the large span of time between the lives of these two men, Jesus claimed that He is the subject of Moses's writings, writings that take us back to the beginning of creation. Again, Jesus makes the correlation that His own words are on the same level of authority and prophetic utterance as the writings of Moses.

Jesus's view regarding the authority of Scripture is clearly seen when He used God's Word to combat temptation while in the wilderness. After having fasted for forty days and nights, the devil tempted Jesus three times, and each time Jesus used Scripture to render the devil ineffective. Jesus's response to each temptation began with, "It is written" (Matthew 4:4, 7, 10). The usage of the words, "It is written" in the Bible is strictly a reference to the Word of God. As Jesus responded to the devil, He quoted Scripture from the Book of Deuteronomy, one of the books of the Torah. In so doing, we see the value that Jesus placed on the written Word of God. His response to the devil in Matthew 4:4 was a direct quote from Deuteronomy 8:3. Jesus said, *"It is written, 'Man shall not live on bread alone, but on every word that proceeds out of the mouth of God.'"* Jesus not only confirmed Scripture as being from God, and therefore, authoritative, but it is so important that every single word of it is necessary for life.

Jesus made other "it is written" statements. When He was asked by the Pharisees and Scribes why His disciples didn't walk according to the tradition of the elders, Jesus replied,

> *"Rightly did Isaiah prophesy of you hypocrites, as it is written: 'This people honors Me with their lips, but their heart is far away from Me. But in vain do they worship Me, teaching as doctrines the precepts of men.' Neglecting the commandment of God, you hold to the tradition of men."* (Mark 7:5-8)

Jesus's response confirmed His view of the Word of God as being given *by God* to the Prophet Isaiah. Then there's the time we see Jesus cleansing the temple. He said,

"It is written, 'My house shall be called a house of prayer';
but you are making it a robbers' den." (Matthew 21:13)

And on another occasion when Jesus was speaking with the Jews, He said,

"It is written in the prophets, 'And they shall all be taught
of God.' Everyone who has heard and learned from the
Father, comes to Me." (John 6:45)

We see from Jesus's use of the words, "It is written," confirms that He believed those Scriptures found within the Law and the Prophets were given by God. Therefore, all Old Testament Scripture has authority.

We also see Jesus asking questions beginning with, "have you not read...?" When Jesus and His disciples were walking through the grainfields on the Sabbath, the Pharisees saw His disciples picking and eating the heads of grain. The Pharisees questioned Jesus as to why He would allow His disciples to do what is not lawful to do on the Sabbath.

But He said to them, "Have you not read what David
did when he became hungry, he and his companions,
how he entered the house of God, and they ate the conse-
crated bread, which was not lawful for him to eat nor for
those with him, but for the priests alone? Or have you not
read in the Law, that on the Sabbath the priests in the
temple break the Sabbath and are innocent? But I say to
you that something greater than the temple is here. But
if you had known what this means, 'I desire compassion,
and not a sacrifice,' you would not have condemned the
innocent. For the Son of Man is Lord of the Sabbath."
(Matthew 12:1-8).

In His response, Jesus was referring to the Book of 1 Samuel, a book that is considered an historical book of the Old Testament. He was questioning the Pharisees' knowledge of God's written Word. Jesus took them back to a specific time in their history, the time of King David. The Pharisees, who were the religious leaders in the days of Jesus, should have been familiar with God's written word surrounding this account of David and the priests. Jesus defended the actions of His disciples by using Scripture to make the point that their act of picking and eating grain on the Sabbath was proper according to God's Word.

In a different instance, Jesus said to the Pharisees and Scribes, *"Why do you yourselves transgress the commandment of God for the sake of your tradition?"* (Matthew 15:3). Jesus never contradicted Scripture and He corrected others when they placed the traditions of men above the authoritative Word of God.

Jesus had many encounters with the religious leaders of His day. Their questioning of His words and actions always centered on whether or not He was adhering to God's Law as given to them in their Hebrew Scriptures. Jesus did not deny that these men taught God's Law as found in the five books of Moses, the Torah.

> *Then Jesus spoke to the crowds and to His disciples, saying: "The scribes and the Pharisees have seated themselves in the chair of Moses; therefore all that they tell you, do and observe, but do not do according to their deeds; for they say things and do not do them."* (Matthew 23:1-3)

Jesus found their teaching of the Law to be accurate. It was their doing of the Law—their behavior—that Jesus rebuked.

> *"But woe to you, scribes and Pharisees, hypocrites, because you shut off the kingdom of heaven from people; for you do not enter in yourselves, nor do you allow those who are entering to go in."* (Matthew 23:13)

Though Jesus called the Pharisees out as hypocrites, He did tell the crowds to obey that which they taught from the Scriptures. Jesus viewed the Pharisees' teachings of the Scriptures as the authoritative Word of God.

On another occasion, Jesus confirmed that what has been written in the Scriptures was given by God. Jesus was asked a question by the Sadducees. In His response, Jesus asked, "Have you not read what was spoken to you by God?" (Matthew 22:31). He then reminded them of a passage of Scripture from the Book of Exodus, the book of the Law. Jesus unequivocally viewed the Bible as God's written Word, thus validating it as having supreme authority.

Jesus Believed in The Precision of God's Word

Let's go back to our passage in Matthew. *"For truly I say to you, until heaven and earth pass away, not the smallest letter or stroke shall pass from the Law until all is accomplished"* (v. 18). Jesus began this statement with the words, "For truly I say to you,...." These words indicate an undeniable statement of Truth. Jesus then stated that not the smallest letter or stroke of the Law shall pass until all is accomplished. This means that God's Word is inspired down to the smallest letter and marking. The smallest letter in the Hebrew language is the *yod*. It is transliterated from the Greek as *iōta*. It is the smallest of all the letters and is equivalent to the minutest part (Strong's G2503). The stroke in the Hebrew language is even smaller than the smallest letter. It is transliterated from the Greek as *keraia*. It's a little extremity, apex, point (Strong's G2762). It would be similar to a stroke we would make in the English language so as to change an F to an E. Jesus said that even the markings that form the words found in Scripture are held in high regard to God, all the way down to the smallest demarcation.

We also see the precision of God's Word concerning verb tenses. The Sadducees, who were critics of Jesus and did not believe in the resurrection, decided to question Jesus on this topic to see if they could trip

Him up. They presented a scenario about marriage in which a woman had married seven times and then asked Jesus whose wife she would be in the resurrection.

> *But Jesus answered and said to them, "You are mistaken, not understanding the Scriptures nor the power of God. For in the resurrection they neither marry nor are given in marriage, but are like angels in heaven. But regarding the resurrection of the dead, have you not read what was spoken to you by God: 'I am the God of Abraham, and the God of Isaac, and the God of Jacob'? He is not the God of the dead but of the living." When the crowds heard this, they were astonished at His teaching.* (Matthew 22:29-33)

Jesus pointed out that they did not understand the Scriptures nor the power of God. He then took them back to the incident found in Exodus 3 when God called out to Moses from the burning bush. Abraham, Isaac, and Jacob lived several hundred years before Moses. When God spoke to Moses in Exodus 3:6, saying, "I *am* the God of...," He was referring to men who had physically died hundreds of years before Moses. Jesus referred back to this event to make the point that there is indeed a resurrection. If there was no resurrection, God would have said, "I *was* the God of...." God hadn't ceased to be their God simply because they had physically died. These men were still alive spiritually. When Jesus responded to the Sadducees, He made it clear that God was speaking to Moses in the present tense. This indicates that Jesus views the Word of God as nothing less than precise and accurate, down to the smallest letter, stroke, and verb tense. When we study the Bible, this is the reason it is wise to dig deep into what is being said and investigate the details of the words themselves.

Jesus Believed in The Preserving Nature of God's Word

Once again, we'll look at Matthew 5:18. *"For truly I say to you, until heaven and earth pass away, not the smallest letter or stroke shall pass from the Law until all is accomplished."* The context of this verse reveals that Jesus was speaking about the preserving nature of God's Word as it related to the end of the present world as we know it. We are told in the Word of God that the present heavens and earth are being reserved for fire, kept for the day of judgment and destruction of ungodly men (2 Peter 3:7). But one day it will come to an end. The heavens will pass away with a roar and the elements will be destroyed with intense heat, and the earth and its works will be burned up (2 Peter 3:10). God will then create a new heaven and a new earth (Revelation 21:1). Until then, Jesus said the unchanging Word of God stands and will continue to do so until all is accomplished. Isaiah 46:10 gives us the assurance that God's plan will be fulfilled and accomplished at the end of the age; … *declaring the end from the beginning, and from ancient times things which have not been done, saying, "My purpose will be established, and I will accomplish all My good pleasure."* Jesus believed that the written Word of God would continue to remain in existence until all is accomplished.

Jesus also let us know that though He is the fulfillment of the Law, the Law has not lost its importance, nor can it be overturned. Jesus said,

> *"But it is easier for heaven and earth to pass away than for one stroke of a letter of the Law to fail."* (Luke 16:17)

On a different occasion, when Jesus was speaking of end times, He said, *"Heaven and earth will pass away, but My words will not pass away"* (Mark 13:31). This statement reiterates for us the powerful, enduring nature of God's Word. His Word is more enduring than both the creation and future destruction of this present world.

We also see several references to the eternal nature of God's Word in the Old Testament. *The sum of Your word is truth, and every one of*

Your righteous ordinances is everlasting (Psalm 119:160). *The grass withers, the flower fades, but the word of our God stands forever* (Isaiah 40:8). The Apostle Peter also quoted that same Scripture found in Isaiah, *"But the word of the Lord endures forever." And this is the word which was preached to you* (1 Peter 1:25). At the time of Peter's writing, over seven hundred years had passed since Isaiah penned those words, yet it was the same Word that Jesus's apostles were preaching in the first century. God's Word had already survived centuries at that point. It has continued ever since and will continue to do so over time. God's Word stands.

Jesus Believed God is Personal and Communicates With Mankind

Jesus taught that the voice of God can be heard and understood by man. When Jesus was speaking to the crowds warning against greed, He told the Parable of the Rich Fool. He spoke of a rich fool who tore down his barns to build bigger ones to store his crops, saying, *"But God said to him, 'You fool! This very night your soul is required of you...'"* (Luke 12:20). We also see that Jesus believed that God's written words can be understood by man. Jesus prayed to the Father regarding His disciples, saying, *"Sanctify them in the truth; Your word is truth"* (John 17:17). Jesus prayed to the Father that His disciples would be set apart to live according to His Word for His purposes. The disciples understood that they were to live by the written Word of God.

Jesus taught that His voice and His words could be understood by man. *"My sheep hear My voice, and I know them, and they follow Me"* (John 10:27). Jesus said that all who belong to Him—His "sheep"— know His voice. When they hear His voice, they understand His words and thus, follow Him. On another occasion, Jesus said, *"It is the Spirit who gives life; the flesh profits nothing; the words that I have spoken to you are spirit and are life"* (John 6:63). Jesus taught that those who have the Holy Spirit living within them have life through His words; His words apply to us personally in our individual circumstances.

We also see Jesus teaching that God relates to us personally.

> *"Ask, and it will be given to you; seek, and you will find; knock, and it will be opened to you."* (Matthew 7:7)

> *"Blessed are those who hunger and thirst for righteousness, for they shall be satisfied."* (Matthew 5:6)

Jesus taught that we are to pray to the Father and be in communion with Him, and when we do so, we will be satisfied. Jesus also taught us to depend on God for what we need every day. We are to ask for those needs in prayer; *"Give us this day our daily bread"* (Matthew 6:11). And Jesus promised that for those who seek first God's kingdom and His righteousness, God, who already knows our every need, will supply those needs (Matthew 7:32-33).

As we look to other Scripture, the writer of Hebrews teaches that God is a rewarder of those who seek Him.

> *And without faith it is impossible to please Him, for he who comes to God must believe that He is and that He is a rewarder of those who seek Him.* (Hebrews 11:6)

God is willing and able to personally reward those who actively pursue Him. We learn in 1 Chronicles 28:9 that if you seek God, God will let you find Him. God says in Jeremiah 29:13, *"You will seek Me and find Me when you search for Me with all your heart."* God loves us and desires for us to be in a relationship with Him. But God is a gentleman. He is not going to force Himself on us. He wants us to come to Him willingly with a desire to know Him. Scripture reveals that God—the very same God who brought all of creation into existence with His spoken words—also fashioned together written words through the hands of His creation (Exodus 34:27; Jeremiah 30:2). His words are His love letter to us, written expressly for the very ones He created. God's words have been written so that we can know Him and be in a relationship with Him.

We are told in Ecclesiastes 3:11 that God has put eternity in our hearts. The eternal God (Deuteronomy 33:27) of all creation, in whose image we are made (Genesis 1:27), has given us an awareness and a longing for Him within our souls. We have a yearning for things eternal, things that stir up our desires to seek and discover the divine. It is that part of us that knows, whether we are conscious of it or not, we are not here by chance. We are here by design and with a purpose. Our hearts are always seeking to know our eternal God. Through His Word, God satisfies that deep, eternal desire within us.

Jesus Believed The Historical Accounts of The Scriptures as Factual

Jesus made several references to some of the stories found in the Old Testament Scriptures, citing them as literal events with actual people. This included some of the more controversial stories in the Bible such as creation, the account of a worldwide flood, and Jonah in the belly of a great fish.

In Matthew's Gospel, Jesus compared the circumstances surrounding His second coming to being similar to the circumstances leading up to the worldwide flood in Noah's day.

> *"For the coming of the Son of Man will be just like the days of Noah. For as in those days before the flood they were eating and drinking, marrying and giving in marriage, until the day that Noah entered the ark, and they did not understand until the flood came and took them all away; so will the coming of the Son of Man be."* (Matthew 24:37-39)

Jesus shows us that the events of Noah and the flood are similar to what will occur just before His second coming. No one knows the day or the hour of it (Matthew 24:42), and many will ignore the warnings of impending judgment. This reference tells us that Jesus believed the written events regarding Noah and the flood.

Jesus also referenced the story of Jonah. God had appointed a great fish to swallow Jonah, and Jonah was in the stomach of the fish for three days and three nights (Jonah 1:17).

> *Then some of the scribes and Pharisees said to Him, "Teacher, we want to see a sign from You." But He answered and said to them, "An evil and adulterous generation craves for a sign; and yet no sign will be given to it but the sign of Jonah the prophet; for just as Jonah was three days and three nights in the belly of the sea monster, so will the Son of Man be three days and three nights in the heart of the earth. The men of Nineveh will stand up with this generation at the judgment, and will condemn it because they repented at the preaching of Jonah; and behold, something greater than Jonah is here.* (Matthew 12:38-41)

Jesus used the story of Jonah and the great fish to illustrate both His coming resurrection as well as His coming judgment upon man. This tells us that Jesus accepted the events of Jonah as historical fact.

We also find that when the Pharisees asked Jesus about divorce, He referenced the account of creation as found in Genesis.

> *And He answered and said, "Have you not read that He who created them from the beginning made them male and female, and said, 'For this reason a man shall leave his father and mother and be joined to his wife, and the two shall become one flesh'?"* (Matthew 19:4-5)

Jesus used the account of Adam and Eve to show us God's intended purpose for marriage; marriage is to be between a man and a woman, and their bond as husband and wife is to be permanent. Jesus accepted the literal existence of Adam and Eve and the account of God, who in the beginning, created them.

Jesus also referred to the cities of Sodom and Gomorrah and the destruction that fell upon them in God's judgment.

> *"Whoever does not receive you, nor heed your words, as you go out of that house or that city, shake the dust off your feet. Truly I say to you, it will be more tolerable for the land of Sodom and Gomorrah in the day of judgment than for that city."* (Matthew 10:14-15)

Jesus used the cities of Sodom and Gomorrah to illustrate that for those who will not accept His message of salvation, judgment will fall upon them. It would fall upon the cities of those days, the same way it did during the days of Abraham and Lot. Jesus believed in the literal destruction of Sodom and Gomorrah.

There are other historical accounts in which we find Jesus referring to the people and events found in the Scriptures. When Jesus was pronouncing *Woe's* to the Pharisees and Lawyers, He referred to Abel (Luke 11:51). Then there is the reference to Lot and his wife (Luke 17:28-32), as well as the time when God sent manna from heaven to the Israelites as they wandered in the wilderness (John 6:32, 49, 58). Jesus left no doubt as to the authenticity of the people and events that literally occurred as recorded in Scripture.

Jesus Established The Validity For The New Testament Writings as Scripture

We have learned that Jesus believed the Old Testament to be the infallible, inerrant Word of God. But what did He think about the

New Testament? The Bible tells us that Jesus is the living Word of God (John 1:1), yet He never actually wrote a single word of Scripture. We remember Jesus's own words, "All authority has been given to Me in heaven and on earth" (Matthew 28:18). Therefore, the words Jesus spoke have the same divine authority as God's words given in the Old Testament. While He never wrote Scripture, it is by His divine authority that He made provision for the New Testament writings.

Under His authority, Jesus sent out His disciples to preach (Mark 3:14). These were men He personally chose to take His message and teach it to others. Jesus instructed His disciples to share His message of salvation with the entire world. They were to make disciples of all nations, teaching them all that Jesus commanded.

> *And Jesus came up and spoke to them, saying, "All authority has been given to Me in heaven and on earth. Go therefore and make disciples of all the nations, baptizing them in the name of the Father and the Son and the Holy Spirit, teaching them to observe all that I commanded you; and lo, I am with you always, even to the end of the age." (Matthew 28:18-20)*

Jesus told His disciples that as they shared His message of salvation, their words would have the same authority as His. Jesus said,

> *"The one who listens to you listens to Me, and the one who rejects you rejects Me; and he who rejects Me rejects the One who sent Me." (Luke 10:16)*

He also said, *"Any place that does not receive you or listen to you, as you go out from there, shake the dust off the soles of your feet for a testimony against them"* (Mark 6:11). And on another occasion, He said, *"Truly, truly, I say to you, he who receives whomever I send receives Me; and he who receives Me receives Him who sent Me"* (John 13:20).

The disciples were also promised that the Spirit of Truth would testify of Jesus, and they, in turn, would then testify to others.

> *"When the Helper comes, whom I will send to you from the Father, that is the Spirit of truth who proceeds from the Father, <u>He will testify about Me, and you will testify also</u>, because you have been with Me from the beginning."* (John 15:26-27)

Jesus told His disciples that He would be giving them further revelation and told them by whom that revelation would be given.

> *"<u>I have many more things to say to you</u>, but you cannot bear them now. But when He, <u>the Spirit of truth</u>, comes, He <u>will guide you into all the truth</u>; for He will not speak on His own initiative, but whatever He hears, He will speak; and He will disclose to you what is to come. He will glorify Me, for He will take of Mine and will disclose it to you."* (John 16:12-14)

Though Jesus said He had much more to say to His disciples, He indicated that those words would be revealed at a later time as they were things they couldn't bear at that moment. There would come a time when Jesus would reveal all He wanted to say, and He would do so through the Spirit. The Spirit would soon become the one to guide them into all Truth. And when the Spirit would come, Jesus promised His disciples the Spirit would teach them and serve as their guide in recounting all that He said.

> *"But the Helper, <u>the Holy Spirit</u>, whom the Father will send in My name, He <u>will teach you all things, and bring to your remembrance all that I said to you</u>."* (John 14:26)

Jesus made these promises to His disciples before He left this world. He assured His disciples, that even after He was no longer living among them, He would continue to speak to them through the Holy Spirit.

Jesus also told us it is by His words that all humanity will be judged on the last day.

> "*He who rejects Me and does not receive My sayings, has one who judges him; the word I spoke is what will judge him at the last day.*" (John 12:48)

It is by the divine and authoritative Word of Jesus Christ that all of mankind—people from every tribe and nation around the globe—will be judged. Given the grave implications of the final judgment, this is a strong indication that Jesus knew a written form of His words would accompany the verbal testimony of His apostles. The Apostle John, under Christ's authority, penned these words:

> "...but *these have been written so that you may believe that Jesus is the Christ,* the Son of God; *and that believing you may have life in His name.*" (John 20:31)

Though John was speaking of the signs Jesus performed when he wrote this, the greater context reveals to the world that Jesus is the Messiah. John wrote his account of Jesus so that we may believe in Jesus and have life in His name.

All the written revelation that God had given us before Jesus was recorded by men who were appointed by God and moved by the Holy Spirit. This written revelation set a precedent. We also see that God chose to speak to us beyond what was written in the Old Testament.

> *God, after He spoke long ago to the fathers in the prophets in many portions and in many ways, in these last days has spoken to us in His Son....* (Hebrews 1:1-2)

After the Old Testament Scriptures had been written, God chose to speak to us through His Son; Jesus only spoke the words of the Father (John 17:8). When Jesus gave His apostles the authority to share His message, He placed no restrictions on the manner in which they were to convey those words and thus, fulfill their commission.

Jesus entrusted His life and ministry to be accurately conveyed by men He chose, upon whom the Holy Spirit would bring to their remembrance all that He said. Jesus Himself even appeared in a vision to the Apostle John while he was exiled on the island of Patmos. He told John to write his vision in a book and gave him instructions as to whom and to where it was to be sent (Revelation 1:11). As the disciples taught and bore witness to others concerning Jesus, it is reasonable to conclude that a written form of the life of Jesus and His message of salvation would be forthcoming. The promises Jesus gave to His disciples assure us that their verbal and written accounts of His life and ministry would be nothing less than an accurate account of all that Jesus said and did.

Though men physically penned the words of God, Jesus affirmed that it is the Spirit who directs the writings of Scripture. In Matthew 22:42-43, Jesus asked the Pharisees whose son they thought the Christ would be. They answered, "The son of David." Jesus then asked, "Then how does David in the Spirit call Him 'Lord?'" In referring back to this psalm of David, we see by Jesus's choice of the words, *in the Spirit*, He knew that David's writings were inspired by the Holy Spirit.

We learn in 2 Timothy 3:16 that all Scripture is inspired by God. The phrase *is inspired by God* is comprised of one word in the Greek, *theopneustos*—a word derived from two other Greek words: Theos, meaning 'God,' and pneo, meaning 'to breathe.' It means the contents of the Scriptures are inspired by God (Strong's G2315). To look at it another way, the words of Scripture are God-breathed.

We also learn in 2 Peter 1:21, *...for no prophecy was ever made by an act of human will, but men moved by the Holy Spirit spoke from God.* The word *moved* in the Greek is *pherō.* It means to carry or bear a burden; to be conveyed or borne, with the suggestion of force or speed, of a gust of wind, or of the mind, to be moved inwardly, prompted; to bring forth by announcing (Strong's G5342). We learn that the Scriptures, though penned by human authors (fallible men), were done so under the divine inspiration of the Holy Spirit (the infallible third person of the Triune God). The Holy Spirit raised up men, who were then borne up and carried by the breath of God, to bring forth God's very own words.

Some of the writers of the New Testament were eye-witnesses and penned the Scriptures based on what they saw and heard.

> *What was from the beginning, <u>what we have heard</u>, what we have <u>seen</u> with our eyes, what we have looked at <u>and touched with our hands</u>, concerning the Word of Life – and the life was manifested, and we have seen and testify and proclaim to you the eternal life, which was with the Father and was manifested to us – what we have seen and heard <u>we proclaim to you</u> also, so that you too may have fellowship with us; and indeed our fellowship is with the Father, and with His Son Jesus Christ. <u>These things we write</u>, so that our joy may be made complete.* (1 John 1:1-4)

Then there was the Apostle Paul. Though not an eye-witness to the life of Christ, he was chosen by Jesus to preach to the Gentiles, to kings, and the sons of Israel (Acts 9:15). Paul had received direct revelation from God regarding Jesus Christ (Galatians 1:16). Through the inspiration of the Holy Spirit, Paul wrote thirteen of the twenty-seven books of the New Testament.

Though not every writer of the New Testament was an Apostle of Christ, the Apostle Paul affirmed some of the writers as prophets (Ephesians 3:5). There was Luke, a Gentile, who penned the Scriptures based on the eye-witness accounts of others.

> *Inasmuch as <u>many have undertaken to compile an account</u>*
> *<u>of the things</u> accomplished among us, just as they were*
> *<u>handed down to us by those who from the beginning were</u>*
> *<u>eyewitnesses and servants of the word,</u> it seemed fitting*
> *for me as well, having investigated everything carefully*
> *from the beginning, <u>to write</u> it out for you in consecutive*
> *order, most excellent Theophilus; so that you may know*
> *<u>the exact truth</u> about the things you have been taught.*
> (Luke 1:1-4)

There was also James, the half-brother of Jesus. Though not numbered among the twelve, Jesus appeared to James (1 Corinthians 15:7) after His resurrection. It was after Jesus's resurrection that we know for certain that James became a follower and believer in Jesus as the Christ. In his writings, James speaks of true faith in Christ and gives us practical wisdom for living out that faith.

The writers of the New Testament, under the divine inspiration and power of the Holy Spirit, with their own flair and personal style, wrote that which testified of Jesus. God raised them up and the wind of His breath carried forth His message exactly where He wanted it to go. God directed their writing through the Spirit as the Spirit guided them into all Truth. God directed it, the Spirit guided it, and men wrote it.

Jesus Believed The Written Word of God Requires Responsibility

> *"Whoever then annuls one of the least of these command-*
> *ments, and teaches others to do the same, shall be called*
> *least in the kingdom of heaven; but whoever keeps and*
> *teaches them, he shall be called great in the kingdom of*
> *heaven."* (Matthew 5:19)

The word *annuls* in the Greek is *lyō*. It means to loosen, undo, dissolve; to do away with, to deprive of authority, whether by precept or act (Strong's G3089). To annul any commandment by God is essentially to reduce it to nothing. It's a disregard of God's authority in which we loose ourselves from His Law or do away with any of the Law's requirements and standards. There is great importance in the Law of God. The Law of God reflects God's character; it is holy and the commandment is holy and righteous and good (Romans 7:12). Though we are no longer under the Law (Romans 6:14; Galatians 5:18), we are held accountable to abide in the law of liberty found in Christ Jesus (James 1:25). Remember, being under the law of liberty does not equate to freedom to sin (Romans 6:1). As followers of Christ, we are to obey the two greatest commandments—loving God with all our heart, soul, and mind, and loving our neighbor as ourselves. Jesus completely fulfilled the moral and legal demands of the Law as His life was in complete obedience to them. By our obedience to the two greatest commandments—a love for God and others—we uphold and fulfill God's Law (Galatians 5:14).

Jesus tells us that anyone who annuls the commandments and teaches others to do the same shall be called least in the kingdom of heaven. There are consequences for disregarding the Law of God. And as seen here, there is a consequence for then teaching others to do the same, whether by way of instruction or by example. Since Jesus's statement indicates a condition or title in the kingdom of heaven, be it least or great, it seems that Jesus may be referring to rewards for believers (1 Corinthians 3:10-15; 2 Corinthians 5:10). Depending upon how a child of God handles the commandments of God—annulling or keeping them and teaching others to do the same—will determine his or her position in the kingdom of heaven. We see a similar warning by John in his second epistle, *Watch yourselves, that you do not lose what we have accomplished, but that you may receive a full reward* (2 John 8).

Jesus taught that our adherence to Him and the Word of God requires a responsibility on our part to obey and to teach others the commandments of God. It is our love for God and others that fuels our obedience to God and *all* that He has commanded of us.

Summary

We have learned that while Jesus did not make a formal statement about His view of the Scriptures, nor wrote a single word, Jesus believed the Scriptures to be the infallible, inerrant, authoritative Word of God— every single word, down to the most minute detail. If we claim to follow Jesus Christ—the Jesus of the Bible—our view of the Bible must be compatible with His.

Chapter 11

HOPE FOR HIS APPEARING

I VIVIDLY REMEMBER A SPECIFIC MOMENT THE day before I married my husband Steve. It occurred during our wedding rehearsal. I was at the back of the church waiting for my cue to begin walking forward when I looked in Steve's direction and saw him smiling as he waited for me at the altar. I'll never forget how excited I was, knowing that in just twenty-four hours I'd be doing this again, except next time, he would become my husband!

The anticipation in my heart at that moment was overwhelming. The hope I had of building a life together with this wonderful man was about to come to fruition. We were soon to be united in holy matrimony and what I had longed for in my heart was about to become a reality.

The Bride of Christ

The Bible tells us that we, the Church, comprised of believers in Jesus, are the bride of Christ. In the Book of Ephesians, the Apostle Paul uses the symbolism of marriage to describe the relationship Christ has with His Church. Paul tells us that husbands are to love their wives as Christ loved the Church and gave Himself up for her (Ephesians 5:25). Jesus, our Bridegroom, out of His great love for His bride, sacrificed Himself *so that He might sanctify her, having cleansed her by the washing of the water with the word, that He might present to Himself the church in all her glory, having no spot or wrinkle or any such thing; but that she would be holy and blameless* (Ephesians 5:26-27). Jesus gave up His life for mankind on the cross so that those who come to Him in repentance and faith—His bride—can stand before God, holy and blameless, and enter into eternal life with our heavenly Father.

An important element of God the Father's predetermined plan and purpose of salvation was to give a bride to His Son. And just like a bride who eagerly waits to be united in marriage with her husband, so too, do we, the Church, long to be united with our Bridegroom, Jesus Christ. We are filled with hope as we look forward to our Bridegroom's return. Upon His return, He will take us to our eternal home where we will be united together in marriage. What a wonderful and glorious time it will be as we rejoice and celebrate the Marriage Supper of the Lamb (Revelation 19:7-9). I can't wait! But wait we must. And while we wait, it is our calling as the bride of Christ to be faithful to Him (2 Corinthians 11:2), keeping ourselves pure just as He is pure (1 John 3:3), so that when we meet Him face-to-face, we don't shrink away from Him in shame (1 John 2:28; 3:2). Our faithfulness to Jesus is to be evident in word and deed, and we are called to use the gifts and talents He has given us to serve Him (Matthew 25:14-30) as we share His message of salvation with a lost world (Matthew 28:19-20).

Ever since I became a Christian, that longing to be with Christ is just as exciting as what I experienced the day before my wedding to Steve. And with each passing day, it only increases. The more I learn about my Bridegroom, the more eager I am for that union to be actualized. This is yet another hallmark that is prevalent among true followers of Jesus—a longing and desire for the soon appearance of our

Lord and Savior, Jesus Christ. It's the longing in our hearts to be united with Christ that causes Christians to abound with great hope; we look forward to His appearing to come and take us home.

> *Now may the God of hope fill you with all joy and peace in believing, so that you will abound in hope by the power of the Holy Spirit.* (Romans 15:13)

Christian Hope

It's important to note there is a clear distinction between Christian hope and the type of hope we commonly hear used in everyday conversation. For instance, we might say, "I hope to be able to complete this task today," or "I hope everything works out as planned." This type of hope is more in line with an outcome we'd like to see come to fruition, but don't necessarily know that it will. It's akin to a strong desire or wishful thinking. But Christian hope is different. Christian hope is based on certainty, a hope based on the promises of God. As discussed in the previous chapter, the Bible is full of prophecy, much of which has already come to pass. Since God is a covenant-keeping God (Nehemiah 9:32), and He never changes (Malachi 3:6), we can know for certain that He says what He means and means what He says. Therefore, the Christian can have complete confidence that everything God has promised will indeed come to pass. Our hope rests in the fact that God keeps His promises.

There are many promises of God that we, His children, are destined to receive given our rightful inheritance as His heirs (Galatians 4:5-7). The Bible tells us, *He who did not spare His own Son, but delivered Him over for us all, how will He not also with Him freely give us all things?* (Romans 8:32). If God was willing to give up His Son for our salvation, it's almost mind-blowing that He would also freely give us *all* things in Christ. Talk about hope! Though we don't know what tomorrow will bring, we do know that we can rest securely in the promises of God as we live out our days on earth. And when the day comes in which we take our final breath, our eternal future with our Savior is a certainty.

Longing For Our Eternal Home

We learn in 2 Corinthians 5:8 that the moment we take our last breath, we will be home with the Lord. As noted in a previous chapter, for all who follow Christ, our citizenship is in heaven (Philippians 3:20). We also learn in Philippians 1:21 that to live is Christ and to die is gain. These three verses tell us that when we die, we'll immediately be at home with the Lord, where our true citizenship lies, and it will be to our advantage. Our experience in heaven will be superior to anything we have known on earth. That alone gives rise to hope beyond what I'm able to imagine. As citizens of heaven, we have so much to look forward to as we spend eternity with our Lord.

Given that this world is not our home (John 17:16), there is a true longing in the hearts of Christians for our Bridegroom to come and take us home. Paul writes about his experience with this longing in his letter to the Philippians.

> *But I am hard-pressed from both directions, having the desire to depart and be with Christ, for that is very much better; yet to remain on in the flesh is more necessary for your sake.* (Philippians 1:23-24)

As believers who rest in the promise of a glorious everlasting life with the Lord, our longing to go to our eternal home is real. Yet at the same time, we are very much aware that while we are still on earth, God is using us for His kingdom purposes. As sons and daughters of the Lord Most High, we earnestly desire in our hearts to accomplish His will. Therefore, we present ourselves to Him, a living and holy sacrifice, to be used according to His purposes until He takes us home. However, that's not always easy. The trials we face in our everyday lives can be quite challenging. That presents a stark contrast to knowing we'll soon be with Jesus in our heavenly home. As such, our longing to go home cannot be extinguished. God has put eternity in our hearts (Ecclesiastes 3:11), and once we become His sons and daughters, we can't escape it. It's the hope inside us for our eternal home with our Bridegroom that fuels the longing within us. And oh, what awaits us! Jesus Himself gave us a glimpse of what we have to look forward to in our heavenly home.

One of my absolute favorite passages of Scripture that speaks to our future with our Bridegroom is found in the Gospel of John. Jesus was speaking to His disciples as He said these words:

> *"Do not let your heart be troubled; believe in God, believe also in Me. In My Father's house are many dwelling places; if it were not so, I would have told you; for I go to prepare a place for you. If I go and prepare a place for you, I will come again and receive you to Myself, that where I am, there you may be also. And you know the way where I am going." Thomas said to Him, "Lord, we do not know where You are going, how do we know the way?" Jesus said to him, "I am the way, and the truth, and the life; no one comes to the Father but through Me." (John 14:1-6)*

Every time I read this passage I inevitably exhale with, "Ahhh...." It's like a breath of fresh air. Jesus told us He is preparing a place for us—a dwelling place in His Father's house. This means Jesus has been preparing a place that is tailor-made for each of us! How exciting is that? I cannot wait to see and experience my dwelling place with Christ.

Death Has Lost Its Sting

As I express my excitement and hope for Christ's soon return, I do want to be clear about something. Though Christians long to be at home with the Lord, it doesn't mean we ought to have a desire to accelerate our death. As previously noted, as long as we still have breath in our lungs, we are called to be faithful to our Bridegroom and to do the work He has called us to do. However, as we abide in Christ and faithfully carry out God's will, our desire to be at home with the Lord seems only to increase. When we are born again, the Spirit goes to work in our hearts. All that the world has to offer begins to lose its appeal and Jesus takes center-stage as we set our minds on the things of Christ.

The more we get to know our great and powerful God, the desires of our hearts take a sharp turn. God becomes supreme and our love for Him and others increases. As a result, our focus shifts from the temporal to the eternal. This doesn't mean we never experience some trepidation over the thought of death. I would guess nearly all people have experienced a fear of dying at some point in their lives. But for the Christian, death has lost its sting (1 Corinthians 15:54-55); it is no longer something to be feared. Jesus defeated sin and death on the cross and His resurrection assures our resurrection (1 Corinthians 15:21). Jesus abolished death and brought life and immortality to light through the gospel (2 Timothy 1:10). Therefore, given that Christians have already passed out of death and into life (John 5:24), that our salvation is sure (1 John 5:13), and we'll meet Jesus face-to-face (1 John 3:2), any feelings of being unsettled about death and dying seem to dim, and our hope in what awaits us for all eternity increases. Our mindset shifts to that which is to come in anticipation of living a resurrected life with Jesus Christ. And for those of us who are steadfast of mind and trust in God, His Word tells us He will keep us in perfect peace; He is our everlasting Rock (Isaiah 26:3-4). As we keep our focus on Christ while we wait for His return, death is not something to be feared. God promises us His peace as we live out the days He has given us. The lack of fear in death and our focus on the eternal frees us up to faithfully carry out His purpose for our lives. As we do so, hope abounds as we look forward to what awaits us the moment we take our last breath.

The Anticipation of The Rapture

Our hope in the life to come is so great, many believers don't want to wait until we die! We eagerly long for the Rapture. Let's take a look at what the Apostle Paul told the believers in Thessalonica regarding the Rapture of the Church. Given Paul's response in his letter, he must have emphasized the soon return of Jesus Christ as he shared the gospel with them during his visit. It seems that after he left, some among them started wondering about their loved ones who had passed away, incorrectly assuming that because they had died, they would miss the return of Jesus Christ and all the glory of that blessed event. Paul responded as follows:

> *But we do not want you to be uninformed, brethren, about those who are asleep* (a common way to denote a person who had died), *so that you will not grieve as do the rest who have no hope. For if we believe that Jesus died and rose again, even so God will bring with Him those who have fallen asleep in Jesus. For this we say to you by the word of the Lord, that we who are alive and remain until the coming of the Lord, will not precede those who have fallen asleep. For the Lord Himself will descend from heaven with a shout, with the voice of the archangel and with the trumpet of God, and the dead in Christ will rise first. Then we who are alive and remain will be caught up together with them in the clouds to meet the Lord in the air, and so we shall always be with the Lord. Therefore comfort one another with these words.* (1 Thessalonians 4:13-18)

And what a comfort this is!

Paul's mention of those who had fallen asleep *in Jesus* was a direct reference to Christians who had died. Paul didn't want those who were still alive to be uninformed about what was going to happen to their loved ones who had already died *in Christ* at the time of Jesus's return. All believers who have died before Christ returns will be caught up to meet Him in the clouds when He comes to get His bride. While we have already learned that our spirits will immediately be with the Lord upon our death, our physical bodies will be left behind. It is at the moment of the Rapture of the Church when the Lord will raise every physical body of believers back to life. Our bodies will be transformed *in a moment, in the twinkling of an eye, at the last trumpet; for the trumpet will sound, and the dead will be raised imperishable, and we will be changed* (1 Corinthians 15:52). What an incredible event we have to look forward to! Our Bridegroom is going to descend from heaven with a shout, and we, His bride, are going to meet Him in the air. I can't even wrap my mind around what that experience will be like, but I know it will be glorious.

Raised in Glory and Power

Given that our human bodies are in a constant state of decay, the thought of having a new, transformed body is exhilarating. What will our new bodies be like? Though we don't know the answer to that entirely, the Bible does tell us that when we see Jesus, we will be like Him.

> *Beloved, now we are children of God, and it has not appeared as yet what we will be. We know that when He appears, we will be like Him, because we will see Him just as He is.* (1 John 3:2)

Let's see what we can learn about what it means to be like Jesus.

Jesus made several appearances after His resurrection from the dead (Acts 1:3). His disciples were among those who had the awesome experience of seeing Jesus in His glorified body. Though Jesus's glorified body was also physical (John 20:17, 27), His was different than ours in that

His body seemed not to be subject to the laws of nature. In a couple of instances, He appeared suddenly in the midst of His disciples while they were in a room, with the doors shut (John 20:19, 26). We see another time in which He suddenly vanished from sight, such as the time Jesus was traveling with two disciples on the road to Emmaus (Luke 24:31). Also, He could quickly transport Himself from one place to another. We see this occur after Jesus had broken bread with those same two disciples. After vanishing from their sight, He appeared among His disciples once again later that evening (Luke 24:36). Yet given the supernatural abilities displayed by Jesus in His glorified body, we also see that He was still able to eat (Luke 24:42-43). And to that...most of us are probably saying, "Hallelujah!" How wonderful that we'll still be able to eat! I can only imagine the feast we'll enjoy at the Marriage Supper of the Lamb. We also see that Jesus's body still bore the marks of crucifixion (John 20:27). Perhaps that is an eternal reminder of His sacrificial love for His bride, in taking upon Himself the punishment for our sin.

Our new bodies are going to be glorious! Our physical earthly bodies will be transformed and redeemed; free of sin, of suffering, and the indwelling sin nature (Romans 8:23). They are going to be imperishable, free from decay (1 Corinthians 15:42); raised in glory and power; raised a spiritual body (1 Corinthians 15:43-44). Amazing!

> *When Christ, who is our life, is revealed, then you also will be revealed with Him in glory.* (Colossians 3:4)

Apart from the marks of Jesus's crucifixion, our bodies are going to be like His body—bodies that allow us to function and live on earth during the Millennial reign of Christ (Revelation 19:14, 20:4), as well as allow us to function and live with Him eternally in the new heavens and new earth (Isaiah 65:17; Revelation 21:1).

This beautiful earth we live on right now is just a preview of the splendor which is to come. And ...*according to His promise we are looking for new heavens and a new earth, in which righteousness dwells* (2 Peter

3:13). The new earth, where only righteousness dwells, will restore what we had at the beginning of creation. God made the heavens and the earth and all living beings, and it was very good (Genesis 1:31). This means the earth will be restored to what it was before the Fall, before the point at which the world and the spirit of man became corrupted by sin. It will be an earth in which God will dwell among us, with no more tears, no more death, no more mourning, or crying, or pain (Revelation 21:3-4). Now that is hope! It's a hope that is only made possible by the redeeming work, and resurrection of, our Lord and Savior, Jesus Christ.

> *Blessed be the God and Father of our Lord Jesus Christ, who according to His great mercy has caused us to be born again to a living hope through the resurrection of Jesus Christ from the dead.* (1 Peter 1:3)

As Christians, we have hope—hope of eternal life, hope of a bodily resurrection, and hope for His appearing. Our hope rests upon God's promises; all He has promised will indeed come to pass. Knowing our eternal salvation is certain allows Christians the freedom to fully live for Christ now. We can rest securely in His promise to faithfully preserve us while we await His return.

> *For the grace of God has appeared, bringing salvation to all men, instructing us to deny ungodliness and worldly desires and to live sensibly, righteously and godly in the present age, looking for the blessed hope and the appearing of the glory of our great God and Savior, Christ Jesus.* (Titus 2:11-13)

Summary

Just like a bride who eagerly waits to be united with her groom, so too, do we, the Church, eagerly wait to be united with our Bridegroom, the Lord Jesus Christ. It's a longing in our hearts that only increases as we faithfully continue to abide in Christ. We wait with great anticipation for His return to come and take us home. *Amen. Come, Lord Jesus* (Revelation 22:20).

Epilogue

"He who is not with Me is against Me;
and he who does not gather with Me scatters." (Matthew 12:30)

T HIS IS THE SAME VERSE I SHARED IN THE opening statement of the Preface. It is profound and carries with it both grave and glorious consequences. According to Jesus, this statement contends there are only two true divisions among the human race, each accompanied by a driving force: those who are *with* Christ (the saved) and gather to Him, and those who are *against* Christ (the unsaved) and scatter away from Him. At some point, we must all decide on which side we stand. Are we *with* Jesus or *against* Jesus? Of all the decisions a person will make in his or her lifetime, this one has the greatest impact, the implications of which, affect us for eternity.

There are both eternal and earthly consequences for this decision. With regard to the eternal, those who reject Christ's sacrifice for their sin will spend eternity separated from God. Those who have put their faith in Christ will spend eternity in the presence of our Lord and Savior. Concerning the earthly consequences, those who reject Christ will never know the joy and peace that comes from a life surrendered to Jesus. They'll never be free from the power of sin in their lives, always a slave to that which leads to spiritual death. As for the Christian, the earthly consequences are often viewed as a "mixed bag" of experiences and circumstances. Some are glorious beyond anything we could ever imagine, and some are riddled with mental, physical, and emotional pain, brought on by trials and tribulations. Whenever we might question our faith and our decision to follow Christ, the trying experiences of the here and now are often that which gives us pause.

The Cost of Following Christ

I also noted in the Preface that following Christ comes at a cost. Jesus Himself summed up the "cost" when He told us what it means to follow Him.

> *And He summoned the crowd with His disciples, and said to them, "If anyone wishes to come after Me, he must deny himself, and take up his cross and follow Me. For whoever wishes to save his life will lose it, but whoever loses his life for My sake and the gospel's will save it. For what does it profit a man to gain the whole world, and forfeit his soul? For what will a man give in exchange for his soul? For whoever is ashamed of Me and My words in this adulterous and sinful generation, the Son of Man will also be ashamed of him when He comes in the glory of His Father with the holy angels." (Mark 8:34-38)*

Whether you've just read these words for the first time or have read them countless times, they tend to sound harsh and unappealing. But Jesus gives us the full picture of what it means to follow Him. We must not let the "sting" of His words detract us from the fact that though there is an earthly cost to following Him, ultimately, our lives will be saved.

228

We learn from Jesus that following Him requires several things: a denial of self, a daily walk with Him in which we carry our cross, and a devotion to following after Him in which we are ready and willing to proudly proclaim our allegiance to Him.

The denial of self Jesus speaks of isn't referring to abstaining from or denying ourselves the comforts or pleasures in this life as a way of "earning" salvation, or a way in which we hope to be "accepted" by Him. Christianity isn't works-based righteousness. We cannot earn, nor merit our salvation.

> *For by grace you have been saved through faith; and that not of yourselves, it is the gift of God; not as a result of works, so that no one may boast.* (Ephesians 2:8-9)

To deny ourselves means we must abandon our own will, goals, and desires and instead, surrender to God's will and authority. This is not to say we must never set goals for ourselves or neglect to make plans for our future. But it does mean that everything we do must be weighed against God's Word and the wisdom He imparts to us. Our daily walk must be guided by His divine authority.

Jesus also said we must "take up our cross." The cross is a symbol of death. We are to die to sin and our selfish ambitions.

> *...for if you are living according to the flesh, you must die; but if by the Spirit you are putting to death the deeds of the body, you will live. For all who are being led by the Spirit of God, these are the sons of God.* (Romans 8:13-14)

Jesus then said, "follow Me." To follow Jesus means we are to adhere to and obey all that He taught. And lastly, we are to follow Him without shame.

Jesus made it clear that following Him requires something from us. We are to deny our will and surrender to God's will, we are to die to our sinful ways and selfish ambitions for His sake and the gospel's sake, and we are to be devoted followers of Him, unashamed of our allegiance to Him, honoring and exalting His reputation more than our own.

Following Jesus comes at a cost. It begins the moment we repent and place our faith in Him. As we have learned throughout this book, once we surrender our lives to Christ, we are no longer the same person we were even one second before. From the moment we are born again, the Spirit moving within us gives rise to new experiences. Depending on what those experiences are and how they affect us, we'll either deem them to be good, bad, or indifferent. We are given some examples in Scripture of what we may experience as followers of Christ. The world will hate us (John 15:18), we'll be persecuted (2 Timothy 3:12), and even members of our households may very well become our enemies (Matthew 10:36), just to name a few! Once again, when we see it laid out like this, becoming a follower of Christ doesn't sound very appealing. Therefore, when we consider the cost, what is it that compels a single one of us to become a devoted follower of Jesus Christ? The answer is simple. It is God's amazing grace!

God's Grace

The word *grace* in the Greek is *charis*. It means goodwill, loving-kindness, favor; of the merciful kindness by which God, exerting His holy influence upon souls, turns them to Christ, keeps, strengthens, increases them in Christian faith, knowledge, affection, and kindles them to the exercise of the Christian virtues (Strong's G5485). God's grace is His unmerited favor toward us. It is immeasurable and never-ending. God's loving-kindness toward us is that which beckons our souls to come and find rest in Him. The fact that we even come to Him at all in repentance and faith is because He draws us in. No one can come to Jesus unless the Father who sent Him draws him (John 6:44). It is only by His grace that we come to a place of recognizing our poverty of spirit and our need for a Savior. Without God's grace, there would be no way by which man could be saved. God justifies us as a *gift of His grace* through the redemption which is found in Christ Jesus (Romans 3:24), forgiving all our trespasses *according to the riches of His grace* (Ephesians 1:7). God's gift of redemption, through His Son, is the height of His amazing love and grace toward us.

> *For of His fullness we have all received, and grace upon grace. For the Law was given through Moses; grace and truth were realized through Jesus Christ.* (John 1:16-17)

As followers of Christ, we are the beneficiaries of all that God graciously bestows upon us. Though following Christ comes at a cost, what we gain and receive as heirs of God is far greater.

> *Jesus said, "Truly I say to you, there is no one who has left house or brothers or sisters or mother or father or children or farms, for My sake and for the gospel's sake, but that he will receive a hundred times as much now in the present age, houses and brothers and sisters and mothers and children and farms, along with persecutions; and in the age to come, eternal life."* (Mark 10:29-30)

Jesus said that in this present age—the time in which we live—what we may lose as a result of following Him, we will receive a hundred times more. And in the age to come, we'll receive eternal life. I believe that if eternal life was all we ever received, that would be enough to turn our lives completely over to Him. Jesus said that it profits us nothing if we live only for the here and now, gaining all that we can from what the world has to offer, yet lose our very souls (Mark 8:36). Therefore, when we consider the cost of following Christ versus what we gain, there is no comparison. The Apostle Paul said that any gain he had in this life, or confidence in his pedigree, or zeal for the Law, was nothing but rubbish when compared to the surpassing value of knowing Christ Jesus as Lord (Philippians 3:8).

Jesus came that we may have life, and have it abundantly (John 10:10). To have the fullness of life that Jesus speaks of, our lives need to be fully surrendered to Him. Without Him, there will always be an emptiness within our souls, like broken cisterns that can't hold water (Jeremiah 2:13). When we surrender our lives to Jesus, we receive all the fullness of life that is found in Him. We get His joy (John 15:11), His peace (John 14:27), His rest (Matthew 11:28), and in Him, we are made complete (Colossians 2:10). Jesus said, *"I am the bread of life; he who comes to Me will not hunger, and he who believes in Me will never thirst"* (John 6:35). This statement alone expresses contentment beyond anything we could ever imagine—a satisfaction that fills the depths of our souls. It is the epitome of a life no longer left wanting.

Psalm 23 gives us a beautiful picture of all that we have in Christ Jesus. It's also a great illustration of how well the Good Shepherd cares for all who belong to Him.

1 The Lord is my shepherd,
I shall not want.
2 He makes me lie down in green pastures;
He leads me beside quiet waters.
3 He restores my soul;
He guides me in the paths of righteousness
For His name's sake.
4 Even though I walk through the valley of the shadow of death,
I fear no evil, for You are with me;
Your rod and Your staff, they comfort me.
5 You prepare a table before me in the presence of my enemies;
You have anointed my head with oil;
My cup overflows.

*6 Surely goodness and lovingkindness will follow me all the days of my life,
And I will dwell in the house of the Lord forever.* (Psalm 23)

We learn from Psalm 23 that with Jesus as our Shepherd, we are filled and satisfied. Psalm 23 tells us the following: We lack for nothing; Jesus provides for all our needs (v. 1). He brings about situations designed to draw us into complete dependence on Him, in which we find rest and peace (v. 2). He restores our souls through the healing of our hearts and minds. He guides us in paths of righteousness because we are His (v. 3). Through times of trials, we need not fear; He is always with us, protecting and comforting us (v. 4). In the midst of our enemies, He lovingly cares for us, filling us more than we need (v. 5). His goodness and loving-kindness will follow us every single day of our lives, and we will forever be with Jesus, in this life and the life to come (v. 6). The truths contained in Psalm 23 affirm there isn't a single need we have that falls outside the realm of what Jesus, the Good Shepherd, provides.

The Covenant of Grace

As we reflect on the hallmarks of a true believer and follower of Jesus Christ, one thing is evident. The impact of God's grace upon the human heart is extraordinary. The hallmarks I've noted that define us as true followers of Christ are a testament to God's grace; none of them would even exist were it not for the grace of God. When we become members of God's family, it is by His grace that every follower of Christ has an internal transformation of the heart. The transformation of our hearts is what produces the desire within us to follow Jesus. It is His Spirit that causes us to walk in His statutes (Ezekiel 36:27). Christianity is never to be mistaken as some kind of performance-based "checklist" of "do's and don't's." It is not bound by law, nor is it defined by rites, rituals, or any semblance of legalism, all of which keep us in bondage to self-serving works of righteousness. *...if it is by grace, it is no longer on the basis of*

233

works, otherwise grace is no longer grace (Romans 11:6). Christianity is about following Jesus.

It is through the shed blood of Jesus Christ that God made a New Covenant with mankind—a Covenant of Grace—in which we are no longer bound by the Law of the Old Covenant (Romans 6:14). Jesus inaugurated the New Covenant on the night He celebrated the last Passover meal with His disciples in the upper room (Luke 22:14-20). At that moment, our worship of God was no longer about animal sacrifices and the keeping of laws. We transitioned out of that old system and into the new system of worshiping God in spirit and truth (John 4:24). God set aside the legal system of sacrifices of the First Covenant, establishing the Second Covenant through the shed blood of His Son, once for all (Hebrews 10:9-10).

The Old Covenant was based on man's performance to keep the Law, yet man lacked the power within his heart to do so. The New Covenant is based on Christ's perfect performance to keep the Law. Jesus lived a sinless life and perfectly upheld the entire Law of God. The New Covenant is a covenant of God's grace, in which our righteousness is now found in His Son (Romans 5:17). When we enter into the New Covenant, God puts His Law within us. He writes it on our hearts (Jeremiah 31:33). God removes our hearts of stone and gives us hearts of flesh (Ezekiel 11:19), making our hearts ripe for transformation. God wants our hearts (2 Chronicles 16:9; Proverbs 23:26). Our worship of Him is about being so in love with His Son that our hearts are fully His. When He has our hearts, it is then that we are pliable and His greatest work is accomplished. We become clay, easily molded in the Potter's hands, yielding to His unique design for each of us as He transforms us into the image of His Son.

God created and designed us with a desire to know and worship Him, a desire that can only be filled and satisfied through Jesus Christ. When we surrender our lives to Christ, everything we need is found in Him. It is in Jesus that our hearts and minds find rest. God forgives us the guilt of our sin (Psalm 32:5) and cleanses our conscience of all the shame that results from a life of sin (Hebrews 9:14). Old things have passed away, and in Him, we are made new (2 Corinthians 5:17). We are free in Christ Jesus (John 8:36)! For all who have been liberated from the chains of guilt and shame, God's grace brings peace and contentment to our souls that allow us to fully live for Him, pursuing all He has called us to (see Ephesians 2:10).

Grace We Have Received, Grace We Are to Give

As followers of Christ who are tasked with sharing God's message of salvation to a lost world, the grace we have so freely received is the same grace we must always remember to extend to others. May we constantly be reminded of our own humble beginnings—our spiritual poverty that brought us to our knees in repentance before a holy God. We were once slaves to sin, walking according to our sinful nature (Ephesians 2:1-2). But God, who is rich in mercy (Ephesians 2:4), compassion, and grace (Exodus 34:6), in His perfect timing, rescued us from the domain of darkness and transferred us to the kingdom of His beloved Son (Colossians 1:13). Amen!

Given that we have been lavished with God's grace (Ephesians 1:7-8), may we always respond with grace toward others. To the unsaved, our job is to never cease planting the seeds of the gospel of Jesus Christ. We are to live in such a way that draws others in, stirring up a hunger inside their hearts to want to know more about the true and living God whom we serve. From there, it is up to God to bring the increase. To our brothers and sisters in Christ, our job is to exhort and encourage one another in ways that deepen and strengthen our faith in Jesus. And during those times in which we might find ourselves in disagreement or concerned about another's walk with the Lord, may we never have a condemning spirit that only serves to tear one another down. Rather, let us offer a spirit of forgiveness as we speak the Truth in love. It is the Spirit of God who will bring conviction to the hearts and minds of those of us who need it, and it is the Spirit who will cause the Truth of

Jesus Christ to resonate within us. Remember, sanctification is a process. It is God who enables us, through the power of His Spirit, to walk in righteousness. So when we stumble and fall, may we be there for one another, sharing the love of Christ and building each other up in the unity of our faith.

Today is The Day of Salvation

As I come to a close, I take us once again to the Preface. My exhortation to you was to examine yourself, to see if you are in the faith. If you are indeed a child of God through His Son, Jesus Christ, my heart is filled with joy knowing we are brothers and sisters in Christ, inextricably bound together as one family for eternity. However, if you have discovered you are not in the family of faith, I exhort you to become a true follower of Jesus Christ, no matter the cost. It is my prayer that you do not let another moment pass without being made right with God. The Bible tells us that today is the day of salvation (2 Corinthians 6:2). Repent and believe in the gospel of Jesus Christ (Mark 1:15). Believe that Jesus is who He said He is—the Son of God who died for our sins, was buried, and then raised to life. Jesus said, *"...for unless you believe that I am He, you will die in your sins"* (John 8:24). Place your faith in the finished work of Jesus Christ and be made right with God (2 Corinthians 5:21). If you do, you will be born of the Spirit and have everlasting life (John 3:16). Your sins will be forgiven (Acts 10:43), and you will be set free from the guilt and shame brought on by a life enslaved to sin. You will be adopted into God's family, no longer a slave but a son, an heir through God (Galatians 4:5-7), with a rich inheritance in the kingdom of God, one that is imperishable and undefiled, and will not fade away (1 Peter 1:4).

For all have sinned and fall short of the glory of God.
(Romans 3:23)

For the wages of sin is death, but the free gift of God
is eternal life in Christ Jesus our Lord.
(Romans 6:23)

God demonstrates His own love toward us, in that while we
were yet sinners, Christ died for us.
(Romans 5:8)

If you confess with your mouth Jesus as Lord, and believe
in your heart that God raised Him from the dead, you will be saved.
(Romans 10:9)

For "Whoever will call on the name of the Lord will be saved."
(Romans 10:13)

Appendix

Definition of Terms

A S NOTED IN THE INTRODUCTION, THERE ARE different words and phrases the Bible uses that identify people as followers of Jesus Christ. Given that they may mean different things to different people, I have defined these words and phrases below. Though each word or phrase may connote something slightly different, essentially they all mean the same thing—they refer to individuals who are true followers of Jesus Christ. Therefore, I use these words and phrases interchangeably; they are synonymous. Every time these words and phrases are used, it is a reference to those who have repented of their sins and have put their faith in Jesus Christ as Lord and Savior. They believe that Jesus is the only begotten Son of God, who lived and died, was buried, and rose again on the third day. They believe that Jesus is Truth, His words are Truth, and without Him, there is no hope of eternal life.

Christian

Many people will identify themselves as Christians. However, the definition of what that means will often vary. As such, a clear definition of the word *Christian* is needed so that its meaning is understood every time you come across it throughout this book. Ultimately, a comprehensive definition will be summed up in this book as a whole.

The first time the word Christian is used in the New Testament is in Acts 11:26. It tells us the disciples were first called Christians in Antioch. Keep in mind that the reference to disciples in this verse does not refer to the original twelve disciples of Jesus, but rather people who were followers and pupils of Christ.

The Greek word for *Christian* is *Christianos*. In short, it means a follower of Christ (Strong's G5546). Vine's states: The word was formed after the Roman style and signified that you were an adherent of Jesus (Vine's Expository Dictionary). As an adherent and follower of Christ, Christians are individuals who attest to Jesus Christ as Lord and Savior. To call Jesus Lord means you believe Him to be your master/owner in whom you obey. To call Jesus Savior means you trust and believe that He is your source of eternal life. As such, Christians are those who have repented of their sins and have put their faith in Jesus Christ as Lord and Savior. The Holy Spirit of God resides within the Christian. As a result of God's Spirit within, a Christian is someone who desires to live a life pleasing to God and exemplifies the nature and character of Jesus Christ as evidenced by a changed life.

Follower

Given that *Christian* in the Greek means a follower of Christ, let's look at what *follower* means. There are two definitions for the word *follow*. The first one is what we see in Matthew 4:19. Jesus asked Peter and Andrew to follow Him. In this verse, it is used as a command. Here, the Greek word is *deute*. It is an imperative and simply means to come here, come now (Strong's G1205). The other definition of *follow* is found in Matthew 16:24. *Then Jesus said to His disciples, "If anyone wishes to come after Me, he must deny himself, and take up his cross and follow me."* The Greek word for *follow* in this verse is *akoloutheō*. It means to join one as a disciple, become or be his disciple, to join his party (Strong's G190). According to Matthew 16:24, to be a follower of Jesus means to become His student and follow His teachings. As such, a person will abandon his or her own will, goals, ways, and desires, and in turn, recognize and surrender to God's will and authority, obeying all that Christ has taught. As I use the term follower throughout this book, it is this second definition that I am referring to.

Disciple

The word *disciple* in the Greek is *mathētēs*. It means a learner; pupil, it denotes one who follows one's teaching (Strong's G3101). Jesus often used this word to refer to His original twelve disciples, but He also used it to refer to all those who would come to a saving faith in Him. Jesus said, *"Go therefore and make disciples of all the nations, baptizing them in the name of the Father and the Son and the Holy Spirit"* (Matthew 28:19). The words *make disciples* in English are represented by one word in the Greek, *mathēteuō*. In this verse, the meaning of the words, *make disciples,* is two-fold: to be a disciple of one, to follow his precepts and instructions, and to make a disciple, to teach, instruct (Strong's G3100). In this command by Jesus, *make disciples* is used to denote not only a student of another, but it also includes a teaching and instructing component. This means that disciples of Christ are not only those who follow His precepts and instructions but also teach His precepts and instructions.

Believer

According to the Merriam-Webster dictionary, *believe* can mean: "to consider to be true or honest, to accept the word of evidence of, to hold as an opinion, to accept something as true, genuine or real, or to have a firm or wholehearted religious conviction or persuasion."[1] Now let's look at the word as used in John 3:16. *For God so loved the world, that He gave His only begotten Son, that whoever believes in Him shall not perish, but have eternal life.* The Greek word for *believe* in this verse is *pisteuō*. It means to think to be true, be persuaded of, and place confidence in, of the thing believed (Strong's G4100). Vine's states: To trust in Jesus or God as able to aid either in obtaining or in doing something: saving faith. "To believe" also "to be persuaded of," and hence, "to place confidence in, to trust," signifies, in this sense of the word, reliance upon, not mere credence (Vine's Expository Dictionary). The word *believe* in John 3:16 isn't simply an acknowledgment of something as being true. It means to fully surrender to, adhere to, rely upon, and put one's trust in.

Let me give you an example of believing in something such that you fully surrender to, rely upon, and trust in it. Consider a parachute. We know, meaning we believe, that a parachute is designed to allow us to free-fall from many feet above the earth's surface, and yet land safely. We believe it will ultimately function in such a way that it will slow our descent as we approach the surface of the earth so that we can land gently enough not to cause any physical harm to our bodies. Now let's say we are given a choice to jump out of a plane. What does our belief in the parachute look like now? Do we trust that the parachute will perform the way we believe it is designed to? If we decide to jump, we have to take what we believe and trust in it to the point we surrender ourselves completely to it. We have to put on the parachute, trust, and surrender to our belief in what it is designed to do, and completely rely upon it to save us from death. This is what is meant by the word *believe* in John 3:16. It means to fully surrender ourselves to the belief that by putting our faith, hope, and trust in Jesus Christ, that our faith in Him will save us from death and thereby grant us eternal life.

---

[1] Merriam-Webster, "Definition of believe," 2020 Merriam-Webster, Incorporated, date accessed December 10, 2020, https://www.merriam-webster.com/dictionary/believe

Born Again

The first time we see this phrase used is in John 3. The word *born* in the Greek is *gennaō*. Simply put, it means to be born. It can be used in two ways: one is to denote a physical birth, and the second is metaphorical, denoting causing something to arise (Strong's G1080). The word *again* is *anōthen*. It means from above, from a higher place, of things which come from heaven or God (Strong's G509). Putting these two words together, *gennaō anōthen* means to be born/arisen from a higher place.

Born of The Spirit

The word *Spirit* in the Greek is *pneuma*. It means the third person of the triune God, the Holy Spirit, coequal, coeternal with the Father and the Son; the disposition or influence which fills and governs the soul; a movement of air (a gentle blast) (Strong's G4151). Whenever the word *Spirit* is capitalized in Scripture, it is a specific reference to the Holy Spirit of God. As such, the translation of *born of the Spirit* is to be born from God, via the Holy Spirit.

The phrases *born again* and *born of the Spirit* denote a literal spiritual birth that comes from God by His Holy Spirit. The Holy Spirit is completely devoid of the corrupt sin nature. When a person is born again/born of the Spirit, that person becomes indwelt with the Holy Spirit of God. The Holy Spirit influences and governs the souls of those in whom He dwells.

Born of God/Born of Him

These two phrases are frequently used by the Apostle John in the Book of 1 John. They mean the same thing as born again and born of the Spirit. These phrases refer to a spiritual birth that comes from God, by His Holy Spirit.

Bibliography

"Strong's Greek Lexicon (nasb95)." Blue Letter Bible. https://www. blueletterbible.org/lexicon/

Vine, W. "Vine's Expository Dictionary of New Testament Words." Blue Letter Bible. Last Modified 24 Jun, 1996. https://www.blueletter-bible.org/search/dictionary/viewtopic.cfm

CPSIA information can be obtained
at www.ICGtesting.com
Printed in the USA
BVHW070415161221
624023BV00012B/1152